PHYSICAL EDUCATION, CURRICULUM AND CULTURE

Deakin Studies in Education Series

General Editors: Professor Rob Walker and Professor Stephen
Kemmis, Deakin University, Victoria, Australia

Deakin Studies in Education Series: 5

PHYSICAL EDUCATION, CURRICULUM AND CULTURE: CRITICAL ISSUES IN THE CONTEMPORARY CRISIS

Edited by
David Kirk and Richard Tinning

 RoutledgeFalmer
Taylor & Francis Group

LONDON AND NEW YORK

First published 1990
By RoutledgeFalmer,
2 Park Square, Milton Park, Abingdon, Oxon, OX14 4RN

Transferred to Digital Printing 2005

British Library Cataloguing in Publication Data
Physical education, curriculum and culture
  1. Educational institutions. Curriculum subjects: Physical
  education. I. Kirk, David. II. Tinning, Richard. III. Series.
  613.707
  ISBN 1-85000-674-1
  ISBN 1-85000-675-X (pbk.)

**Library of Congress Cataloging-in-Publication Data
is available on request**

Jacket design by Caroline Archer

Set in 10½/13pt Bembo by
Graphicraft Typesetters Ltd, Hong Kong

Contents

Contents

General Editors' Introduction

The Deakin Studies in Education Series aims to present a broad critical perspective across a range of interrelated fields in education. The intention is to develop what might be called a 'critical educational science': critical work in the philosophy of education, curriculum, educational and public administration, language education, and educational action research and clinical supervision. The series strives to present the writings of a rising generation of scholars and researchers in education.

A number of researchers based at Deakin University have been closely associated with the development of the critical perspective across these fields. For such reasons, people in the field have sometimes spoken of a 'Deakin perspective'. We do share some common views from which we hope to contribute to contemporary debates about the future development of educational enquiry; at the same time, our disagreements seem as fruitful for us as our agreements.

The Deakin Studies in Education Series provides an opportunity for extending this debate about the nature and future development of education and educational enquiry. It will include the writings of a variety of educational researchers around the world who, like ourselves, are interested in exploring the power and limitations of the critical perspective in the analysis of educational theory, policy and practice.

The central themes of the series will not be dictated by the alleged boundaries between 'foundational' disciplines in education, nor by an unexamined division of the tasks of education and educational research between 'practitioners' and 'theorists', or between 'practitioners' and 'policy-makers'. On the contrary, one of the tasks of the series is to demonstrate, through careful research and scholarship across a range of fields of practical, political and theoretical endeavour, just how outmoded, unproductive, and ultimately destructive these divisions are both for education and for educational research. Put positively, the central themes and questions to be addressed in the series include:

> the unity of educational theory and practice — expressed, for example, in the work of educational practitioners who research their practice as a basis for improving it, and in the notion of collaborative, participatory educational research, for example, in educational action research;
>
> the historical formation, social construction and continual reconstruction of education and educational institutions and reforms through processes of contestation and institutionalization — expressed, for example, in the work of critical researchers into the curriculum and educational reform; and
>
> the possibilities of education for emancipation and active and productive participation in a democratic society — expressed, for example, in the development of critical pedagogy and the development of communitarian perspectives in the organization of education.

These are enduring themes, touching upon some of the central questions confronting our contemporary culture and, some would say, upon the central pathologies of contemporary society. They are all too easily neglected or obscured in the narrow and fragmented views of education and educational research characteristic of our times. Yet education is one of the key resources in what Raymond Williams once described as our societies' 'journey of hope' — the journey towards a better, more just, more rational and more rewarding society. Education has always aimed to nurture, represent, vivify and extend the values and modes of life which promise to make the best in our culture better. Finding out how this can be done, interpreting our progress, and appraising and reappraising the quality of our efforts at educational improvement are the tasks of critical educational research. They are the tasks of this series.

Stephen Kemmis and Rob Walker

Acknowledgments

As in any collaborative project involving so many people, there are always a number of debts of gratitude to be acknowledged. Each of the authors who has contributed to this volume has included a note of thanks directly following his or her own chapter where this has been appropriate. It falls to us as Editors to acknowledge the assistance and support of those people who helped us to put this book together. First of all, we want to thank the authors collectively for the energy they put into this project and their willingness to meet our often demanding deadlines. We also wish to thank Professor Rob Walker and the Deakin Institute for Studies in Education for their encouragement to go ahead with the book. Thanks also to Fran Dickson at Deakin University for her excellent work in typing a number of the chapters.

David Kirk and Richard Tinning
School of Education, Deakin University

Chapter 1

Introduction: Physical Education, Curriculum and Culture

David Kirk and Richard Tinning

All of a sudden, it seems, school and community physical activity pro-grammes are newsworthy items. Research agencies in various countries, some of them government sponsored, are busily engaged in conducting or planning physical fitness surveys of school children and adults, and school physical education is featuring in the pages of the popular press and on serious current affairs television programmes. Meanwhile, the chatter surrounding the fate of international sports performers is ever present, the volume and acrimony rising sharply as the latest failure on the international scene is scrutinized and dissected, and physical educators once again find themselves included in the hunt for scapegoats. Many of these events have been taking place in Britain over the past five years, where a very public debate about school physical education has been conducted, a debate that has been more subdued in other countries, but, as we will see from the contributions to this book, has nevertheless being going on there too. What is clear from the attention that has been directed at physical education is that it has been implicated in wider societal events at a time when we are faced with an ever-growing number of crises. Those of us who read the daily press will be very well aware of the current upheavals in the world economy, with the concomitant instability in political life and chronic large-scale unemployment. We are faced regularly with distressing reports of impending environmental catas-trophe caused by holes in the ozone layer and the threat of diseases like AIDS reaching epidemic proportions. There can be little doubt that we live in unsettled and unsettling times, where words like 'crisis', 'turmoil' and 'unrest' are certainly not out of place.

In this context, as Evans and Davies (1988) have argued, it is hardly surprising that there is unrest, change and dislocation within education and schools. Education has been a hot political topic since the early 1960s in its function as a major plank in the post-Second World War 'social reconstruction' of a number of Western countries. Now, suddenly, physical education and related activities like physical fitness, health, sport and recreation are on stage, and willing or not have become star performers in what Stuart Hall (1983) has called 'The Great Moving Right Show'. Suddenly, the cultural significance of physical activity, and its symbolic relationship to political ideologies in particular, have been exposed as politicians and other ruling class agents have sought out and found powerful media for their messages (Fitzclarence, 1987). While physical educators within their own professional contexts have been excited by a range of new ideas such as health-based physical education and concepts like 'lifestyle', 'fitness' and 'health', there has been little critical analysis to date of these trends and their relationships to events in wider society. As Tinning (1984) has recently pointed out to Australian physical educators, most of the critique that does appear in the pages of physical education journals is aimed at other physical educators. We lack a critical tradition in our field, and tend to view conflict and criticism as always destructive, intensely personal, rarely objective and never constructive. We seem to be more concerned with following trends, with showing that we can fit whatever role society requires of us, and we take the subservient view that we shouldn't 'bite the hand that feeds us'. Social responsiveness is important, but so is social critique, for without it we allow ourselves to be implicated in cultural movements that may not always be for the good of the few or the many, and which may actually undermine some of the things our profession values.

Critical awareness of events in society at large does not mean, as one recent commentator has implied (Saunders, 1985), that we take on political lobbying on environmental issues, the nuclear arms race or some other social issue as a professional function. Our interests instead, as physical educators, must be focused on how these wider movements in society circumscribe and interfuse our work in school physical education. This means that we cannot go on blissfully measuring the happenings inside physical education classes, counting students' 'motor-engaged' time or the amount of time teachers devote to managerial matters, without also taking account of the forces outside schools that are actively shaping the very substance of what we teach and, indeed, why we think such measurements might be important in the first place. If school physical education is such big news, we are not likely to find the answers why in micro-analyses of physical education lessons alone. The studies brought together in this volume attempt to look out and look in at the same time, to note the substantive issues in physical education and at the same time locate these within the ebb and flow of cultural movements and processes. The key focusing concept in each is knowledge, and how it is selected, organized, appropriated, legitimated and evaluated. The rest of this introduction is an attempt to explain why critical studies of curriculum issues in physical education are important, our motivations as editors for putting this book together, and to identify in summary form the issues each chapter addresses.

Physical Activity and Knowledge

Many readers and most of the contributors to this book, who have at some point in their lives undergone a course of teacher training in physical education, will be sympathetic to the idea that there is much to learn and know about physical activity and the body. Most of us will be familar with some of the rudimentary objections to the orthodoxy of mind/body dualism and as physical educators would be likely to reject the notions that engaging in physical activity is in some sense a 'non-cognitive' activity, as educational philosophers of the 1960s like Richard Peters (1966) would have it, and that physical education in schools is inferior to other curriculum topics due to its eminently practical nature. Some of us occasionally may have felt a sense of injustice at the emphasis placed on 'intellectual' pursuits within Western educational practice and frustration at the persistent denigration of physical education by some of our administrators, policy-makers, academics and colleagues.[1]

Despite this tradition of dualism within educational practice, however, organized physical education has survived in both public and private school systems.[2] It has developed in a number of countries from humble beginnings into a fully fledged school subject and increasingly with a cadre of four-year trained graduate teachers. Given the alleged intellectualist bias in educational systems, physical education's continued existence and in places its expansion are on the face of it a remarkable feat, and suggest at least a paradox. How can a subject that has occupied a 'marginal' educational role in the curriculum for so long begin to grow at an unprecedented rate and in such a relatively unfavourable environment?

There are several possible answers to this question. One that may spring most readily to mind for some people is that physical education has finally been able to demonstrate its scientific basis and so its worth as a respectable intellectual pursuit. Indeed, this would seem to constitute the basis of the received or dominant view which presently informs the organization of the study of physical activity in tertiary institutions. However, while it may account for the current growth in tertiary level 'human movement science' degree courses and examinable subjects in secondary schools, this response leaves the place of actual physical activity in this context problematic (see e.g. Best, 1978; Arnold, 1979; Kirk, 1988). This trend toward science as a basis for the study of physical activity is also in itself a problematic issue, a matter that is discussed in the chapters by Bain, Kirk, Dewar and Fitzclarence and Tinning in this volume.

Another response may be that the main criteria for the inclusion of a subject in the school curriculum are not necessarily 'educational' (in the sense outlined by philosophers such as Peters, 1966), and that schools themselves must now fulfil a complex range of functions (cf. Kemmis, 1983). In this respect physical education's continuing presence in the school curriculum is to serve purposes other than educational ones, such as maintaining students' fitness and health, providing them with leisure-time skills for adulthood or with sports skills for elite performance. This is a much more complex position than the 'evolution to science' argument since it brings into play the relationship between schools and society, rather than merely considering the place of one subject within the school, college or university as a closed system. There may be other possible explanations of the paradox that physical activity courses in educational institutions represent, but while these are locked within restricted cognitivist views of 'education' as an exclusively intellectual activity, it is unlikely that we will achieve any kind of satisfactory resolution to this apparent conundrum. Consideration of the complexity of the relationship between school knowledge and wider societal interests makes any clear and unequivocal explanation of the role of physical activity in the curricula of educational institutions less likely, but it does suggest an important direction in which to focus our attention in search of powerful and more penetrating insights into this apparent paradox. One radical alternative to the orthodox cognitivist view of the role of physical activity in educational contexts is suggested in the work of the French historian of ideas, Michel Foucault.

The Body, Movement and Culture

Foucault (1980) has argued against the widespread notion that Western civilization has neglected the body in preference to the intellect. He suggests, on the contrary, that control and repression of the body have played a fundamental part in the establishment and maintenance of power required for the growth of industrial capitalism since the eighteenth century. In the early days of industrial capitalism, when a vast and disciplined workforce was required as a prerequisite to industrial production, a range of institutions was invented — schools, hospitals, factories, barracks, asylums — where the same regime of physical repression and control was applied. It is no coincidence that the substance and conduct of physical education was framed within repressive, quasi-militaristic forms in the context of compulsory mass education in the late nineteenth century, a legacy that has remained with physical education until as recently as the 1960s. Foucault suggests that since the late 1950s this 'heavy, ponderous, meticulous and constant' investment of power through the subjection of the body has undergone dramatic transformation in train with changes in the structure of contemporary capitalism, and that a new, much more individualistic and less obvious regime of corporeal control has begun to develop. Foucault's central point is that, far from neglecting the body, society has since at least the eighteenth century recognized the crucial significance of the body and movement in relation to the exercise of power.[3] The fact that the body has been positioned in particular ways within educational discourse, as irrelevant to intellectual development for example, is not inconsistent with Foucault's thesis, since the roles allocated to physical activity within schools have served purposes that rarely challenged this logic of corporeal control.

What is important about Foucault's work in relation to the body and power is that it shows the physical dimension of our beings to be infused with social and cultural significance. This is a difficult notion to come to terms with at first, not least because of the ways in which a variety of discourses in education, the military, work, religion, medicine and science has represented the body as a biophysical object to be manipulated, disciplined, repressed, punished and treated. The recent rise to prominence of scientific functionalism in 'human movement science', discussed in the chapters by Kirk, Dewar, Bain and Fitzclarence and Tinning in this volume, has done much to extend this way of looking at the body, leaning heavily as it does on the logic of experimental science and scientific medicine. Within this discourse of scientific functionalism, the moving body is depersonalized, represented as an object which obeys the laws of gravity, which generates force in its own right, and which is made up of 'systems' of muscles, bones, nerves, tendons and other specialized tissue which function in many instances independently of what people think and feel. Within this discourse, comparisons of the body's functioning to that of a computer or some other machine seem to be accurate and apt descriptions, an issue that is elaborated in the chapters by Bain and Colquhoun. Such analogies will be familiar to many readers who have trained as physical educators. However, it is this very familiarity that sometimes makes it difficult for us to think of the body and movement in other terms.

The fact that movement and the body are of crucial social and cultural significance is not so difficult to appreciate, however, when we begin to consider mass culture and the media. Sport, as a major institutionalized form of physical activity, is used regularly by advertisers to sell a diverse range of products. In many advertisements, direct associations are made between the qualities inherent in sports performance and their products, qualities such as excitement, dynamism, just reward for hard work, competitiveness and success. The series of Australia and New Zealand Bank advertisements discussed in the chapter by Fitzclarence and Tinning shows how effectively analogies are being drawn between techniques for successful performance in sport and successful conduct in life. Sport is a pervasive feature of everyday life that appears at many levels of society, albeit in different forms, and so it resonates with many people's mainly pleasurable experiences. More than this, success in sport is much more easily and unproblematically measured than in other areas of life, and so acts as a simple metaphor for the 'good life'. The sheer physicality of many sports is a major part of their attraction and power, and it is this power that draws so many advertisers to use sport to sell their messages and products.

In a similar way, the slender body achieved widespread prominence as a metaphor for health, well-being and affluence in the print and electronic media. Fatness, on the other hand, particularly in women, elicits moral reproof. Overweight or obese people are represented as lazy, emotionally weak and sexually unattractive. These representations of the body in advertising and other media forms can have such a powerful impact on people precisely because they go beyond rational descriptions of desirable weight and shape to become moral imperatives. Picking up the thread of Foucault's analysis, we might suggest that this may be one of the new forms of corporeal control he alludes to, where the locus of control has shifted from the masses and punitive external sanctions and repressions to become internalized within the individual and located within a moral category of guilt and reproof. Certainly, as writers like Crawford (1986) and others such as Colquhoun in this volume have suggested, the widespread occurrence of eating disorders such as anorexia nervosa and bulimia, which are both underwritten by an obsession with weight and body shape, illustrates two contradictory imperatives within contemporary capitalism to consume and abstain. The incoherence of these requirements of capitalism, when worked out in the lives of individuals, is aptly illustrated in the tragedy, waste and misery of the lives of victims of these disorders.

The Interconnectedness of Physical Education and Culture

In this context of the social and cultural significance of movement and the body, physical activity programmes in educational institutions occupy an important position in defining, transmitting and legitimating forms of human movement that are thought to be useful, socially permissible and morally sound.[4] The kinds of physical activities that make up physical education programmes are the resultants of a number of structural and practical forces, in particular tradition, conscious selection and planning, and a range of pragmatic factors such as facilities, equipment and teacher expertise. However, whether programmes are mainly the outcome of conscious planning or history and tradition, their constitution is in neither case 'accidental'. Given the interconnectedness of physical activity, the body and culture, the work of physical educators takes on enormous significance as a key moment in the process of cultural production.[5] Just as movement and the body are socially constructed, so physical education is itself deeply implicated in this process of construction. The forms of human movement that make up physical education programmes exist because they are important to the interests of some groups of people somewhere in society. This is not to suggest a monolithic or deterministic imposition of alien values on the receivers of physical education in schools, but merely to make the point that these activities have not been generated out of nothing. They exist in school programmes because, in some convoluted way or another, they service the interests of some people often at the expense of others. It is, for example, no coincidence that physical educators around the world are currently developing health-based physical education programmes at a time when there is a popular mass cultural movement towards physical fitness and health, environmental sickness that can be linked directly to human illness, and a deepening crisis in Western capitalism signalled by world-wide recession and mass, chronic unemployment.

Political Projects, Cultural Critique and Substantive Concerns

The nature of this interconnectedness, however, between physical education, physical activity and culture, or between fitness, corporeal control and chronic unemployment for that matter, is neither obvious nor straightforward. While we believe it is essential for research to incorporate and utilize a concept of 'social structure' in any analysis of physical education policy, programmes and practice, we suggest that it is neither helpful nor accurate to draw simplistic lines of connection between wider social processes and events in schools and classrooms. In their worst form, such analyses engender a 'radical pessimism', a sense of hopelessness in the face of overpowering forces and predetermined events. At the same time, micro-analyses of teaching and other educational action that focus exclusively on the minute and idiosyncratic can also be dangerously blind to forces that exist outside the direct control of individuals or groups of people.[6] In putting together this collection of papers, we have attempted to solicit studies that show a sensitivity to structures in society and at the same time pay close attention to the detail of practice in physical education, and to the interconnections that run between each point of focus. In pursuing this project our activities as editors and contributors have been directed by three major concerns.

Our first concern was to frame the project from the outset within an explicit and coherent political position. It is now commonplace among all but the most petulantly scientistic physical educationists to acknowledge the pervasiveness of values in all of our professional activities as educators. It has been well demonstrated that far from being above values, it would be a strange educator indeed who was not prepared to communicate to students knowledge s/he believed in. This does not mean that we must travel to that other extreme, from a spurious neutrality to irrational prejudice, or that we must politicize education. Education is already 'political'. As Habermas (1972) has pointed out, all of our knowledge is insolubly linked to the pursuit of particular human interests, whether these be the need to maintain the conditions for our survival, communication with each other, or to move beyond our current circumstances to new understandings. We as researchers are as much caught up in the world of values and beliefs as educationists in other contexts like schools, and so it makes little sense to us to suggest that our research can somehow be above and beyond this world. We also believe, however, that it is a certain kind of dishonesty, a form of self-deception, to refrain from attempting to articulate as coherently as we are able what our leading values and beliefs are, as far as we are conscious of them.

This political position is most appropriately outlined in substantive detail by each of the authors in this volume, in direct reference to particular issues and problems in physical education. Readers will find little discussion of the ideologies and policies of major political parties, of 'right', 'left' or 'middle', except where it is required by the integrity of the analysis to locate issues in physical education within recognizable party-political frames. What readers will find instead are explicit discussions of 'the other politics', or what Sparkes refers to in his chapter as the 'micropolitics' of everyday life, of the concerns and beliefs and values that are expressed in and through our actions. In these terms the political project of this book is to open up to critical scrutiny the things we do, say and think about physical education with the express purpose of doing, thinking and saying those things better, and to create the possibility of changing these practices when the need arises. By opening up our professional practices to scrutiny, by ourselves and our peers, we create the possibility of turning each of these areas of practice into 'sites of contestation' (Kirk, 1988) where we can begin to address, practically and specifically, issues and problems that are driven by forces beyond our own immediate and local situations. Each of the papers in this book was commissioned as part of this political project, with the aim of opening up for critical scrutiny a range of curriculum issues in physical education, and of projecting these as potential sites of contestation. Each attempts to treat abstract matters such as power, sectional interests and cultural change in ways that have the potential to inform and empower practitioners within their own spheres of action. In addition, each is underwritten by a concern to contribute to an ongoing process of cultural change by helping to realize education, in schools and through other agencies, as an empowering and emancipatory experience for learners, an issue that is explored in some detail in the chapters by Gore, Bain, Fitzclarence and Tinning and Evans.

In our pursuit of this political project two further concerns followed. Our second concern was to develop critiques of the taken-for-granted assumptions that underwrite forms of educational and organizational practice in physical education. Critique is more than mere criticism in the sense of 'destructive comment'. We use this term here to refer to the effort to stand back from events and practices that are very familiar to us as physical educators, in an effort to gain sufficient analytic space to see beyond the obvious and everyday. Once we have been able to penetrate the sometimes opaque layers of meaning in social life, critique then enables us to position the events under scrutiny within the larger context of which they are a part. For instance, in the case of Derek Colquhoun's chapter we can begin to see the health-based physical education programmes and texts he analyzes as part of definitions of health and its relationship to exercise and body shape that are in themselves crucially important indicators of shifts in social values, norms and practices. In each of the papers that make up this collection authors have attempted to take us, the readers, beyond the obvious and taken-for-granted, and to locate their analyses where appropriate within broader cultural movements and trends.

Our third concern was to present studies that treat the substance of physical education in some detail. This is a matter of considerable importance since the success of the effort to communicate the insights the author has gained from her or his work stands or falls by the extent to which the phenomena being critiqued are actually recognizable to readers. Moreover, as we suggested earlier, it is important that events and practices in physical education are worked through in some detailed, and are not glossed over. It is important that we combine our critical efforts with a view from the inside, with an attempt to understand the values and intentions and meanings of what people do from their perspectives. If the major purpose of our work is to understand what we do and to do it better, we can see little value in research that owes allegiance first and foremost to analytic categories, such as 'class, race and gender'. This is not to say that such categories are irrelevant to understanding organizational and educational practice in physical education, and indeed they figure prominently in the chapters by Evans, Bain, Gore, Dewar and Kirk. However, by treating the substance of physical education, it is more likely that appropriate action based on this research can result. What we have attempted to do is to encourage authors to begin with actual problems in physical education, and to continue to refer to these issues as their analyses develop.

Critical Issues in Physical Education

In substantive terms the central preoccupation of the contributors to this collection of papers is knowledge in physical education and how it has developed in different contexts such as school and teacher education programmes, how it has been organized, the conditions and circumstances in which it has been acquired and appropriated by both teachers and pupils, and the ways in which these processes are circumscribed and interfused by social forces. There are recurrent and interrelated themes in relation to knowledge in physical education that appear and are worked through by the authors in these different contexts.

An issue of central concern and one that surfaces repeatedly in the chapters of this book is that of the increasing dominance of scientism or scientific functionalism, both in physical education and in Western society more generally. Arguably, scientific functionalism is currently the dominant paradigm or world-view in physical education, and is characterized by an unquestioning belief in the status of quantitative, objective information focusing on the physical and physiological functioning of the body, as the ultimate category of knowledge of relevance to physical education. Fitzclarence and Tinning and Colquhoun show how a version of scientific functionalism, in the form of biophysical knowledge, has become the basis of programmes and texts in primary and secondary schools in Australia, while Bain discloses its presence in US schools in the form of what she calls 'technocentric ideology', which involves an extension of technological and economic criteria into judgments of political, moral, social and ethical issues relevant to physical education. Sparkes discusses a similar manifestation of scientific functionalism in his chapter where these technological criteria are applied to the process of curriculum change and development, while Gore critiques the scientism underwriting the notion of teacher effectiveness that dominates much research on teaching. Finally, the chapters by Dewar and Kirk reveal the extent to which scientific functionalism has saturated professional preparation and discourse in physical education and effectively elevated patriarchal values to a dominant position within the profession, in the process alienating many female physical educators.

This association between scientific functionalism and patriarchal dominance raises another pervasive issue, which is the problem of gender equity and the production of gender identity in and through physical education. The chapters by Dewar, Evans, Gore, Bain and Kirk treat this issue in some detail, showing that female teachers and students are discriminated against in physical education by the very structure of physical education activities, which tend to emphasize and celebrate masculine values like physical size and strength, competitiveness and aggression. The extent to which knowledge in physical education programmes is gendered and favours males is strongly portrayed by Dewar and Gore in relation to teacher education programmes, by Bain in terms of non-sexist and anti-sexist strategies such as co-educational school physical education and the problematic outcomes of these for girls, and by Evans and Kirk who highlight female teachers' differential treatment beside men in relation to their opportunities to develop comparable careers and gain positions of leadership and influence.

The celebration of competitiveness and motor elitism in physical education programmes is another recurrent concern in the work of a number of authors. Bain argues that despite the lack of attention to achievement in physical education classes in contrast to school sport in the United States, and clear structural inequalities based on race, class and gender, a meritocratic ideology thrives in schools. Physical education simultaneously fails to offer a challenge to meritocratic school sport, and is marginalized because of its alleged ineffectiveness in realizing this ideal. Evans makes a similar point in relation to British schools, suggesting that the introduction of innovations like teaching games for understanding and health-related fitness, which purport to champion egalitarian ideals, make little difference to teachers' or pupils' experiences of physical education, since both focus on individual rather than social solutions to the structural inequalities inherent in the state school system and worked through in turn in school physical education. Sparkes adds substance to the claims of Bain and Evans in his account of the failure of a Head of Department to overcome the elitist sporting ideology of some of his staff. Even though he managed to establish mixed-ability games lessons and so apparently alter his teachers' practices, he had little effect on their deeply rooted beliefs about the nature and purpose of physical education which for them was centrally concerned with excellence in competitive sport.

Sparkes also highlights in his work a fourth issue that appears consistently in each of the other chapters, which is the major part that human action plays in the construction of knowledge in physical education. Sparkes illustrates the political processes integral to change, in contrast to a Head of Department's belief in the political neutrality and rationality of the process, while Fitzclarence and Tinning identify the various cultural and political factors that have an impact on the process of curriculum writing and that circumscribe the agency of the writer. The chapters by Colquhoun and Evans also show how a range of political and cultural forces has been influential in shaping the construction of school programmes and materials in Britain and Australia, while Gore emphasizes the socially constructed nature of knowledge in a teacher preparation course in her account of the various 'readings' of the text that constituted her and her students' structured actions. Kirk's chapter highlights the way in which knowledge and the definition of physical education itself was bitterly contested in British physical education in the period immediately following the Second World War, and how the lines of struggle were drawn by gender and to a lesser extent the social class of the protagonists and their conflicting world-views. Dewar elaborates Kirk's theme in her discussion of the role of gender in defining worthwhile knowledge in a Canadian teacher preparation course, while Bain seeks to build on the potential of human agency to create change by arguing for the development of critical and emancipatory pedagogy in physical education, whereby pupils can be empowered to recognize the social constructedness, and overcome the partiality, of school knowledge and create the possibility of a more equitable and just society.

These four issues are the threads that run through the chapters of this book, and while they are treated in varying detail by each author, they demonstrate the important similarities and commonalities in physical education programmes in Britain, Australia and North America. The fact that there are issues common to each of these countries is important because they provide an antidote to parochialism and illustrate the extent to which international capitalism is able to generate mass culture across national boundaries. At the same time sensitivity to the form these issues take at different levels in educational systems and within different class, ethnic, gender and other cultural traditions is also important, because, as we have already remarked, it is only through close attention to detail that we can begin to gain insights into the *meaning* of episodes, issues and trends for particular groups and individuals. While the chapters share a common focus on the organization, contestation, negotiation and appropriation of knowledge in physical education at an abstract level, they are loosely sequenced on the basis of their substantive concerns.

Linda Bain (Chapter 2) usefully identifies and previews research on three major dimensions of the hidden curriculum of physical education programmes in the United States — meritocracy, technocentric ideology, and social relations — which also underwrite some of the more specific concerns of the other chapters in this volume. Bain argues that meritocracy is sustained by the two-tiered US system of sport and physical education. While sport is explicitly elitist, physical education is characterized by an emphasis on control and order rather than achievement. Bain suggests that while there is some resistance from teachers to meritocracy, their individualistic alternatives pose little challenge to the meritocratic ideology of the school as a whole, due to physical education's perceived marginality. In contrast, in the case of technocentric ideology, the second hidden dimension, a preoccupation with ends over means, is actively reinforced through physical education practices. Bain cites the objectification of the body, and the reduction of health to functional issues such as physical fitness, as examples of this technocentric ideology in operation. The third dimension is social relations, and in particular what students learn through peer interaction in physical education classes. Bain draws on research that has focused on interaction between students in multiracial and mixed-sex classes to suggest that while physical educators have generally ignored the issues raised by racial mixing in schools, their practices continue to contribute to the maintenance of institutionalized patriarchal dominance. By highlighting meritocracy, technocracy and racial and gender relations as hidden dimensions of physical education programmes, Bain is able to demonstrate how structured practices in society at large manifest themselves in physical education programmes and classes.

The next four chapters by Kirk, Dewar, Gore and Evans focus on teachers and their relationship to and role in the construction of knowledge in physical education. In Chapter 3 David Kirk documents the fate of gymnastics in British physical education discourse between 1945 and 1965 in an attempt to show how the form and content of physical education programmes were negotiated and defined by rival coalitions working within a range of social and cultural forces. Kirk highlights the ways in which the definition of the subject was contested by two rival factions, one predominantly female and the other male. Men did not begin to enter physical education teaching in substantial numbers until the years immediately following the Second World War. Until that time women constituted the vast majority of trained physical educators and held a virtual monopoly over the standards and qualifications required for entrance to the profession. The introduction of mass secondary schooling through the Butler Education Act of 1944 created a demand for trained teachers that easily surpassed supply, and many men embarked on physical education teaching careers straight from the army. Their entrance into the profession in such relatively large numbers and in such an abrupt fashion had a dramatic impact on physical education, and initiated a clash of ideologies that was to influence the way physical education was conceived, defined and practised in the years that followed the war. No one issue reflected the fracture between female and male versions of physical education better than the question of how gymnastics should be taught. The female faction, strongly influenced by the work of Rudolf Laban, promoted child-centred educational gymnastics, while the males advocated an appoach to gymnastics influenced by competitive sport and the new 'scientific' knowledge relating to fitness and skill development. The ensuing debate was conducted at a high level of emotional intensity and with rancour, revealing a profession riven by fundamental disputes over first principles, of what their subject was and how it should be taught. Kirk argues that the male definition became the dominant one because it was consistent with broader educational, political and cultural trends that were rising to ascendancy in the 1950s. He suggests, in addition, that there is much contemporary physical educators can learn about curriculum debates from this example, particularly in relation to the contested nature of curriculum change and structuring of this process by wider social and cultural forces.

The rise of scientific functionalism and the extension of patriarchal dominance in physical education were not confined to post-war Britain, but have been a significant force in contemporary professional preparation programmes in North America also. Alison Dewar (Chapter 4) draws on descriptive data from a case study of a Canadian university physical education programme to show how conceptions of pedagogy and 'really useful knowledge' were underscored by patriarchal and scientistic values that led to the further privileging of already privileged white, bourgeois males. She argues that both the new science of sports pedagogy and biobehavioural knowledge dominated the programme, combining to authorize and legitimate an unproblematic world-view, in which the purpose and practice of physical education are seen to be self-evident and factual. Dewar takes the case of the portrayal of gender as a biobehavioural variable in sports performance and a natural, genetic limitation for women as a potent example of this process, contrasting this with the less popular view among students presented in sociocultural courses of gender as a social construct that is itself complicit in the definition of successful sports performance. Within this context the students negotiated their own gender identities, and Dewar describes in detail the forms that emerged from this process of negotiation, each of which was ultimately circumscribed by patriarchal definitions of physical education and encapsulated in the term 'jock', even those of a female group of 'non-jocks'. Dewar argues that these students' experiences of their physical education programme and the patriarchal and scientistic conceptions of pedagogy that it conveyed must play a crucial part in shaping their own projections of what physical education is in their teaching.

In Chapter 5 Jennifer Gore's self-reflective study of a teacher preparation course in Australia elaborates the issues raised by Kirk and Dewar, and emphasizes the active role student teachers take in interpreting and reconstructing knowledge. Gore draws on her experience of teaching and researching an introductory course in physical education pedagogy to critique existing orientations to research on teaching in physical education. The course attempted to rework traditional ways of presenting physical education subject matter by locating this 'established' and 'authoritative' knowledge within an investigative, peer teaching mode. Through this Gore offers a sophisticated and complex account of teaching and learning to teach physical education that is able to accommodate the reality of multiple 'readings', which in themselves reflect social, cultural and political factors that have a bearing on this process. Attempting to move beyond the dominant technical orientation which emphasizes teaching skills in isolation from social, cultural and political factors, and the emergent inquiry orientation built on ideology critique which she suggests inclines towards vitriol and dogmatism, Gore develops the notion of 'pedagogy as text'. Through this notion she establishes the necessity of interpreting or reading social action in context and on the basis of particular subjectivities, which renders the possibility of generalized readings highly problematic. The diversity of readings of the text of the course by students revealed that conventional notions about physical education subject matter and generally accepted views of gender-appropriate activities and behaviour and values such as competitiveness and aggression became problematic for many of them. She further illustrates the notion of pedagogy as text in a detailed account of her attempts to research her own teaching, and shows how her original analyses of her teaching, framed within the inquiry orientation, led to a number of unwarranted or contentious assumptions. By reading the results of her research again, this time employing the notion of text, Gore argues that a more sophisticated, complex, but less certain and prescriptive account of the students' experiences of her course can be delivered, one that denies the possibility of a 'preferred' reading by focusing more squarely on the students' subjectivities.

Extending and elaborating Dewar's and Gore's investigations of knowledge and student teachers in tertiary programmes, John Evans (Chapter 6) focuses on the ways in which the abilities and career opportunities of physical education teachers and the status of the subject in schools have been influenced by recent developments in Britain both within and outside physical education. Evans locates his analysis in recent right-wing attacks on comprehensive schooling and the values it is supposed to promote such as equality of opportunity. The outcome of these attacks, he suggests, has been a widespread reappraisal of physical education in schools by physical educators and the emergence of two curriculum initiatives, health-related fitness and teaching games for understanding, which together form what he calls the 'new physical education'. While these initiatives appear to have the potential radically to alter traditional practices, built on patriarchal values and meritocratic ideals, Evans argues that they do little to change the status of physical education alongside other 'academic' subjects, or the existing power hierarchies in physical education departments which men dominate. Like Bain, Evans contends that these innovations are mired in individualistic notions of perseverance and determination, free will and choice, and within the health-related fitness literature in particular, that achieving lifetime fitness is ultimately the responsibility of the individual. Evans recognizes that the 'new physical education' is not a homogeneous phenomenon, and that there are elements within each innovation, such as a critique of excessive competition and elitism, which offer a radical challenge to traditional practices. But he suggests that these changes are largely concerned with meeting the abstracted needs of individuals rather than tackling the institutionalized and structured inequalities that lie behind individual pupils' dissatisfaction and recusance. Evans concludes that since the 'new physical education' is incapable of moving beyond a politically limited version of liberal individualism, definitions of teachers' abilities and opportunities are also likely to be hemmed in by voluntaristic and individualistic perspectives.

The chapters by Fitzclarence and Tinning, Sparkes and Colquhoun are concerned with trends and developments in physical education in Britain and Australia, and in particular with the processes of curriculum construction and appropriation at primary and secondary school levels.

In each case the authors amplify many of the issues raised in previous chapters, in particular the domination of scientific functionalism in school programmes and the social construction of knowledge in physical education. Lindsay Fitzclarence and Richard Tinning (Chapter 7) draw on their experiences as curriculum writers for the Victorian Certificate of Education (VCE) physical education course in Australia to outline some of the leading issues currently facing the development of physical education as a secondary school subject. They explain how the VCE initiative was inspired by a reconceptualization of the entire secondary school curriculum in train with greater retention rates among senior students and a consequent wider spread of ability and interest, and a commitment on behalf of the Victorian Labor Government to principles of equity and social justice. They add to this account a brief analysis of the ways in which physical activity and the body are increasingly presented, through advertising for instance, as metaphors for Australia's performance in the international market place and symbols of the qualities of corporate efficiency and competitiveness that are considered necessary to developing a 'winning edge'. Fitzclarence and Tinning show that the established physical education programme which the VCE course was to replace failed to meet many of the requirements for the VCE by virtue of its domination by propositional knowledge which drew almost entirely on scientific knowledge of the functioning of the body. In addition, while the previous programme had almost eliminated physical activity, most of the students attracted to study physical education were motorically competent males. While the course was formally and self-consciously mimetic of established 'academic' subjects, its domination by scientific functionalism led to an unreflective celebration and endorsement, rather than a critique, of contemporary representations of physical activity and the body. Fitzclarence and Tinning locate the production of the new VCE physical education course within this constellation of factors and forces, and argue that the curriculum writers' attempts to reunite theoretical and practical knowledge in physical education, to redress the imbalance of biologically-based knowledge by incorporating sociocultural elements, and to assist students to achieve a level of independence and freedom from reliance on 'authoritative' knowledge which had been at the root of the previous curriculum, each constitute profoundly political actions which are part of attempts to come to terms with the role of physical activity and physical education programmes in the current phase of capitalism. More than this, they argue that physical educators everywhere need to begin to critique the ways in which physical activity and sport are currently and increasingly being drafted into the service of the nation-state in the international capitalist market place, if values and qualities other than those determined by economic imperatives are to occupy a place in their teaching.

In a study of the micropolitics of curriculum change Andrew Sparkes (Chapter 8) shifts our attention from the system level and the curriculum writer to the school level and the attempts of one teacher to bring about change. Sparkes' major concern is to document in some detail the outcomes of a belief in the power of rational planning to bring about change. He draws on data from a study of a Head of Department's attempts to institute mixed-ability teaching in games and the inclusion of greater numbers of individual in place of team activities in his school programme. The Head of Department, 'Alex', encountered opposition to his plans, despite his aspirations to set out his case for change in a rational manner, and to provide a democratic forum for debate in staff meetings. In the face of his inability to persuade other teachers to his way of thinking Alex progressively resorted to the use of a range of political tactics to outmanoeuvre his opponents, including a selective definition of the terms of the debate in a way which advantaged Alex and disadvantaged his staff. While Alex finally won the day, Sparkes suggests that he lost the war, since there was innovation without change. Through his analysis Sparkes reveals the complexity of the process of curriculum change, and the need for sophisticated strategies that move beyond naive rationalistic, scientistic and apolitical models of change.

In Chapter 9 Derek Colquhoun takes us further into the practices of school physical education by examining images of healthism in physical education curriculum materials, extending Evans' analysis of the health-related fitness component of the 'new physical education' in Britain, and Bain's concerns over the technocentric nature of fitness and exercise initiatives in the United States. He argues that health has become an important cultural category in contemporary society, symbolizing normality, well-being and success. The view of health that is promoted through a variety of media including curriculum materials is one in which individual responsibility for the resolution of health and lifestyle problems is emphasized to the point where other causes of illness outside the individual's sphere of action are masked or trivialized. On the basis of an analysis of physical education materials and practices in schools Colquhoun argues that this reduction lies at the heart of health-based physical education initiatives. These initiatives draw on mechanistic analogies of the body's functioning and on biological knowledge. The net effect of this knowledge base, Colquhoun suggests, is to deflect attention from the broader social dimensions of health and illness, thus reinforcing the individualism at the centre of healthism and health-based physical education, and marking school physical education as a key site of production of healthism, a view of health as unproblematically achievable given 'responsible' behaviour by individuals, and an exaggerated belief in health as a metaphor for well-being in other areas of life.

While each of these chapters illustrates the diverse range of practical curriculum issues currently facing physical education, the continuities between them also suggest a certain commonality of experience in Britain, North America and Australia. In each it is difficult not to detect at least some rumblings of the various crises — environmental, political, economic, social — that are increasingly having an impact on our everyday lives in the present and shaping our thoughts and plans for the future. As we have gone to some lengths to stress in this introduction, physical education is a part of social life, and is probably more than ever before a key site for the production and legitimation of important cultural mores, values and symbols. In several chapters in this book authors have called for action on the part of physical educators, irrespective of whether they work in schools, colleges, universities or in the recreation or fitness sectors, that acknowledges the interconnectedness of physical education and culture and our responsibilities as professionals in this field to attend to matters that manifest themselves in our local situations, but which have their source in broader societal movements and trends. We are used to thinking of ourselves as largely autonomous from our colleagues who work in different sites, in schools, universities and so on. What the studies in this collection show quite clearly to the contrary is that the entire world of physical education consists of a number of 'separate' sites in a very limited sense only, and that each site forms a crucial part of a dynamic whole, which is itself interwoven into many other institutions in society. The issues confronting the profession today are common to all sites in which physical educators work, and developments in one unavoidably have consequences in others. If nothing else, this realization of our interdependence should encourage us to look beyond our own local concerns to seek out the threads that bind us together, and to begin to locate our work as physical educators in broader contexts than we invariably if unknowingly influence.

Notes

1 The debate over the 'educational status' of physical education has been a particular preoccupation of British philosophers and physical educationalists, but has nonetheless raised issues of relevance to physical education in other countries. The debate generated quite a large and diverse literature during the 1960s and 1970s that has yet to be brought together in a comprehensive overview. Some of the key texts are Carlisle (1969), Carr (1979, 1983a, 1983b), Thomp-

son (1980). The use here of the descriptor 'educational' in relation to a curriculum topic is consistent with its use within this body of literature, which was itself framed by the work of philosophers like Peters (1966). Peters' criteria for an 'educationally worthwhile activity' were based on a cognitivist view of school knowledge as an exclusively intellectual pursuit. For an extended discussion of some of this work in relation to physical education's educational status see Kirk (1988, pp. 43–81).

2 It is important to acknowledge that physical education's place in the school curriculum has been under threat in some countries, see e.g. Siedentop (1981), Crum (1982), Tinning (1988), Evans (1987).

3 Fitzclarence (1986) makes a very similar point about 'soft' methods of control. Drawing on an analysis of the rise of affluence in Japan since the Second World War, he points out the significance of corporeal and sports metaphors as concomitant with the process of commodity production. In this respect the body itself becomes a commodity, and its uses, shapes and activities are governed by the same logic that controls capitalist production.

4 Our formulation of this relationship between school knowledge and society has much in common with the position taken by Evans and Davies (1988).

5 See Johnson (1983) for a useful outline of the process of cultural production.

6 It is significant to note that much of the 'official discourse' in research on teaching in physical education that has championed micro-analysis has also presented a conservative view of change; see Kirk (1989), McKay, Gore and Kirk (in press) and the chapters by Dewar and Sparkes in this collection.

References

ARNOLD, P. (1979) *Meaning in Movement, Sport and Physical Education*. London: Heinemann.

BEST, D. (1978) *Philosophy and Human Movement*. London: Allen and Unwin.

CARLISLE, R. (1969) 'The Concept of Physical Education.' *Proceedings of the Philosophy of Education Society of Great Britain*, Vol. 3, January.

CARR, D. (1979) 'Aims of Physical Education.' *Physical Education Review*, 2 (2), 91–100.

CARR, D. (1983a) 'The Place of Physical Education in the School Curriculum.' *Momentum* 8 (1), 9–12.

CARR, D. (1983b) 'On Physical Education and Educational Significance.' *Momentum* 8 (3), 21–4.

CRAWFORD, R. (1986) 'A Cultural Account of 'Health': Control, Release and the Social Body,' in MCKINLEY, J. (Ed.), *Issues in the Political Economy of Health Care*, pp. 60–103. London: Tavistock.

CRUM, B. (1982) 'Over de gebruikswaarde van bewegingsonderwijs' ('Concerning the Usefulness of Physical Education'), NKS cahier 14, *Bewegen op school enwat daama?* Den Bosch: Nederlandse Katholieke Sportfederiate, 16–24.

EVANS, J. (1987) 'Teaching for Equality in Physical Education?' Paper presented at the Ethnography and Inequality Conference, St Hilda's College, Oxford, September.

EVANS, J. and DAVIES, B. (1988) 'Introduction: Teachers, Teaching and Control,' in EVANS, J. (Ed.), *Teachers, Teaching and Control in Physical Education*, pp. 1–19. Lewes: Falmer Press.

FITZCLARENCE, L. (1986) 'Physical Education and the Controlled Society.' *ACHPER National Journal*, 112, 25–6.

FITZCLARENCE, L. (1987) 'The Physical Education Curriculum: The Right Direction?' *Education and Society*, 5 (1 and 2), 79–85.

FOUCAULT, M. (1980) *Power/Knowledge: Selected Interviews and Other Writings, 1972–1977*. Edited by Colin Gordon. Brighton: Harvester Press.

HABERMAS, J. (1972) *Knowledge and Human Interests*. London: Heinemann.

HALL, S. (1983) 'The Great Moving Right Show,' in HALL, S. and JACQUES, M. (Eds), *The Politics of Thatchersim*, pp. 19–39. London: Lawrence and Wishart.

JOHNSON, R. (1983) 'What Is Cultural Studies Anyway?' *Anglistica*, 26 (1/2), 7–31.

KEMMIS, S. (1983) 'Getting Our Thinking Straight! Three Views of Education.' *Advise*, 37, April, 1–3.

KIRK, D. (1988) *Physical Education and Curriculum Study: A Critical Introduction*. London: Croom Helm.

KIRK, D. (1989) 'The Orthodoxy in RT-PE and the Research/Practice Gap: A Critique and an Alternative View.' *Journal of Teaching in Physical Education*, 8 (2), 123–30.

MCKAY, J., GORE, J. and KIRK, D. (in press) 'Beyond the Limits of Technocratic Physical Education.' *Quest*.

PETERS, R. (1966) *Ethics and Education*. London: Allen and Unwin.

SAUNDERS, J. (1985) Guest Editorial. *ACHPER National Journal*, 108, 2–3.

SIEDENTOP, D. (1981) 'Physical Education: An Endangered Species,' in *Teaching Physical Education Reader*, pp. 30–7. Geelong, Deakin University, 1987.

THOMPSON, K. (1980) 'Culture, Sport and the Curriculum. *British Journal of Educational Studies*, 28 (2), 136–41.

TINNING, R. (1984) Social Critique in Physical Education.' *ACHPER National Journal*, 103, 10.

TINNING, R. (1988) 'The "Good Ship Physical Education": A View from the Crows Nest.' *Plenary Papers*, 17th ACHPER National Biennial Conference, Canberra, January, 10–14.

Chapter 2

A Critical Analysis of the Hidden Curriculum in Physical Education

Linda L. Bain

The daily life of physical education teachers and students is filled with routines: dressing for activity, taking attendance, forming teams, doing warmups, practising skills, playing games. While the substance of the lesson changes from week to week, the routines and the interactions which accompany them often retain remarkable consistency. The term 'hidden curriculum' has been used extensively in educational literature since the early 1970s to refer to 'what is taught to students by the institutional regularities, by the routines and rituals of teacher/student lives' (Weis, 1982, p. 3). The concept of the hidden curriculum has been analyzed in relation to physical education (Bain, 1975, 1985a; Dodds, 1983, 1985) and has served as a useful framework for interpreting research on the operational curriculum.

Contemporary discourse about curriculum includes recognition that curricula can be analyzed at many levels and from many positions. McCutcheon provides the following definition: 'By curriculum I mean what students have an opportunity to learn in school, through both the hidden and overt curriculum and what they do not have an opportunity to learn because certain matters were not included in the curriculum' (McCutcheon, 1982, p. 19). Gore, in Chapter 5 in this volume, suggests that one cannot talk about *the* hidden curriculum because pedagogical practices have different meanings depending on the position of the interpreter. Nevertheless, the value of the term 'hidden curriculum' is that it draws attention to interpretations that have received little recognition in explicit curriculum discourse and which may serve as alternatives to what Gore calls the 'preferred meanings'. This chapter will examine such interpretations of the curriculum in physical education in the United States of America.

US schools explicitly endorse the principle of merit: all students should be provided with equal opportunity, be encouraged to work hard and be rewarded for their achievements. Differences in outcome are expected but are viewed as the inevitable result of variations in ability and motivation. The belief is that the system is fair as long as equal opportunity is guaranteed. However, critics have suggested that beneath the 'facade of meritocracy' lies a system which reproduces and legitimates existing economic inequalities (Bowles and Gintis, 1976, p. 103). Others, while sharing a concern about the political dimensions of education, have cautioned against a deterministic view of education which ignores the contradictions and contestation which occur within the school (Apple, 1982). A more complete understanding of how ideologies work in schools requires examination of day-to-day school life (Apple and Weis, 1983). This chapter will draw upon observational research in physical education classes in the USA to examine ideological issues. Pedagogical researchers in the US have conducted extensive observational research in school physical education programmes. Much of that work has been based on a natural science model and has attempted to identify effective teaching behaviours. However, qualitative studies describing the curriculum in action or 'life in the gym' provide a basis for examination of ideological issues.

US schools provide instruction in physical education for all students as well as interscholastic athletic competition for highly skilled performers. General curriculum requirements are established by each of the fifty states but local school districts develop the specific curriculum. Most states require physical education, but the number of years of instruction and the amount of time per week vary greatly among the states. In the elementary school (ages 5–11) most children have physical education two or three days per week. The instruction may be provided by a physical education specialist, who frequently travels to two or more schools, or by a classroom teacher with a degree in elementary education. In the middle school (ages 12–13) and high school (ages 14–18) students are more likely to have daily physical education taught by physical education specialists, but that instruction frequently ends after ninth or tenth grade (ages 14–15). Interscholastic athletic programmes generally begin in middle school but may begin in the upper elementary grades. Most schools offer a range of sport teams for boys and girls. Because of the large number of coaches needed, the teams are coached both by physical education teachers and by other teachers with an interest in sport, but generally no specialized training in coaching. Athletics plays an important role in the social life of the American high school (Coleman, 1965) and many events, especially boys' basketball and football games, draw large crowds. Coaches devote considerable time to their athletic duties and their job security is more dependent on their coaching success than their teaching performance

(Sage, 1989). Many students, especially boys, also participate in community youth sports programmes conducted by volunteer coaches.

The analysis in this chapter will rely primarily on research conducted in physical education classes, but some reference will be made to research conducted in athletic and youth sport programmes. Research on the curriculum in action is based on observation of day-to-day practices which characterize life in the school or, in this case, the physical education programme. Rarely have researchers specified the theoretical perspective underlying the work. Some of the studies appear to be derived from a functionalist perspective which assumes that implicit values learned in school prepare students for participation in adult society. Much of the research seems to be based on an interactionist or interpretive perspective which describes patterns of behaviour and examines the meanings that teachers and students attach to those experiences. A few studies have adopted a critical theory stance and have attempted to examine how meanings and values are negotiated in physical education programmes and to identify opportunities for transformation of social reality. This chapter will not attempt to describe each of the studies completed since such a review is available elsewhere (Bain, 1989). Rather this work will analyze three themes which emerge from studies of the hidden curriculum in physical education: meritocracy, technocentric ideology, and the construction of social relations.

Meritocracy

Sport and physical education provide a complex and sometimes contradictory picture of the meritocratic ideology basic to society in the USA. Competitive sport programmes are highly visible as extracurricular activities of the school and seem to function as symbols of meritocratic principles despite historical inequities based on race and gender. Coaches in interscholastic athletic settings and community youth sport programmes emphasize effort and achievement (Bain, 1978; Coakley, 1980; Dubois, 1986; Fine, 1987; Harris, 1983, 1984). Within these settings two definitions of achievement emerge: winning and losing, and knowing how to play the game (Harris, 1983). Although the relative emphasis on each varies across competitive sport situations, the overall focus on achievement is greater than that found in physical education classes.

One of the apparent contradictions in physical education programmes is that despite a subject matter that involves competitive sport, relatively little emphasis is placed on achievement. Research indicates that achievement receives little attention in the instructional planning of physical education teachers (Goc-Karp and Zakrajsek, 1987; Placek, 1983, 1984). Teachers do not focus on student learning, but direct their planning to provide for student enjoyment and participation and avoid incidents of misbehaviour. Placek (1983, p. 49) suggests that the teachers 'seemed to define the teaching situation in terms of keeping students busy, happy, and good.' Observational research in physical education classes also reveals a lack of emphasis on learning and achievement in instructional and evaluation practices (Bain, 1976, 1978; Tousignant and Siedentop, 1983; Veal, 1988b).

Physical education programmes seem to be characterized by emphasis on order and control rather than achievement. Teachers tend to evaluate their success and non-success in teaching based on student participation and enjoyment and the absence of student non-compliance (Arrighi and Young, 1985; Placek and Dodds, 1988). This affects the activities they choose to teach (Placek, 1984) and class organization and regulations (Bain, 1976, 1978). The emphasis on order and control also influences teacher interactions with students. Based on his research on teacher expectations, Martinek (1983, p. 65) suggests that 'teachers appeared to have a more positive bias toward students who were conforming, cooperative, orderly, and high-achieving.' This focus on order and control is accompanied by an emphasis on the importance of effort. Perceptions of student effort affect teacher expectations (Martinek, 1983) and their interactions with students (Tousignant and Siedentop, 1983). Evaluation procedures tend to focus on student participation and effort (Imwold, Rider and Johnson, 1982; Kneer, 1986; Veal, 1988b). Teachers judge their teaching success based largely on student motivation, interest and involvement (Placek and Dodds, 1988). In summary, teachers plan activities based on their perceptions of student interests. Students are expected to exhibit compliance by participating in the activities. However, participation is not enough; a successful student must demonstrate effort and enthusiasm.

The greater emphasis on achievement in athletics and the provision of more instruction and other resources for these programmes than for physical education suggest what Dodds (1986) labelled 'motor elitism'. Skilful performance is a valued commodity, but only high ability students are entitled to quality instructional and competitive programmes. Physical education programmes for the ordinary students are designed to keep them 'busy, happy, and good'. The physical education programmes appear to be more recreational than instructional, but tend to be adult-controlled and rule-governed, lacking the player autonomy and action-centred qualities characteristic of informal play (Coakley, 1980). For this reason physical education programmes seem to regulate and constrain play even in the absence of instructional goals. Such a two-tiered system seems to reinforce the ideology of meritocracy without providing equal opportunity to develop physical skills or fitness. Bowles and Gintis (1976, p. 107) question the validity of limiting access to educational programmes to the most able based on the assumption that they will be most capable of benefiting themselves and society. Ironically, they use physical exercise to illustrate their point; 'education is something like physical exercise: some people are more talented than others, but all benefit equally from athletic involvement and instruction.' The physical education programme which presumably provides broad access to instruction seems instead to teach the importance of effort in the absence of noticeable benefits.

Student responses to such expectations vary (Bain, 1985b; Griffin, 1983, 1984, 1985a; Kollen, 1983; Tousignant and Siedentop, 1983). In some cases students put forth effort because they enjoy the activity. In other cases students learn impression management; that is, they learn to fake participation and perhaps even effort and enjoyment. Other students engage in strategic non-compliance which may include modifying the teacher-planned activity or engaging in 'off-task' behaviour. Some of this off-task behaviour may be viewed by the teacher as deviant and be negatively sanctioned. Other instances may be what King (1983) labels illicit play involving unsanctioned interactions that oppose the explicit rules and expectations of work; examples include whispering, poking other children and clowning around. Teachers evaluate student effort based on informal observations of student behaviours such as 'hustle during a game, getting to class early, working on skills instead of talking to friends, giving positive verbal indications of effort, not hiding during games, and being energetic and enthusiastic' (Veal, 1988b, p. 333). These assessments, which form the basis for daily interactions with students and for the assignment of grades, serve to keep resistance within limits. Students generally seem to accept the privileges and attention bestowed on athletes. Research indicates that being an athlete is a primary source of status for boys, and to a lesser extent for girls, within the American high school (Coleman, 1965; Eitzen, 1975). Thus while students may resist the meaninglessness of the physical education programme, most (but not all) appear to believe that athletes have earned their higher status based on a meritocratic system which rewards outstanding performance.

Teachers as well as students may demonstrate resistance to meritocracy. The data suggest that some physical educators reject universalistic values which judge all students by the same criteria. These teachers may emphasize effort and improvement as indicators which take into account individual differences in ability. Earls (1981) found that physical education teachers who had been identified as 'distinctive' had abandoned an 'athletic mentality' and evidenced unconditional positive regard for children of all types. Veal (1988a, 1988b) found that teachers individualized evaluations of student achievement based on effort, ability, improvement and past experience. These teachers seemed to adopt a common-sense version of attribution theory (Brawley and Roberts, 1984) in which they saw effort as the factor influencing achievement over which they and their students had some control. Teachers assume that if students participate and 'try harder', they will learn. If teachers design lessons which engage students, learning will follow even though specific instructional goals have not been identified. This research suggests that some physical education teachers, rather than endorsing meritocratic principles which evaluate and reward all students according to the same criteria, have adopted a perspective which emphasizes individual differences. Physical educators may be permitted or even encouraged by school authorities to adopt this humanistic stance because of the marginal status of physical education within the school (Goc-Karp, Kim and Skinner, 1985; O'Sullivan, 1989; Templin and Schempp, 1989). Since physical education may not be viewed as essential to the academic mission of the school, normative evaluation of student performance is seen as unimportant and many schools have adopted pass-fail grading in physical education.

However, the emphasis within physical education on effort, improvement and individual differences has not constituted a serious challenge to the meritocratic ideology of the school. Physical educators have not initiated an attempt to change normative grading practices in other subject areas. The result seems to be that the emphasis on effort rather than achievement in physical education does not challenge the overall meritocratic principles of the school but reinforces the marginal status of the field and the underlying assumptions of mind-body dualism. Because physical education is viewed as unimportant, procedures which would not be permitted in athletics or academic subjects have been allowed. Such procedures have had little effect in changing either the practice or the ideology of the school. In part this lack of impact may be due to the technocentric ideology of the school which limits most educational discourse to questions of efficiency, not fundamental values.

Technocentric Ideology

The technological society tends to be sustained by an ideology in which ends or goals are taken-for-granted and unexamined and attention is focused on the development of increasingly effective and efficient means for achieving the goals. Within such a technocentric ideology people are viewed as 'human resources' who are educated so as to maximize their productivity, especially their economic productivity. Education is judged by the technological criteria of efficiency and effectiveness in producing measurable outcomes (Eisner, 1985). The political, moral, ethical and aesthetic value of the goals and of the educational process remain unexamined. For this reason technocentric education tends to reproduce rather than challenge existing social arrangements. In an analysis of technocentric ideology in physical education Charles (1979) suggests that physical educators view 'man [sic] as machine' and aim to produce the most efficient machine measured in terms of performance. One result is that the body may become reified and be viewed as an instrument and object for manipulation (Broekhoff, 1972). The body tends to become a commodity to be exchanged for admiration, security or economic gain. The basis for this exchange differs by gender; for women, appearance of the body is the valued commodity, while for men, action and performance tend to be valued (Orbach, 1978).

Much of the analysis of technocentric ideology in physical education has focused on the production of top level performers in sport and dance (Blumenfeld-Jones, 1987; Kirkland, 1986; Lapchick, 1986). The picture that is drawn is that of the coach or the choreographer treating the athlete or dancer as an instrument with which to achieve the desired performance. In many cases the participant learns to view his or her body as an instrument to be trained, manipulated and in some cases drugged for the sake of performance. These events present a strong ideological statement to the general population and especially to aspiring athletes and dancers. However, they have little direct relevance to physical education classes because of the relative lack of emphasis on achievement and performance in those classes. The area of the physical education curriculum in which technocentric ideology seems to have a more direct impact is exercise and fitness. Because fitness provides an outcome that is easily defined and measured, it often provides the central justification for physical education programmes in a technological society.

The stated goal of most exercise programmes is to use exercise as a means to enhance health. Consistent with technocentric ideology, the meanings and definitions of health are not critically examined. A healthy body is often equated with performance or appearance. The social construction of images of the body and the relationship of those images to gender relations are not explored (Turner, 1984). Factors relating to gender, race and class differences in body size (Bain, 1986) are rarely discussed. Little attention is given to the risks of obsessive concern with body size manifested in eating disorders or compulsive exercise. Students are not introduced to debates within the medical profession regarding whether moderate overweight or constant dieting is the greater health hazard (*Harvard Medical School Newsletter*, 1986). Health and fitness remain unexamined educational goals.

Recent literature distinguishes between the process of physical activity and the product of physical fitness and debates the relative health benefits of each (Meredith, 1988; Simons-Morton, O'Hara, Simons-Morton and Parcel, 1987). Despite recommendations that emphasis be placed on participation not performance, many exercise programmes continue to equate fitness with health and to define fitness as performance on a fitness test. The appearance dimension is incorporated by inclusion of a body composition measure in the test (usually a per cent body fat estimate based on skinfold measures). The view that a physically active person with mediocre performance and moderate overweight might be healthy is rejected without debate by most physical educators. Observational studies confirm the dominance of a technocentric view of health and fitness. Research in exercise classes for college students and adults indicates that a high proportion of the participants are female and that their concerns often centre on appearance rather than health (Bain, 1985b; Bain, Wilson and Chaikind, 1989; Kenen, 1987; Kotarba and Bentley, 1985). The body is viewed as an object to be slenderized and toned in order to increase its value. Fitness is often equated with appearance, and perceptions of physical attractiveness are closely associated with self-esteem, especially for females (Fox, 1988). Large women in exercise programmes report feelings of embarrassment and concerns about being judged by others and often drop out (Bain, 1985b; Bain *et al.*, 1989). Measures of fitness performance and especially of body fatness are seen not as providing useful information but as a public confirmation of one's lack of worth.

Instructors in exercise programmes may use varying strategies to motivate students to achieve desired levels of fitness. Some programmes, especially commercial programmes aimed at women, make a direct appeal to concerns about appearance (Kenen, 1987). Some employ a technical-rational perspective that assumes that information will change behaviour and ignores the subjective-affective concerns of students (Bain, 1985b). Others imply a moral obligation to maintain health and fitness and use guilt to motivate (Kotarba and Bentley, 1985). In elementary and secondary school programmes fitness awards have been used to motivate students. Recently questions have been raised about these awards, but the debate has been framed as a technological question of effectiveness, not as a moral and ethical question of values (Corbin, Whitehead and Lovejoy, 1988).

The language employed in technological discussions of health and fitness has been limited to an instrumental perspective of using physical activity as a means to an end. Increasing attention is being given to providing for enjoyment of activity in order to increase voluntary participation (Meredith, 1988). However, even those who have proposed more emphasis on enjoyment and fun have seen movement as a means to an extrinsic goal, not as an intrinsically important activity. Although a few physical educators have expressed concerns about the instrumental perspective and mind/body dualism (Kleinman, 1986), the possibility that movement is not only a means to health but a form of healthful and integrated living has received little attention within a 'fitness' discourse dominated by a technocentric ideology.

Because issues of health and fitness have been viewed as technological concerns and not value questions, the arena has been dominated by experts in physiology, measurement and psychology. Their discourse assumes a positivistic stance of objectivity, but Vertinsky (1985, p. 73) suggests that health promotion programmes may be characterized as 'imposing values packaged in scientific wrapping'. Pellegrino (1981, p. 373) cautions not to confuse technical authority with moral authority, saying 'experts have no special prerogative entitling them to make value judgements for the rest of humankind.' Ingham (1985) suggests that the framing of health issues in terms of personal lifestyle diverts attention from political issues regarding the state's responsibilities for health care. Despite these efforts to open a moral and political dialogue, there is little indication that the technocentric ideology at the centre of the fitness movement is being critically examined or challenged by most physical educators. This may reflect, in part, the conservatism of those who select a career in physical education (Sage, 1980). In addition, the fitness movement and its association with preventive medicine may provide a source of prestige for a field with marginal status. The fitness movement also represents an expanding industry whose profiles depend on marketing healthy lifestyles to individual consumers (Ellis, 1988). This expansion of the fitness industry has provided new career opportunities for physical educators at a time when there is an oversupply of physical education teachers. This growing industry invests heavily in promoting an ideology which will enable it to market apparel, equipment and services. Because the status of the field of physical education is closely linked to the fitness movement, those in the field have tended to be uncritical supporters of the movement.

Social Relations

The definition of curriculum as what students have an opportunity to learn includes what they learn from their peers. An important aspect of the hidden curriculum is the way in which social relations are constructed within the school setting. Patterns of interaction among students and between teacher and students constitute social practices which may reproduce or challenge existing power relations. Although most of the observational research in physical education classes has focused on technical aspects of instruction, a few studies have examined patterns of social interaction based on race or gender. Two early studies of the hidden curriculum in physical education examined patterns of interaction in multiracial settings. Tindall (1975) observed boys' basketball classes and an interclass tournament in a community with Mormon and Native American students. He found that the style of play differed between the two cultures. In games where the players were predominantly Native American the games were structures of individual performances, while Mormon games were strategic organizations of group effort. His study suggests that the meanings attached to specific activities are culturally structured. Wang (1977) conducted a participant observation study of a fifth grade physical education class in a school in North Carolina that recently had been racially integrated. She discovered a teacher-sponsored curriculum and a separate, contradictory student-imposed curriculum. The teacher-sponsored curriculum promoted an ideal of integrated, democratic living in which rules of individual worth were tempered with emphasis upon cooperation, equality and social responsibility. The student-imposed curriculum revealed patterns of discrimination based on gender, race, social class, personality and skills. Skilful sport performance had a property-like nature in the student society. Wang suggested that more active instruction in skills might be the most effective way to counter discrimination.

Despite the issues raised by these early studies and the increasing number of multiracial schools in the USA, no additional research examining such settings was published for almost a decade. Griffin's (1985c) study of an urban, multiracial physical education programme found that white, middle-class teachers received little help in learning to deal with student diversity and felt powerless to control contextual factors which affected their teaching. Cultural, racial and gender differences in student behaviours results in a complex pattern of diversity which teachers found overwhelming. Despite the difficult circumstances, teachers tended to blame themselves for not implementing the type of programme viewed as desirable. The response of the physical education profession to multiracial diversity and racism within the USA seems to be to ignore the issue. Despite the high rate of participation by blacks in competitive sport, the physical education profession has remained primarily white and middle-class. Teachers are given little preparation for teaching in multi-racial settings, and teaching conditions in many urban physical education programmes are poor (Locke and Griffin, 1986). Efforts to improve school physical education programmes tend to focus on improving teachers' pedagogical skills or redesigning the curriculum rather than addressing contextual constraints. This seems to ignore the political nature of institutionalized racism.

The topic of gender relations in physical education has received more attention than race, perhaps because women are substantially represented in the profession while blacks and hispanics are not. Until the 1970s physical education programmes in the USA were generally segregated by sex, although boys and girls might be taught together in the primary grades. The content of the two programmes differed based on perceptions of gender-appropriate activities. Men and women teachers attended different teacher preparation programmes and tended to differ in programme emphasis and teaching styles (Spears and Swanson, 1978). After the passage of Title IX in 1972 and its implementation in physical education and sport in 1978 physical education programmes were required to be co-educational with the exception of participation in contact sports. While separate athletic programmes for boys and girls were permitted, the programmes were required to provide equal support and opportunity. The effects of Title IX on school physical education and teacher education programmes have been dramatic. Athletic programmes for girls have expanded. Many school physical education programmes are now co-educational. However, that aspect of the law has been met with resistance by teachers who found it difficult to implement and resented the arbitrary nature of mandated change. Most university physical education programmes are now co-educational, and separate men's and women's physical education departments have been merged.

The recent merger of programmes does not imply that issues of sex equity have been resolved. The traditional definition of sport as a male domain continues to predominate (Theberge, 1985). Although increased sport participation by women has challenged male domination, women's quest for equality in sport remains contested and ambiguous (Messner, 1988). Co-educational physical education classes constitute a relatively new set of practices in which relationships between gender and sport are being negotiated. Observational research provides an important source of information about the construction of gender relations in these classes. Despite the considerable attention given to Title IX and gender issues,

Table 1. Participation Patterns of Middle School Students

| Gymnastics[1] | | Team Sports | |
Boys	Girls	Boys[2]	Girls[3]
1 Serious	1 Serious	1 Machos	1 Athletes
2 Frivolous	2 Exploratory	2 Junior machos	2 JV players
3 Reluctant	3 Reluctant	3 Nice guys	3 Cheerleaders
		4 Invisible players	4 Femmes fatales
		5 Wimps	5 Lost souls
			6 System beaters

Sources: 1 Griffin (1983).
2 Griffin (1985a).
3 Griffin (1984).

relatively little observational research has been conducted. This is in part a result of pedagogical researchers' concentration on teaching effectiveness research. In addition, the dominance of the liberal feminist perspective focused attention on girls' and women's access to sport and physical education, not on how meanings and social relations were negotiated within those settings (Boutilier and SanGiovanni, 1983). The major piece of observational research in this area was a three-month case study examining a co-educational middle school physical education programme in a white, middle-class community in New England conducted by Griffin (1983, 1984, 1985a, 1985b). Based on observations and interviews with teachers, Griffin classified student participation patterns in gymnastics and team sports classes (see Table 1). Her observations revealed considerable variation in participation both within and between sexes. Participation style seemed to be affected by the nature of the activity, personal characteristics such as size and skill and the reactions of other students.

Patterns of interaction among the students seemed to be heavily influenced by gender. The most frequent boy-to-girl interaction was verbal or physical 'hassling' (Griffin, 1983). Girls rarely initiated interactions with boys and generally responded to hassling by acquiescing, ignoring or separating from the boys. Interactions among boys tended to be physical and combative, with much public clowning. In contrast, girls' interactions with each other were mostly cooperative, verbal and private. The interactions among students differed based on the participation styles of the particular students, but the aggressive actions of boys and the non-assertive behaviour of girls were the characteristic patterns observed. There were examples of resistance to the pattern of male domination, particularly among girls with higher skill levels, but participation in co-educational instruction did not change the overall pattern of male domination. The interaction patterns exhibited in the physical education setting did not differ substantially from those in other instructional settings (Everhart, 1983). However, the research indicated that assumptions that co-educational physical education would change traditional gender relations were naive (Griffin, 1989). The research also revealed a need to understand how teachers as well as students understand gender. Teachers tended to respond differently to the different groups of students (Griffin, 1985b). Even if there were only a few 'machos', 'junior machos' and 'wimps' in a class, they received most of the teacher's attention because they were involved in more class disruption. The teachers believed that the wimps, who were the most visibly ridiculed by other students, brought the teasing on themselves. On occasion teachers attempted to distribute participation among students or to intervene in inequitable student interactions. These efforts produced changes in student behaviour, but repeated reminders were required to sustain the changes. Teachers expressed reservations about whether or not student sex typical behaviour could be changed and viewed non-conforming behaviour as a problem. Griffin (1989) has recently suggested that efforts to attain sex equity by mixing boys and girls in co-educational classes and training teachers to use different methods were simplistic and ineffective. She states that 'though grouping by abilities, using a variety of teaching styles, avoiding sexist language, and restructuring game play all are excellent teaching strategies, they also are superficial changes without an accompanying shift in how teachers conceptualize gender and the role of physical education and sport in gender construction.' There is little indication that the underlying conceptualizations of gender or sport are changing in physical education programmes. Patriarchy and the oppression of women are supported ideologically not only by gender differentiation but by compulsive heterosexual relations (Rich, 1980). Femininity and masculinity are socially constructed gender ideologies which serve to constrain individual choices. The reactions of teachers and peers to the 'wimps' and 'overaggressive' girls illustrate the power of these constraints. The gendered social structures in physical education and sport affect the lives of both men and women while contributing to the maintenance of institutionalized heterosexual relations and a sexual division of labour that is the foundation of patriarchal power (Hall, 1988).

Critical Pedagogy

Schooling is not merely an academic experience, it is an intensive experience in institutional living (Silberman, 1971). The routines and rituals of daily life in the school constitute important social practices which communicate basic principles and assumptions about the culture. The messages are powerful because they are pervasive and continuously repeated. The fact that the messages remain unspoken and unacknowledged may make them even more powerful by making them seem natural and inevitable. The behaviour of teachers and students is often the expression of tacit beliefs that are so 'taken-for-granted' that they cannot be recognized or verbalized. A major value of the research on the hidden curriculum is that it may provide a mirror in which physical educators can see their own programmes. The hidden curriculum in physical education seems to endorse a meritocratic ideology in which status is dependent on effort and ability. Consistent with this view, quality instructional and competitive experiences are provided only for the highly skilled athletes while other students are urged to try harder. This meritocratic ideology is complemented by a technocentric ideology in which ends or goals are unexamined and attention is focused on the development of increasingly effective means for achieving the goals. This technocentric perspective views the body as an instrument to be trained and manipulated for the sake of performance or appearance. Images of the body and social relations within physical education classes differ by gender and race and reproduce practices which contradict the assumptions of equal opportunity underlying the meritocratic ideology.

Changing the hidden curriculum is a difficult task because it requires changing behaviour that is habitual and reflects deeply held beliefs. The task often involves transforming not merely the programme or the school but challenging existing social conditions which contradict principles of democracy and justice. This is not easy, but as Giroux (1981, p. 218) states, 'while it would be naive and misleading to claim that schools alone can create the conditions for social change, it would be equally naive to argue that working in schools does not matter.' Research on the lived culture of the school reveals contradictions and resistance that can serve as the starting point for emancipatory education. Emancipatory education is based on the belief that education is a dynamic process in which students and teachers are active agents in the creation of the social conditions of their lives (Greene, 1978). Within the constraints of culture, context and biography, individuals have the power of choice. The actions they choose have the potential to modify the constraints. That is, people, individually or collectively, can reinterpret experience in order to change their circumstances and possibilities. Within such a conception the goal of education is to encourage critical reflection and self-awareness, thus empowering teachers and students to create a better, more just society. Emancipatory pedagogy requires that students be included in critical discourse in which assertions about knowledge and values are viewed as problematic (Cherryholmes, 1988). The basic premise of proposals for critical pedagogy in physical education is that teachers and students should examine social issues related to sport and physical education and question taken-for-granted assumptions and practices. However, few examples of such pedagogy can be cited, especially in elementary and secondary school physical education.

Two potential models for critical pedagogy in physical education are available in the literature. Hellison (1973, 1978, 1985) has developed and disseminated a model for social development in physical education in which students are encouraged to be reflective, but his work focuses on individual development rather than social change. Some of his work with delinquency-prone youth (DeBusk and Hellison, 1989; Hellison, 1978) could be interpreted as encouraging adjustment to the existing social system rather than criticism of the system. However, his model has the potential to be extended to reflect a critical stance. The advantage of using Hellison's model for developing a critical pedagogy is that his work is field-based and therefore has high credibility with teachers. A second model which has the potential to serve as the basis for critical pedagogy in physical education is action research. Action research is a collaborative, participatory process in which participants attempt to improve a situation by improving their understanding of what is occurring. Although most examples of action research in physical education have related to the pre-service and in-service education of teachers, the method could be used to foster critical discourse in physical education classes (Bain, 1988). However, Grundy (1987) cautions that action research which seeks more efficient ways of reaching objectives without examining the goals themselves may be technological, not critical. If action research is used as a basis for critical pedagogy, participants in the research process must examine goals as well as the means for achieving them. The work of Bain, Wilson and Chaikind (1989) with exercise for overweight women represented an effort to employ such an action research model.

In a discussion of approaches to critical pedagogy a word of caution seems necessary. A focus on pedagogical change creates a risk that the political nature of the current reality will be ignored. Educational reformers often portray teachers as the source of problems in the school system and direct their reforms at the improvement of teacher performance. Critical theorists need to avoid this trap of blaming the teachers and to work with teachers to empower them to effect changes in the social structure of schools. Griffin (1985c, p. 165) suggests, 'if there is to be real hope for change, it lies not in finding the right pedagogical stuff but in acting on the right political stuff.'

References

APPLE, M.W. (1982) *Education and Power*. Boston, Mass.: Routledge and Kegal Paul.

APPLE, M.W. and WEIS, L. (1983) *Ideology and Practice in Schooling*. Philadelphia, Pa: Temple University Press.

ARRIGHI, M. and YOUNG, J. (1985) 'Teachers' Perceptions about Effective and Successful Teaching.' *Journal of Teaching in Physical Education*, 6 (2), 122–35.

BAIN, L.L. (1975) 'The Hidden Curriculum in Physical Education.' *Quest*, 24, 92–101.

BAIN, L.L. (1976) 'Description of the Hidden Curriculum in Secondary Physical Education.' *Research Quarterly*, 47, 154–60.

BAIN, L.L. (1978) 'Differences in Values Implicit in Teaching and Coaching Behaviors.' *Research Quarterly*, 49, 5–11.

BAIN, L.L. (1985a) 'The Hidden Curriculum Re-examined.' *Quest*, 37, 145–53.

BAIN, L.L. (1985b) 'A Naturalistic Study of Students' Responses to an Exercise Class.' *Journal of Teaching in Physical Education*, 5, 2–12.

BAIN, L.L. (1986) 'Issues of Gender, Race and Class in Health Promotion Programs.' Paper presented at the 12th Conference on Research on Women and Education, Washington, D.C., November.

BAIN, L.L. (1988) 'Beginning the Journey: Agenda for 2001.' *Quest*, 40 (2), 96–106.

BAIN, L.L. (1989) 'Implicit Values in Physical Education,' in TEMPLIN, T.J. and SCHEMPP, P.G. (Eds), *Socialization into Physical Education: Learning to Teach*, pp. 289–314. Indianapolis, Ind.: Benchmark Press.

BAIN, L.L., WILSON, T. and CHAIKIND, E. (1989) 'Participant Perceptions of Exercise Programs for Overweight Women.' *Research Quarterly for Exercise and Sport*, 60 (2), 134–43.

BLUMENFELD-JONES, D.S. (1987) 'Dilemmas of Detachment: Educating Dancers,' in CARNES, M. and STUECK, P. (eds), *Proceedings of the Fifty Curriculum Theory Conference*. Athens, Ga: University of Georgia.

BOUTILIER, M. and SANGIOVANNI, L. (1983) *The Sporting Woman*. Champaign, Ill.: Human Kinetics Publishers.

BOWLES, S. and GINTIS, H. (1976) *Schooling in Capitalist America*. New York: Basic Books.

BRAWLEY, L.R. and ROBERTS, G.C. (1984) 'Attributions in Sports Research Foundations, Characteristics, and Limitations,' in SILVA, J.M. III and WEINBERG, R.S. (Eds), *Psychological Foundations of Sport*. Champaign, Ill.: Human Kinetics Publishers.

BROEKHOFF, J. (1972) 'Physical Education and the Reification of Human Body.' *Gymnasium*, 9 (2), 4–11.

CHARLES, J.M. (1979) 'Technocentric Ideology in Physical Education.' *Quest*, 31, 277–84.

CHERRYHOLMES, C.H. (1988) *Power and Criticism: Poststructural Investigations in Education*. New York: Teachers College Press.

COAKLEY, J. (1980) 'Play, Games and Sports: Developmental Implications for Young People.' *Journal of Sport Behavior*, 3 (3): 99–118.

COLEMAN, J.S. (1965) *Adolescents and the Schools*. New York: Basic Books.

CORBIN, C.B., WHITEHEAD, J.R. and LOVEJOY, P.Y. (1988) 'Youth Physical Fitness Awards.' *Quest*, 40 (3), 200–18.

DeBUSK, M. and HELLISON, D. (1989) 'Implementing a Physical Education Self-responsibility Model for Delinquency-prone Youth.' *Journal of Teaching in Physical Education*, 8 (2), 104–12.

DODDS, P. (1983) 'Consciousness Raising in Curriculum: A Teacher's Model for Analysis,' in JEWETT, A.E., CARNES, M.M. and SPEAKMAN, M. (Eds), *Proceedings of the Third Conference on Curriculum Theory in Physical Education.* Athens, Ga: University of Georgia.

DODDS, P. (1985) 'Are the Hunters of the Function Curriculum Seeking Quarks or Snarks?' *Journal of Teaching in Physical Education*, 4, 91–9.

DODDS, P. (1986) 'Stamp Out the Ugly 'Isms' in Your Gym,' in PIERON, M. and GRAHAM, G. (Eds), *Sport Pedagogy*. Champaign, Ill.: Human Kinetics Publishers.

DUBOIS, P. (1986) 'The Effect of Participation in Sport on the Value Orientations of Young Athletes.' *Sociology of Sport Journal*, 3, 29–42.

EARLS, N.F. (1981) 'Distinctive Teachers' Personal Qualities, Perceptions of Teacher Education and the Realities of Teaching.' *Journal of Teaching in Physical Education*, 1, 59–70.

EISNER, E.W. (1985) *The Educational Imagination*. New York: Macmillan.

EITZEN, D.S. (1975) 'Athletics in the Status System of Male Adolescents: A Replication of Coleman's "The Adolescent Society".' *Adolescence*, 10, 267–76.

ELLIS, M.J. (1988) *The Business of Physical Education*. Champaign, Ill.: Human Kinetics Publishers.

EVERHART, R.B. (1983) *Reading, Writing and Resistance: Adolescence and Labor in a Junior High School*. Boston, Mass.: Routledge and Kegan Paul.

FINE, G.A. (1987) *With the Boys: Little League Baseball and Preadolescent Culture*. Chicago, Ill.: University of Chicago Press.

FOX, K.R. (1988) 'The Self-esteem Complex and Youth Fitness.' *Quest*, 40 (3), 230–46.

GIROUX, H. (1981) 'Pedagogy, Pessimism and the Politics of Conformity: A Reply to Linda McNeil.' *Curriculum Inquiry*, 11 (3), 211–22.

GOC-KARP, G. and ZAKRAJSEK, D.B. (1987) 'Planning for Learning — Theory into Practice?' *Journal of Teaching in Physical Education*, 6, 377–92.

GOC-KARP, G., KIM, D.W. and SKINNER, P.C. (1985) 'Professor and Student Perceptions and Beliefs about Physical Education.' *Physical Educator*, 43 (3), 115–20.

GREENE, M. (1978) *Landscapes of Learning*. New York: Teachers College Press.

GRIFFIN P.S. (1983) 'Gymnastics is a Girls' Thing: Participation and Interaction Patterns in Middle School Gymnastics Classes,' in TEMPLIN, T.J. and OLSON, J.K. (Eds), *Teaching in Physical Education*, pp. 71–85. Champaign, Ill.: Human Kinetics, Publishers.

GRIFFIN, P.S. (1984) 'Girls' Participation Patterns in a Middle School Team Sports Unit.' *Journal of Teaching in Physical Education*, 4, 30–8.

GRIFFIN, P.S. (1985a) 'Boys' Participation Styles in a Middle School Physical Education Sports Unit.' *Journal of Teaching in Physical Education*, 4, 100–10.

GRIFFIN, P.S. (1985b) 'Teacher Perceptions of and Reactions to Equity Problems in a Middle School Physical Education Program.' *Research Quarterly for Exercise and Sport*, 56 (2), 103–10.

GRIFFIN, P.S. (1985c) 'Teaching in an Urban Multiracial Physical Education Program: The Power of Context.' *Quest*, 37, 154–65.

GRIFFIN, P.S. (1989) 'Gender as a Socializing Agent in Physical Education,' in TEMPLIN, T.J. and SCHEMPP, P.G. (Eds), *Socialization into Physical Education: Learning to Teach*, pp. 219–34. Indianapolis, Ind.: Benchmark Press.

GRUNDY, S. (1987) *Curriculum: Product or Praxis?* Lewes: Falmer Press.

HALL, M.A. (1988) 'The Discourse of Gender and Sport: From Femininity to Feminism.' *Sociology of Sport Journal*, 5 (4), 330–40.

HARRIS, J.C. (1983) 'Interpreting Youth Baseball: Players' Understandings of Attention, Winning and Playing the Game.' *Research Quarterly for Exercise and Sport*, 54, 330–9.

HARRIS, J.C. (1984) 'Interpreting Youth Baseball: Players' Understandings of Fun, and Excitement, Danger and Boredom. *Research Quarterly for Exercise and Sport*, 55, 379–82.

Harvard Medical School Newsletter (1986) Cambridge, Mass.: Harvard University, September.

HELLISON, D. (1973) *Humanistic Physical Education*. Englewood Cliffs, N.J. Prentice-Hall.

HELLISON, D. (1978) *Beyond Balls and Bats*. Washington, D.C.: American Alliance for Health, Physical Education, Recreation and Dance.

HELLISON, D. (1985) *Goals and Strategies for Teaching Physical Education*. Champaign, Ill.: Human Kinetics Publishers.

IMWOLD, C., RIDER, R. and JOHNSON, D. (1982) 'The Use of Evaluation in Public School Physical Education Programs.' *Journal of Teaching in Physical Education*, 2 (1), 13–18.

INGHAM, A.G. (1985) 'From Public Issue to Personal Trouble: Well-being and the Fiscal Crisis of the State.' *Sociology of Sport Journal*, 1, 43–55.

KENEN, R.H. (1987) 'Double Messages, Double Images: Physical Fitness, Self-concepts and Women's Exercise Classes.' *Journal of Physical Education, Recreation and Dance*, 58 (6), 74–6.

KING, N.R. (1983) 'Play in the Workplace,' in APPLE, M. and WEIS, L. (Eds), *Ideology and Practice in Schooling*. Philadelphia, Pa.: Temple University Press.

KIRKLAND, G. (1986) *Dancing on My Grave*. New York: Doubleday.

KLEINMAN, S. (Ed.) (1986) *Mind and Body: East Meets West*. Champaign, Ill.: Human Kinetics Publishers.

KNEER, M.E. (1986) 'Description of Physical Education Instructional Theory/Practice Gap in Selected Secondary Schools.' *Journal of Teaching in Physical Education*, 5, 91–106.

KOLLEN, P. (1983) 'Fragmentation and Integration in Movement,' in TEMPLIN, T.J. and OLSON, J.K. (Eds) *Teaching in Physical Education*, pp. 89–93. Champaign, Ill.: Human Kinetics Publishers.

KOTARBA, J.A. and BENTLEY, P. (1985, August) 'Social Psychological Factors in Corporate Wellness Compliance.' Paper presented at the annual meeting of the Society for the Study of Social Problems, Washington, D.C.

LAPCHICK, R.E. (Ed.) (1986) *Fractured Focus: Sport as a Reflection of Society*. Lexington, Mass.: D.C. Heath.

LOCKE, L.F. and GRIFFIN, P. (Eds) (1986) 'Profiles of Struggle.' *Journal of Physical Education, Recreation and Dance*, 57 (4), 32–63.

MCCUTCHEON, G. (1982) 'What in the World Is Curriculum Theory?' *Theory into Practice*, 21, 18–22.

MARTINEK, T.J. (1983) 'Creating Golem and Galatea Effects during Physical Education Instruction: A Social Psychological Perspective,' in TEMPLIN, T.J. and OLSON, J.K. (Eds), *Teaching in Physical Education*, pp. 59–70. Champaign, Ill.: Human Kinetics Publishers.

MEREDITH, M.D. (1988) 'Activity or Fitness: Is the Process or the Product More Important for Public Health?' *Quest*, 40 (3), 180–6.

MESSNER, M.A. (1988) 'Sports and Male Domination: The Female Athlete as Contested Ideological Terrain.' *Sociology of Sport Journal*, 5 (3), 197–211.

ORBACH, S. (1978) *Fat Is a Feminist Issue.* New York: Berkley Books.

O'SULLIVAN, M. (1989) 'Failing Gym Is Like Failing Lunch or Recess: Two Beginning Teachers' Struggle for Legitimacy.' *Journal of Teaching in Physical Education*, 8 (3), 227–42.

PELLEGRINO, E.D. (1981) 'Health Promotion as Public Policy: The Need for Moral Groundings.' *Preventive Medicine*, 10, 371–8.

PLACEK, J.H. (1983) 'Conceptions of Success in Teaching: Busy, Happy and Good?' in TEMPLIN, T.J. and OLSON, J.K. (Eds), *Teaching in Physical Education*, pp. 46–56. Champaign, Ill.: Human Kinetics Publishers.

PLACEK, J.H. (1984) 'A Multi-case Study of Teacher Planning in Physical Education.' *Journal of Teaching in Physical Education*, 4, 39–49.

PLACEK, J.H. and DODDS, P. (1988) 'A Critical Incident Study of Pre-service Teachers' Beliefs about Teaching Success and Nonsuccess.' *Research Quarterly for Exercise and Sport*, 59 (4), 351–8.

RICH, A. (1980) 'Compulsory Heterosexuality and Lesbian Existence.' *Signs: Journal of Women in Culture and Society*, 5 (4), 631–60.

SAGE, G.H. (1980) 'Sociology of Physical Educator/Coaches: Personal Attributes Controversy.' *Research Quarterly for Exercise and Sport*, 51 (1), 110–21.

SAGE, G.H. (1989) 'Becoming a High School Coach: From Playing Sports to Coaching.' *Research Quarterly for Exercise and Sport*, 60 (1), 81–92.

SILBERMAN, M. (Ed.) (1971) *The Experience of Schooling.* New York: Holt, Rinehart and Winston.

SIMONS-MORTON, B.G., O'HARA, N.M., SIMONS-MORTON, D.G. and PARCEL, G.S. (1987) 'Children and Fitness: A Public Health Perspective.' *Research Quarterly for Exercise and Sport*, 58 (4), 295–302.

SPEARS, B. and SWANSON, R.A. (1978) *History of Sport and Physical Activity in the United States.* Dubuque, Iowa: Wm C. Brown.

TEMPLIN, T.J. and SCHEMPP, P.G. (Eds) (1989) *Socialization into Physical Education: Learning to Teach.* Indianapolis, Ind.: Benchmark Press.

THEBERGE, N. (1985) 'Toward a Feminist Alternative to Sport as a Male Preserve.' *Quest*, 37, 193–202.

TINDALL, B.A. (1975) 'Ethnography and the Hidden Curriculum in Sport.' *Behavioral and Social Science Teacher*, 2 (2), 5–28.

TOUSIGNANT, J. and SIEDENTOP, D. (1983) 'A Qualitative Analysis of Task Structures in Required Secondary Physical Education Classes.' *Journal of Teaching in Physical Education*, 3 (1), 47–57.

TURNER, B.S. (1984) *The Body and Society*. New York: Basil Blackwell.

VEAL, M.L. (1988a) 'Pupil Assessment Issues: A Teacher Educator's Perspective.' *Quest*, 40, 151–61.

VEAL, M.L. (1988b) 'Pupil Assessment Perceptions and Practices of Secondary Teachers.' *Journal of Teaching in Physical Education*, 7, 327–42.

VERTINSKY, P. (1985) 'Risk Benefit Analysis of Health Promotions: Opportunities and Threats for Physical Education.' *Quest*, 37 (1), 71–83.

WANG, B. (1977) 'An Ethnography of a Physical Education Class: An Experiment in Integrated Living.' *DAI, 38,* 1980A. (University Microfilms No. 7721750)

WEIS, L. (1982) 'Schooling and the Reproduction of Aspects of Structure.' *Issues in Education: Schooling and the Reproduction of Class and Gender Inequalities*, pp. 1–16. Occasional Paper #10. Buffalo, N.Y.: State University of New York at Buffalo.

Chapter 3

Defining the Subject: Gymnastics and Gender in British Physical Education*

David Kirk

Physical education programmes in British schools have been the subject of a vociferous public debate in the latter half of the 1980s. The major point of contention has been whether an insidious undermining of competitive sport in schools by 'progressive' physical educators has been taking place. Usually debates over the contents and teaching methods of physical education are contained within the profession. At least we have tended to think of curriculum development as an in-house issue, of interest to policy-makers and a few researchers perhaps, but certainly unlikely to attract the attention of anyone else. However, in this case the debate not only attracted the interest of the media, politicians and sporting bodies, it was to a large extent initiated by them, and the strength of feeling the debate generated took many physical educators by surprise. Details of the terms of the debate, the circumstances surrounding it and its likely impact on schools are now beginning to emerge,[1] and these analyses provide insights into the changing nature of sport and organized physical activity in British society and the extremely important role of school physical education within this process.

However, this episode also projects in a dramatic fashion another, not unrelated, issue that has been preoccupying curriculum researchers and sociologists of school knowledge over the past decade, and that is the ways in which school subjects develop and change over time, and in train

---

* This paper is an early product of a large and long-term research project. Many of the issues touched on here are treated more thoroughly in a forthcoming book, *Defining the Subject: The Social Construction of Physical Education in Britain 1945–1965*. These include the nature of progressivism of which educational gymnasts were a part, the nature of scientific functionalism and its links with competitive games and sport, and health and fitness.

with this interest how certain kinds of knowledge are selected and how other kinds are left out of the school curriculum. The work of Ivor Goodson and his colleagues has been particularly useful in demonstrating the role of subject communities and other groups in shaping the form and content of school subjects and in so doing promoting their own sectional interests.[2] At least two key insights emerged from this work. One was that the shape and content of school subjects are in constant process, and that this process is characterized by contestation and struggle between rival groups to gain the right to define the 'correct' version of the subject. A second was that school subjects do not therefore evolve in an apolitical manner, but are instead shaped by the active involvement of people in specific social, cultural and political environments. These insights are radical insofar as they challenge the received wisdom of rational curriculum developers and also common-sense notions about the apparent stability of school subjects.[3]

The contemporary debate over physical education in British schools is an excellent example of the process of contestation and struggle to define the subject as it is characterized by Goodson and his colleagues. However, the existence of conflict in relation to the selection, organization and legitimation of knowledge in physical education is not restricted to this contemporary episode. Indeed, the history of institutionalized physical education in schools since the mid-nineteenth century is marked by struggles over the 'correct' form and content of physical education.[4] These more distant struggles are quite relevant to the contemporary debate, but there are more recent antecedents in the immediate post-Second World War era that illuminate the underlying themes of the present struggles. The period immediately following the Second World War represents a watershed in the development of physical education in British schools. It was then that the definition of 'physical education' was contested by two rival groups, one predominantly female, the other male. The fact that gender was one of the main dividing lines between the opposing groups is particularly important in the light of recent feminist critiques of physical education and sport as a male preserve.[5]

This chapter focuses on gymnastics as one crucial site of contestation between these competing factions. It identifies the various discourses that existed in physical education,[6] examining how the conditions and contexts in which these arose structured and so assisted, and yet at the same time set limits on, their development. These struggles are important for contemporary curriculum practice in physical education because the alternative discourses articulated and contested by rival factions were not merely linguistic contests, conducted according to the rules of rational academic debate, but reflected actual power struggles located in particular physical and symbolic sites. They therefore worked at a number of levels, particularly in terms of institutionalizing 'correct' practice in physical education, and establishing the ideas that in the process of socialization into the profession we come to accept as right and proper. Though gymnastics was only one of several activities that made up physical education programmes at this time, it played a crucial role in reflecting the most fundamental assumptions physical educators made about their version of the subject. Indeed, male and female physical educators considered gymnastics to be the foundation for all other physical education activities. My concerns will mainly be to draw out the characteristics of each group's perspectives and locate these in the broader social, educational and political climate of post-war Britain. I begin with a description of three versions of gymnastics that were competing for curriculum time in British schools at the end of the Second World War. From there I will discuss briefly the demise of the formally dominant Swedish system as a way of previewing two new discourses, one represented by the female educational gymnasts and the other by the predominantly male scientific functionalists. Finally, I will attempt to show how the conditions under which each discourse was nurtured and developed also set limits on the potential for progress of these versions of gymnastics, and of physical education as a school subject more broadly.

Three Versions of Gymnastics

By the end of the Second World War three distinct versions of gymnastics were competing for teaching time in school physical education programmes. The first of these, Swedish (or Ling) gymnastics, had been the traditional hallmark of the professional female physical educator between the late 1890s and the 1930s, and the version of physical education officially approved by the then Board of Education for use in its elementary schools. The Swedish system was invented by Per Henrick Ling in the early decades of the nineteenth century and consolidated into a system of physical training at the Central Gymnastic Institute in Stockholm which he founded. It involved mostly free-standing exercises set out in tables that sought to exercise systematically each part of the body through increasingly intricate flexions and extensions. It also involved some apparatus work such as vaulting. Teaching within the Ling system was highly formalized and, in the beginning especially, movements were performed to militaristic commands such as 'at the double!' and 'fall in!', and was easily practised with large groups in confined spaces. The Swedish system was boosted in Britain in the 1880s through the work of

Swedish gymnasts appointed by the Board of Education to organize physical education in its elementary schools. One of these organizers was Madame Bergman-Osterberg, who in 1885 formed her own college of physical training for women.[7] Swedish gymnastics formed the foundation of the women's professional training, which was supplemented by massage, remedial exercises and games.

The second form of gymnastics, which was witnessed in its modern form for the first time by British physical educators at the 1948 London Olympic Games, was German or Olympic gymnastics. German gymnastics had been around at least as long as Ling's system, and involved work on apparatus such as the rings, parallel bars and pommel horse. At the beginning of the twentieth century it had vied with the Swedish system for selection as the official system of physical training by the Interdepartmental Committee set up by the Royal Commission on Physical Training (1903) to produce a *Syllabus of Physical Exercises* for British schools. It lost that contest, and suffered the stigma of its German origins after the First World War to be neglected by all but a handful of enthusiasts in Britain until the 1940s. After the boost given by the 1948 Olympics, however, which presented gymnastics as a competitive sport made up of the six activities of floor-work, vaulting, rings, bars, beam and pommel horse, there was an increasing level of interest in this version of gymnastics with growing advocacy for its inclusion in school programmes from the early 1950s.[8]

The third form was educational gymnastics, and it had made a rapid and dramatic impact on female physical education from the first appearance of Laban's ideas on movement and dance in Britain in the 1930s. Modern dance was built on a radical critique of 'unnatural' movement patterns in industrial society that had, in Laban's opinion, much to do with the presence of mental illness and other personality disorders. In the spirit of other psychologistic critiques of contemporary industrial society by people like R.D. Laing and Wilhelm Reich, Laban's philosophy argued for the release of dangerously pent up and inhibited energies through free, spontaneous movement. Although Laban's main concerns were focused on the theatre and industry, his ideas were very quickly applied to gymnastics by female physical educators during the late 1930s and through the war years. Educational gymnastics borrowed from modern dance a concern for the qualitative dimensions of movement experience and selectively adopted some of the rhetoric and ideas of the fast growing and fashionable child-centred progressivism in British educational circles of the time, particularly those associated with humanistic liberal individualism.[9]

The Demise of Swedish Gymnastics

By the end of the Second World War Swedish gymnastics was under siege on several sides. The Butler Education Act of 1944 was the product of a war-time coalition government, but the Labour Government that came to power the following year was quick to employ its egalitarian proposals for secondary education for all as a central plank in its policy for social reconstruction.[10] In a climate of national optimism in the immediate post-war period the work of the Swedish gymnast seemed to have little place, and indeed it was the provision of facilities for games playing and their role in helping to rebuild the nation that occupied the attention of professional publications like *The Times Educational Supplement* in most references to physical education between 1945 and 1965.[11] It is significant, for instance, that in the decade preceding the war the Ling Association had little formal involvement in the mass Keep Fit movement in the north of England and the Women's League of Health and Beauty in the south. At the end of the 1930s there were no Swedish gymnasts invited to sit on any of the government committees formulating policies concerning youth and recreation.[12] These examples suggest that the Swedish gymnasts did not have a public profile that was in tune with the events of the time.

Their fall from grace began in the 1930s, at a time when Swedish gymnastics was firmly established as the basis for the professional training of female physical educators, and had begun to play the same role in the new specialist colleges for men that appeared during the 1930s at Glasgow, Leeds and Loughborough. There had been challenges from inside the subject itself, through the introduction of musical accompaniments to exercises by Irene Marsh, an innovation resisted staunchly by the Ling Association for many years,[13] and the modification of exercises by Elli Bjorksten in Finland and Elin Falk in Sweden to include rhythmic activities.[14] But these had done very little to challenge the firmly rooted orthodoxies of the system.

However, in a series of articles that appeared in the *Journal of Physical Education* in 1945 and early 1946 it is clear that the Swedish gymnasts were by that time fighting a rearguard action. The articles attempted to defend what one author called 'formal movements, or gymnastics movements proper' from a number of challenges.[15] These centred on the claim that Swedish gymnastics involved formal, mechanical and therefore 'unnatural' movements, and that these were 'non-creative and dull, merely a sequence of unnatural movements put together without meaning'. The responses to this criticism reveal some of the assumptions the Swedish gymnasts made about their version of physical education. According to M.E. Squire, Principal of Anstey Physical Training College, it 'is the only form of physical education which systematically attempts to affect bodily structure and to remedy possible defects of posture; therefore it should be the basis of all physical education in that it prepares a sound movable instrument upon which all other forms of physical education should play harmoniously.'[16] This statement conveys with certainty and conviction the idea that formal gymnastics is the fundamental form of human movement, and this in a manner that is clearly not open to question. Another author, discussing the role of vaulting and agility work within the Swedish system, communicates the same notion of the fundamentality of formal exercises in saying that 'the relationship of free standing exercises to vaulting and agilities is as grammar is to composition.'[17] The use of a descriptor like 'systematic' betrays something of the Swedish gymnasts' concerns for precision, physicality and for the functionality of movement. Similarly, their stress on harmony and their close attention to posture confirm the importance of intervention in the physical development process.

On the basis of this view of physical education the gymnasts were unimpressed by the Laban-inspired educational gymnasts' criticism of formal exercises, and in the final paragraph of her 1945 article M.E. Squire fired this exasperated broadside.

> If we only move in the natural directions with natural co-ordination there is a danger of working various sets of muscles only in one direction and range, and lessening the power of the individual to respond alertly to unexpected demands. If we never hold the body in a straight line or shew a precise position we shall lose much that is of value in self discipline, and this I think is the real danger in the modern gymnastic work. There is too much 'Do as you please as long as you move', too much so-called experimental work and no real training value.... Can we not get back a little more discipline both mental and physical and keep our aim of achieving easy poise in movement on the most perfect possible structural foundation?[18]

This criticism of the lack of discipline and precision in educational gymnastics was to resurface time and again in future years from a variety of sources. However well founded though, it was too late to save Swedish gymnastics, and over the next decade it was to disappear completely from the curriculum of the specialist training colleges.[19] Well before its eventual demise in the 1950s alternative versions of gymnastics were already waiting in the wings to take its place. Even though the Swedish system had been the hallmark of the female physical educator until the 1930s, it had been taken on enthusiastically in the early days of the specialist colleges for males.[20] After 1945, however, the meaning of gymnastics would depend, as one contemporary commentator noted, 'on the sex of the individual'.[21]

Child-centred Progressivism and the Female Creed

The female physical educators had begun, as early as the 1930s and still within the confines of the Swedish system, to critique the negative influence of modern industrial society on the quality of human life. Maja Carlquist, a Swede who had worked closely with Ellen Falk in the 1920s and 1930s, argued that rhythm was an essential quality in movement that 'through civilisation with its industrialisation, mechanisation and technology...has become more and more dulled.... Look at the people in the streets; stiff feet — stiff restricted movements — stiff expressions on their faces.... Here one can truthfully talk of the melody which was lost.'[22]

This comment could easily have been made by a Laban-inspired educational gymnast. Laban himself did not commit his ideas on the place of movement education in wider society until 1948, when he published *Modern Educational Dance*. He had by then carried out research in industry, and had become convinced of the detrimental effects of simple, repetitive movement sequences of many factory-based occupations on the worker's emotional and intellectual health.[23] These ideas were eventually to find their way, in largely unaltered form, into the discourse of the educational gymnasts, as we can see from this remark from an influential spokeswoman for the educational gymnasts, Ruth Morison: 'The limitations imposed by contemporary life tend to disrupt natural harmonious movement and produce stilted, restricted, isolated actions, and to develop bad habits of movement and carriage which in their turn cause tensions, cramps and the resultant ills.'[24]

This critique of modern industrial civilization, translated into the language of child-centred progressivism, was in tune with popular educational discourse in the 1940s and 1950s, particularly in the primary sector, though also in some of the new secondary modern schools.[25] Progressivism was not unique to this period, of course, but the form it took in Britain at this time had a particular flavour that owed much to a fusion of liberal humanism and socialist ideology.[26] By the 1950s and 1960s this ideology had become the new orthodoxy in political discourse on education, and in the process the radicalism that promoted and sustained it had been largely neutralized.[27] Nevertheless, the notion of equality of opportunity that came to symbolize both political and educational progressivism in post-war Britain had a pervasive and powerful influence on the thinking of many teachers, and the radical Laban-inspired values of the educational gymnasts were in places quite consistent with this new idealism, particularly in relation to its humanist elements.

By the early 1950s the educational gymnastics movement was in full forward motion, and had received important official support from the then Ministry of Education in England through the publication of the two curriculum guides *Moving and Growing* and *Planning the Programme*.[28] These guides appeared in 1952 and 1953, and were intended to replace the 1933 syllabus in primary school physical education. While neither of the guides mentions Laban explicitly, both are clearly and strongly influenced by his ideas and the work of the educational gymnasts. Given that Laban himself only set out his ideas in written form as late as 1948, the guides represented the first authoritative statement of the educational gymnasts' creed.

With the publication of these guides they had achieved official recognition for their work. But this recognition was almost exclusively within the rarified environment of female physical educators in schools, colleges and the Inspectorate. Taking the specialist educational press as an indicator, there is virtually no acknowledgment of this 'radical' reorientation of physical education to 'progressive' views outside physical education circles,[29] and certainly no celebration of it. This apparent indifference on the part of the wider teaching profession, never mind the general public, was to have detrimental influence on the continuing progress of the educational gymnasts. Also their version of gymnastics was 'radical' and 'progressive' more in relation to what had gone before than in any political sense. At least their allegiance to humanistic individualism was more in keeping with bourgeois politics than with the collectivism of the Labour left in 1940s Britain.

Many of the women who practised educational gymnastics in the 1940s through to the 1960s did so with a high level of conviction and emotional intensity. It is not uncommon to find them being referred to as 'devotees' or 'disciples', 'a mystic cult of female groupies' idolizing Laban and accepting his ideas indiscriminately and uncritically.[30] Like their predecessors the Swedish gymnasts, many of these women continued to work in the insular and elite circles of their colleges and grammar schools, displaying that 'curious blend of therapeutic, upper-crust and feminine values' associated with the tradition set in motion in the 1880s by Madame Bergman-Osterberg.[31] There were disputes among the educational gymnasts over issues such as the difference between dance and gymnastics or whether quality or shape of movement was more important, as we can see in the following comment on the boundaries between dance and gymnastics. 'There is the danger that, because the terminology is the same, girls may "dance" in the gymnastic lesson. This may not offend all, but I'm sure that it will offend many and it should be stamped out the moment it arises, as its presence suggests a confusion of attitude.'[32] While such issues were no doubt worthy of serious attention and discussion, the tone of the educational gymnasts' debates still had an air of certainty and authority that had also characterized the Swedish gymnasts.

Pleas for Moderation

It was this apparent intensity, assuredness and accompanying zealousness of the educational gymnasts that prompted various pleas for proportion in the professional press in the late 1940s and early 1950s. Most of these calls for moderation were stimulated by what their authors saw as excessive zeal in following through the tenets of movement education. One writer, in an open letter in the *Journal of Physical Education*, decried the imposition of problem-solving on all children:

> We have, at the moment, I think, in the field of physical education, a tendency to force originality and initiative from children beyond what is right and proper — to lose, in fact, our sense of proportion about it.... Do we not, perhaps, in our phobia against 'Teacher Direction' (which some of us seem to regard as the ultimate heresy) urge originality and experimentation in the physical sphere upon the child whose medium of expression may be the writing of verse or the painting of a picture?[33]

This letter prompted a string of responses supporting the plea for moderation, one of which highlighted the problem of balancing inventiveness and discovery in and through movement with the consolidation of skills.

> There seems to be too much emphasis on variety in the 'new' way and the child executes many beautiful movements which can never become known to him because he does not repeat them sufficiently. The children become absorbed in thought rather than in the quality of their efforts and the mechanics of the movements. Consequently, it seems doubtful whether they will absorb the same principles concerning movement as quickly as children under the 'old' way.[34]

This criticism of the lack of specificity and practice within education-al gymnastics was to become a popular stick with which to beat the Laban-oriented women in subsequent years. The challenge did not lie in a return to the 'old way' though, but in the new knowledge derived from scientific measurement that was being produced in the university depart-ments of physical education. It was at this point, in the early 1950s, and perhaps not coincidentally at a time when the educational gymnasts had received official approval of their work from the Ministry, that alterna-tive perspectives began to articulate their concerns.

Scientific Measurement and the Male Perspective

Hard on the heels of the pleas for proportion published in the *Journal of Physical Education* came the first flickerings of open antagonism in Scot-land. As a result of a National Conference on Physical Education held in Edinburgh in 1954 involving both male and female physical educators, the organizers set up a special committee to carry out an investigation into the content of the gymnastic lesson for boys. The dispute revolved around which of the three versions of gymnastics should be taught in Scottish schools.[35] After four one-day meetings the committee decided to support traditional Swedish gymnastics which had had a strong foothold in the Scottish School of Physical Education (SSPE), the male college, since its establishment in 1932. What is interesting about this decision is the rejection of educational gymnastics on the grounds that it would undermine the traditionally high standards of gymnastic skill at the SSPE, an issue that was to form the cornerstone of the male critique of educa-tional gymnastics.

Meanwhile, south of the border, A.D. Munrow's influential *Pure and Applied Gymnastics* was published in 1955, and this book became the mouthpiece of male opposition to the progressive trend in physical education.[36] Munrow eloquently articulated the views of the coming force of scientific measurement, and how this new knowledge could be applied to physical education. Gymnastics, for Munrow, involved exer-cises designed to have particular effects on the body, and while his definition excluded many of the activities that made up Olympic gymnas-tics, we will see that the logic underlying his view supported this version of gymnastics over educational gymnastics. The book was significant not only for the distinctly alternative position that it stated in relation to the educational gymnasts, and thus its influential role representing the male philosophy, but also by virtue of the fact that it was read by many of the educational gymnasts and so formed one of the few avenues of communication between the rival parties.[37]

University departments of physical education had been established at Edinburgh, Liverpool, Manchester, Birmingham and Leeds during the 1930s. Their initial role was to provide recreational programmes for the students,[38] but they soon added to this a research function. In 1949 physical education became a specialism within the BA degree at Birmingham, and this institution along with Leeds in particular appointed staff with research orientations. Most of these staff were male, and all of the directors of the university physical education departments were male. By 1955 Munrow was expressing a widespread feeling among male physical educators of the time in saying that while physical education was an art, 'it does however aim to be systematic and scientific in its statement of principles.'[39]

In adopting the perspective and discourse of scientific measurement, the university physical education departments were following another trend in post-war British society in the same way that the educational gymnasts had fallen in with the progressive movement. There is no doubt that the Second World War gave the technology of fitness development and the acquisition of skill[40] a boost comparable to other technological developments such as the use of radar in commercial aviation, radio isotopes in medicine and the widespread use of penicillin.[41] Certain techniques like circuit training had been shown to be an effective way of improving troops' physical fitness for warfare.[42] But more significantly, the whole of British culture was suffused with enthusiasm for the power of science to bring about change for the better. The effects of scientific research could be seen everywhere, in all aspects of people's lives. Indeed, the rapid advance of technology hand-in-hand with increasing affluence after the austerity of the immediate post-war years had its most profound impact in the home. Over a relatively short time people's day-to-day lives were revolutionized by labour-saving devices like washing machines and vacuum cleaners, by motor cars and by television. Scientific advances were made somewhere 'out there', in the laboratories of the universities and research institutes that few undoubtedly ever stopped to think of or consider, but the results of this work were nevertheless felt directly and personally by people throughout society.[43]

The educational sector was strongly implicated in the 1950s in the rise of technology to these new levels of influence. Schools were soon to become, in the 1960s, a cornerstone in Britain's survival as a major industrial power, and a technologically-oriented curriculum was the way this was to be achieved.[44] The 'systems approach' began to be adopted by curriculum developers keen to promote educational innovations in schools. Science also played an important part in sustaining and legitimating the new selective tripartite system of secondary schooling instituted by the 1944 Education Act, through the mental measurement school of educational psychology and its construction of IQ tests for the 11+ exam. It was in this wider social and political context that the male physical educators began to see their subject as being scientifically-based. By the middle of the 1950s experimental studies of exercise, skill acquisition and sports technique were well on their way to establishing the basic core of knowledge in physical education, and thus supplying the support for a competitive form of gymnastics that demanded high levels of skill.

Inside the Debate

There were two major issues that help to focus the debate that was developing through the 1950s and 1960s in the wake of the demise of the Swedish system between the female educational gymnasts and the males with their functional scientific perspective. The first was the controversy surrounding the level of specificity required for skill development and the problem of transfer of training. The second related closely to this first matter, and concerned the application of objective standards to gymnastic performance and the place of competition in the gym. Both issues revealed the essential nature of the differences between the female and male philosophies and practices.

In *Pure and Applied Gymnastics* Munrow presented a definition of gymnastics that was narrowly physical and functional. He argued that physical educators had in the past placed too strong an emphasis on Swedish gymnastics skills, and had neglected skills in other sports and games. This emphasis was doubly misplaced since these formal gymnastics exercises had a very high skill threshold level before competent performance became possible. In moving away from the Swedish system after the Second World War, he suggested that male and female physical educators had reacted in different ways to this problem. 'The men have made overt acknowledgement that other skills are as important and have "diluted" the gymnastic skill content of gymnasium work so that now boys may be seen practising basket-ball shots and manoeuvres, carrying out heading practices or practising sprint starting.'[45] Munrow's definition limited gymnastics to the exercises which were designed solely for their 'effect on particular parts of the body'. These effects were the development of strength, suppleness, stamina and skill; the muscles, joints, heart and lungs, and nervous system being the parts of the body affected. Skill could be developed through simplified skill drills which Munrow regarded as a form of gymnastic exercise. Miming a tennis serve would be an example of a gymnastic practice designed to 'groove' a tennis skill. Munrow contrasted the male response to the female reaction:

> The women, in the main, have...'diluted' the traditional gymnastic skills by a quite different device. They have ceased both to name and to teach them. Instead, a description is given, in general terms, of a task involving apparatus and individual solutions are encouraged. A much wider range of solutions is thus possible; some may include traditional skills but many will not.[46]

The problem with the female alternative to the Swedish system, as Munrow saw it, was that pupils rarely had the chance to consolidate their skills. Nor were they able to extend them, and this led into the second contested issue in the debate, over standards and competition. The child's own imagination and creativity set the limits on what could be achieved, because intervention by the teacher was interpreted by the educational gymnast as an imposition that not only set a standard against which the pupils' success could be measured, but also where their failures and inadequacies could be revealed. In Munrow's view this double-edged quality to objectively set standards was unavoidable: 'If we attempt too much to shield the child from failure we shall also shield him from real success. For success that all can have for the asking is not worth having.'

The educational gymnasts' response to Munrow's challenge appeared six years later in 1961 in Marjorie Randall's *Basic Movement*. In the opening chapter of the book Randall immediately went on the offensive to contest Munrow's functional definition of gymnastics, suggesting that 'the masculine approach...has become largely outmoded so far as women's work is concerned.' She claimed that 'women's gymnastics... have been emancipated from the restricted practices of stereotyped patterns of movements based upon anatomical classification. The physiological and anatomical ends...are incidentally served.'[47]

The major aim was the achievement of what Randall called 'body awareness', which included (merely physiological) nervous control combined with a higher level kinaesthetic awareness that could be developed through experience into an intuitive control of movement. She added to this a concern to engage the child cognitively in contrast to the male approach which she accused of stressing only the physical effects of exercise. 'The masculine approach to gymnastics', she claimed, 'separates content from method. Munrow's gymnastics exercises can be directly and formally taken or informally taken. Movement gymnastics requires the intelligent co-operation of the child, rendering command-response methods obsolete...this represents a big break-away from the traditional approach of the "see this" and "do it this way" school of thought.'[48]

The notion of body awareness ran directly counter to the new knowledge being produced by motor learning theorists. The educational gymnasts claimed, in much the same way as the Swedish gymnasts had before them, that the movement experience they had to offer was a general foundation upon which more specific skills could be built. The notion of body awareness expressed this idea of a generalized kinaesthetic control. Motor learning theorists, on the other hand, argued that transfer of training was most likely to occur when the tasks in questions were similar, and so the best way to learn a specific action was to perform that action repeatedly over a period of time.[49] Other new knowledge that focused on the physiological parameters of performance, expressed in concepts such as 'progressive overload', came into physical education directly from what had been learned about strength and endurance training during the war.[50] From Randall's earlier comments we can see that this emphasis on functionality and physicality would have been antithetical to the educational gymnasts' approach.

This matter became more acutely focused when the new scientific knowledge was used to enhance performance in competitive sport. In response to Munrow's view that standards were a necessary and important means of challenging pupils to strive for excellence, Randall suggested that girls, particularly in adolescence, had quite different needs from boys. She argued that the growing boy 'derives considerable prestige and social prominence through physical advantage in competitive games which his increase in height, weight and strength gives him.' Girls, on the other hand, may have little to gain from competitive sport during the adolescent period, and so

> In the gymnastic lesson let her be free from all this competition and let her progress at her own rate and find joy and satisfaction in the slow but sure progress of controlling her body. Through her pride in the mastery of her body in the gymnasium will grow a certain independence, security and emotional stability.... Teaching must be geared to the individual; it must be flexible and tolerant of a wide range in aptitude...no longer is her worth in the gymnasium measured by whether she can get over the box in long fly or whether she can put her head on her knees keeping her legs straight; but rather can she work to surpass her own standards without being harrassed or harried because she cannot conform to a common one.[51]

The aims of 'independence, security and emotional stability' contrast sharply with the desire to develop strength, endurance, flexibility and particular skills, and to use these attributes in competitive situations. What these contrasting aspirations reveal are quite different frames of reference and values that were not so much diametrically opposite points of view on the same set of issues; more accurately, the agendas of each group were in themselves so vastly different that there were few points of contact or overlap where the same language could be used and communication could be possible. In all of this each group's position in relation to gender is significant. Munrow's views are only weakly framed, as if the gender of the pupils was irrelevant. This in itself is an important statement, however, since there seems to be the assumption that 'the sex of the individual' is far from being a leading consideration in defining gymnastics. Randall's comments, on the other hand, are much more gender-specific and explicitly concerned with feminine qualities. At the same time each operates with a clear view of physical education's role in fitting boys and girls for boys' and girls' futures, the former for sports participation and the latter for marriage and motherhood. In this sense their agendas *are* the same, since they do little to challenge the orthodoxies of male and female roles and relationships.

The Social Context of Defining the Subject

In 1969 Bob Carlisle read a paper at the Annual Conference of the British Philosophy of Education Society entitled 'The Concept of Physical Education'. This paper was firmly located in the new orthodoxy of conceptual analysis initiated and popularized by the influential writings of Professors Peters and Hirst, and Carlisle was essentially preoccupied with the question, 'What does the term physical education mean?' In pursuing this question, and following the Peters/Hirst line, Carlisle neglected to take into account something he would have undoubtedly known, which was that the answer depended on whether the question was asked of a female or a male physical educator.

Carlisle's paper was itself a response to the struggle over the meaning of the subject that had its roots in the immediate post-war era. I have tended to characterize the rival philosophies as polarities, and of course as the pleas for moderation in the early 1950s indicate, there have been many shades of opinion between these poles. Nevertheless, the gap between the perspectives of female and male physical educators was so vast in terms of what the term 'physical education' meant, constituting almost entirely separate discourses where communication was virtually impossible, that contrasting them in such stark terms is justified and appropriate. What the gymnastics debate reveals is how these alternative and contested definitions of the subject were manifest within sets of conditions that simultaneously promoted and set limits on their future progress.

The educational gymnasts, on the one hand, thrived within an already existing female tradition in physical education. They had institutions to practise and develop their art, schools in which to apply it, and a progressive educational movement to legitimate it. Their ideas were also extremely influential in the state primary sector, and through this educational gymnastics developed a base of support and gained official government backing. However, these very conditions that fostered their version of physical education also limited its ability to move beyond a certain point.

The insularity of their institutions, for one thing, restricted to those women who could afford to pay their fees, worked against them in the late 1940s when the government began to demand more teachers than they could possibly hope to supply.[52] They found they could not compete with the larger institutions being set up to meet this demand, and there resulted a series of takeovers, amalgamations and closures that had almost entirely undermined their professional infrastructure by the 1960s.[53] Perhaps this process could have been slowed but for two other forces that were also built in to the context in which educational gymnastics developed.

The first of these was their influence in the state sector primary schools and the fact that educational gymnastics very quickly came to be associated with primary school physical education. Because of the continuities between its non-competitive, aesthetic and creative features and the child-centred movement that was bringing about sweeping changes in primary classrooms, educational gymnastics was championed by teachers of younger children, particularly infant teachers.[54] The way towards status and prestige, however, lay in the new secondary schools modelled on the subject-oriented grammar schools. While the arrival of mass secondary schooling had given the primaries more scope to experiment, it was the secondary sector that was expanding rapidly, and it was there that the various Labour and Conservative governments in the late 1950s and the 1960s focused their attention, particularly on the transitional period from school to work and higher education. Progressivism in the primary school also worked against the achievement of an enhanced status and influence for the educational gymnasts' version of physical education by its very non-proprietariness, stressing instead the value of an integrated curriculum which attempted to dissolve subject boundaries.

This was little short of disastrous for a curriculum topic that could not present a coherent and unified public image of what physical education was and the knowledge it encompassed.

The second force at work lay in wider social and political trends. While the educational gymnasts were promoting humanitarian ideals focused on the notion of individual worth, the radicalism of post-war social reconstruction was proving to be a sham.[55] Beneath the consensual politics of right and left, Britain was moving during the 1950s into a consumer-oriented materialism that sprung from the new technologically produced affluence. Equality of opportunity came to mean something quite different in Labour educational policy from what it had meant to the child-centred progressives.[56] The early radical intent of leftist policy for social change through the raising of a collective consciousness and personal enrichment through the acquisition of liberal culture, was drowned in the clamour of voices from the middle and right of the Labour Party which in contrast adopted a purely quantitative conception of equality based in the fair distribution of educational goods. As one recent commentator put it, the doctrine of equality of opportunity within Labour educational policy in the late 1950s and early 1960s 'endorsed the principle that education, like society itself, is a competition, a process that produces winners and losers. The purpose of [educational] policy is to ensure that the rules of the competition are fair — that everyone has an equal chance.'[57]

This conception of equality of opportunity was quite at odds with the liberal humanism of the educational gymnasts where 'each girl in the class should work individually, trying to improve her own standard but not unduly conscious of or worried by the greater abilities of the girls around her.' The problem for the educational gymnasts was that the ideals of both liberal and radical progressivism were marginalized in the consensual educational policies of the day, and 'equality' became a slogan masking a profound materialism. Thus the discourse of progressivism in educational gymnastics, and the version of the subject it presented, had little support in the realities of broader educational policy and practice.

The male orientation, on the other hand, grew out of a different set of circumstances, and these created a contrasting set of possibilities to those of the educational gymnasts'. Their functional, scientific and competitive discourse from the start was in tune with a number of powerful trends. One of these was the widespread popular acceptance of competitive sport in schools and its role in the promotion of national prestige. Whereas the educational press was relatively quiet on issues that concerned the educational gymnasts, it was vociferous in relation to the provision of playing fields for sports and games, and for the development of sport in education in the national interest.[58]

The great demand for teachers to meet the needs of mass secondary schooling was a particularly significant event for male physical educators. In the years immediately following the war there were fewer of them compared to the women, and so greater attention was given to meeting this shortfall.[59] The institutional settings in which scientific functionalism was fostered, in the universities, large teacher training colleges and secondary schools, were therefore relatively unhindered by tradition and the men were in a better position than the women to respond to contemporary challenges. These factors helped the males to maintain a higher profile in relation to developments in the wider educational arena and in society at large. Furthermore, universities with their increasing bias towards technology and the secondary schools with their subject-specific organization provided a fruitful environment in which to pursue professional status.

And what of Olympic gymnastics? Little has been said about this version of gymnastics up to this point, and this is for the reason that it was not, at first, so closely aligned with the male perspective as educational gymnastics was with the female. However, while as many women as men did participate in this sport as its popularity grew through the 1960s, the new knowledge that sustained it owed little to the educational gymnasts or the female tradition. The males' focus on the development of physical fitness fitted them well for the task of preparing elite sport performers. This version of gymnastics was an international competitive sport that demanded exactly what the male physical educators could provide — knowledge of how to develop strength, muscular endurance, agility and high levels of precision skills. Thus Olympic gymnastics was fostered within the emerging discourse of scientific functionalism, even though many females actively participated in the sport.

Conclusion

In conclusion, I suggest that the conditions in which the scientific functionalist discourse arose created a range of possibilities that were denied to the female tradition of physical education. In a field that until the late 1940s had been dominated by women for almost fifty years the rise of this male discourse to power and influence during the twenty years between 1945 and 1965 was little short of dramatic. I have already outlined some of the conditions of emergence of this discourse, in terms of the establishment of institutions and ideologies and how these followed some of the wider social, educational and political trends of the times. However, none of this entirely explains why such disparate discourses emerged and, more to the point, why they were so firmly identified with 'the sex of the individual'.

This is not to deny that some women were appointed to the university departments,[60] nor to deny that some men did teach educational gymnastics, and indeed as the monopoly of the private women's colleges was broken in the early 1960s, the distinctiveness of the two discourses did begin to blur at the edges. Perhaps the insularity and elitism of the female tradition were important in allowing two distinctly different discourses to exist, but while this explains how their conditions of emergence were dissimilar, it does not tell us why it was that the women as a group chose to move away from the functionalism of Swedish gymnastics towards a humanistic child-centred form of the subject, while the men reformulated the functionalism of the Swedish system within a scientific discourse. Perhaps, as Fletcher suggests, the quite disparate experiences of men and women during the Second World War, and the male experience of armed combat, were crucial in drawing female and male physical educators so far apart.

Perhaps more to the point is the nature of patriarchal norms and practices in which the events that have been discussed here were embedded. Scratton and Hargreaves both suggest that while the female discourse formed a radical alternative to the male version of physical education in one sense, in another it did little to challenge women's roles as wives and mothers.[61] Scratton claims that while, on the one hand, girls' physical education presented a radical challenge to Victorian notions of the frail, illness-prone and delicate constitution of the female, on the other girls' activities were still framed and limited by patriarchal views of correct conduct, biological capacity and emotional instability.[62] Hargreaves lends support to this line of argument in her claim that from the beginning of the female tradition in physical education the gymnasts' support for female emancipation was based on 'a nationalistic sentiment, confirming the contemporary Social Darwinistic position about the vital importance of motherhood to evolution, and the encompassing belief that educational arrangements should be geared to the role of women as mothers.'[63] Thus the family emphasis of the Victorian era based on patriarchal authority and a strict hierarchy of command and definition of roles was, as Fletcher has shown in her study of Bedford Physical Training College, still present in the women's colleges in the 1950s. The fact that educational gymnastics came to be associated with the physical education of girls and small children in itself says much about the limits set by patriarchal structures on the extent to which any oppositional group may be permitted to form radical alternatives.

This example holds a number of lessons for understanding the contemporary debate. The first is that contestation and struggle over the form and content of the subject are the *normal* state of affairs, not, as much of the curriculum development literature would have us believe, the exception. In this process the influences of rival groups wax and wane and the substantive details of the debate shift and change. But the dynamics of the process remain essentially the same. The second lesson is that the form and content of physical education now, as in the period covered by this study, are shaped in important ways by the broader educational, social and political events of the time. This suggests that physical educators must be aware of and in touch with these trends and events if they are to play a decisive part in shaping the substance of their subject and through this their day-to-day working practices. The third lesson is that contemporary physical education programmes both reflect *and produce* the constitution of society at large. The forces of capitalist accumulation, consumer culture and the nation-state are therefore far from irrelevant to the work of physical educators. Physical education programmes clearly show these forces at work, through competitive sport and the importance of representative competition at all levels from inter-school to international, and the rise to prominence of health-related programmes focusing on individual fitness, appearance and well-being. These are substantive representations of powerful forces in society.

At the beginning of *Pure and Applied Gymnastics* Munrow offered his definition of gymnastics, and following academic convention proceeded to argue his case in support of it. In her response in *Basic Movement* Randall was quick to point out that, notwithstanding the logic of Munrow's defence of his definition, the meaning of the term 'gymnastics' differed according to the gender and nationality of the gymnast. Her point, if not her intention, is clear; one cannot simply define or argue a particular meaning of a subject into existence. In drawing out the conditions of emergence of each of the rival discourses that surrounded gymnastics teaching, it should by now be clear that the alternative conceptions of physical education each discourse embodied were not open to rational choice. Nor had each an 'equal' or 'fair' chance to demonstrate what they had to offer to pupils within an educational setting. This is because the debate among the Swedish, educational and Olympic gymnasts, and their attempts to define the subject, were struggles over the operations and conduct of tertiary institutions and schools, and over the hearts and minds of physical educators. In such a context the rules of the debating society certainly do not apply.

Notes

1 See the papers in J. Evans (1988) *Teachers, Teaching and Control*, Lewes: Falmer Press, Evans' own contribution to that volume, and Chapter 6 in this book.
2 I.F. Goodson (1983) *School Subjects and Curriculum Change*, London: Croom Helm; I.F. Goodson and S.J. Ball (1984) *Defining the Curriculum: Histories and Ethnographies*, Lewes: Falmer Press; I.F. Goodson (1985) *Social Histories of the Secondary Curriculum: Subjects for Study*, Lewes: Falmer Press.
3 B. MacDonald and R. Walker (1976) *Changing the Curriculum*, London: Open Books and L. Stenhouse (1975) *An Introduction to Curriculum Research and Development*, London: Heinemann contain excellent critiques of the rational planning approach to curriculum development and change. See also Sparkes' chapter in this book.
4 This can be seen clearly in J.A. Mangan (1981) *Athleticism in the Victorian and Edwardian Public School*, Cambridge: Cambridge University Press, and in a more muted form in P.C. McIntosh (1968) *PE in England Since 1800*, 2nd ed., London: Bell.
5 There has been a growing volume of feminist literature recently concerned with physical education and sport. See, for example, the collection of papers on the 'Gendering of Sport, Leisure and Physical Education' in the special issue of the *Women's Studies International Forum*, 19 (4), 1987; also S. Fletcher (1984) *Women First: The Female Tradition in English Physical Education 1880–1980*, London: Althone; J. Hargreaves (1985) 'Playing Like Gentlemen While Behaving Like Ladies: Contradictory Features of the Formative Years of Women's Sport,' *The British Journal of Sports History*, 2 (1), 40–52; S. Scratton (1986) 'Images of Femininity and the Teaching of Girls' Physical Education, in J. Evans (Ed.), *Physical Education, Sport and Schooling: Studies in the Sociology of Physical Education*, pp. 71–94, Lewes: Falmer Press.
6 The term 'discourse' is used here in a broad sense to denote ways of thinking and talking about, and practising physical education. Discourses project the meaningfulness and significance of physical education for the people who articulate them, and so can be read at a number of different levels, literally, symbolically, figuratively and so on.
7 The college was permanently housed at Dartford ten years later from 1895.
8 See W. Saunders (1951) 'Why Exclude Olympic Gymnastic Apparatus Work?' *Journal of Physical Education*, 43, 85–8.
9 For discussions of progressivism in British education see D. Hamilton (1986) 'Some Observations on Progressivism and Curriculum Practice,' Unpublished paper, University of Glasgow; K. Jones (1983) *Beyond Progressive Education*, London: Macmillan; and M.E. Finn (1983) 'Social Efficiency, Progressivism and Secondary Education in Scotland, 1885–1905,' in W.M. Humes and

H.M. Paterson (Eds), *Scottish Culture and Scottish Education 1800–1980*, pp. 175–96, Edinburgh: John Donald.

10 Centre for Contemporary Cultural Studies (1981) *Unpopular Education*, London: Hutchinson.

11 For example, between 1945 and 1955 Scandinavian gymnastics are mentioned in *The Times Educational Supplement* on only four occasions — 12 June 1948, 31 July 1948, 31 March 1950, 22 April 1955 — which contrasts starkly with the frequent comments on the promotion of games and sports, and the provision of playing fields.

12 Although the Central Council for Recreative Physical Training (later the Central Council for Physical Recreation) was formed through the collaboration of the Ling Association with the National Playing Fields Association in 1935.

13 See Fletcher (1984), *op. cit.*

14 M. Carlquist (1955) *Rhythmical Gymnastics*, London: Methuen.

15 C.M. Read (1945) 'Gymnastics and Physical Education II,' *Journal of Physical Education*, 37, 130–2.

16 M.E. Squire (1945) 'Gymnastics and Physical Education I,' *Journal of Physical Education*, 37, 101–4.

17 G.M. Cox (1946) 'Gymnastics and Physical Education III,' *Journal of Physical Education*, 37, 57–60.

18 Squire (1945), *op. cit.*, p. 104.

19 See Fletcher (1984), *op. cit.*, p. 113 on the fate of Swedish gymnastics at Bedford Physical Training College.

20 R.B. Small (1976) 'The Effects of Individuals on, and Developments within, the Scottish School of Physical Education in the 20th Century.' Unpublished paper, Jordanhill College of Education, Glasgow.

21 M. Randall (1961) *Basic Movement: A New Approach to Gymnastics*, London: Bell.

22 Carlquist (1955), *op. cit.*, p. 2.

23 R. Laban (1948) *Modern Educational Dance*, London: MacDonald and Evans.

24 R. Morison (1969) *A Movement Approach to Educational Gymnastics*, London: Dent, p. 6.

25 D. Rubinstein and B. Simon (1966) *The Evolution of the Comprehensive School, 1922–1966*, London: Routledge and Kegan Paul.

26 See Note 9.

27 See Jones (1983), *op. cit.*, for a discussion of this issue.

28 Ministry of Education (1952) *Moving and Growing: Physical Education in the Primary School, Part 1*, London: HMSO; Ministry of Education (1953) *Planning the Programme: Physical Education in the Primary School, Part 2*, London: HMSO.

29 See *The Times Educational Supplement*, 31 March 1950 and 11 September 1953.

30 See Fletcher (1984), *op. cit.*, pp. 134, 136.

31 *Ibid.*, p. 128.

32 See Randall (1961), *op. cit.*, p. 16.

33 J. O'Dwyer (1951) 'Open Letter — A Plea for Proportion,' *Journal of Physical Education*, 43, 46–7.

34 E. Karn (1952) 'The "Old" and the "New" in Physical Education,' *Journal of Physical Education*, 44, 64–5.

35 The conference topic was 'Physical Education Today and in the Future' and was organized by the Scottish Joint Consultative Committee on Physical Education which was made up of representatives of the separate male (Scottish Physical Education Association) and female (Scottish League of Physical Education) associations. There is a report on the conference in *The Leaflet*, 56(1), 1955.

36 A.D. Munrow (1955) *Pure and Applied Gymnastics*, London: Arnold. Munrow was the first Director of the Department of Physical Education at Birmingham University.

37 In the second edition of *Pure and Applied Gymnastics*, published in 1963, Munrow commented on the debate around his definition of gymnastics presented in the first edition.

> Certainly the impact of the word 'artificial' in the definition has been unfortunate, especially on supporters of Modern Educational Gymnastics. Some of them might subscribe to the present definition of 'systematised exercises designed to produce particular effects on the body'.... Thus a small area of agreement could be found on which to stand together and discuss what are likely to be substantial areas of disagreement. (p. 22)

38 See McIntosh (1968), *op. cit.*

39 Munrow (1963), *op. cit.*, p. 282.

40 See, for instance, Squadron-Leader W. Winterbottom (1945) 'Physical Training in the Royal Air Force,' *Journal of Physical Education*, 37, 9–11, and Brig. T.H. Wand-Tetley, CBE (1946) '"Purposeful" Physical Training in the Army,' *Journal of Physical Education*, 38, 140–3.

41 A. Marwick (1982) *British Society Since 1945*, Harmondsworth: Penguin.

42 Further developed at Leeds University by Morgan and Adamson after the war. See R.E. Morgan and G.T. Adamson (1957) *Circuit Training*, London: Bell.

43 As one historian has commented, 'there evolved a technological civilization of a sort not previously seen in Britain...now the concept of one unified technology, based on what its apostles termed the "systems approach", was beginning to influence every aspect of social organisation.' See Marwick, (1982), *op. cit.*, p. 114.

44 See Centre for Contemporary Cultural Studies (1981), *op. cit.*

45 Munrow (1963), *op. cit.*, p. 276.

46 *Ibid.*

47 Randall (1961), *op. cit.*, p. 12.

48 *Ibid.*, pp. 25–6.

49 B. Knapp (1963) *Skill in Sport*, London: Routledge and Kegan Paul, pp. 110, 166.

50 Morgan and Adamson (1957), *op. cit.*

51 Randall (1961), *op. cit.*, pp. 20–2.

52 McNair Report (1944) *Teachers and Youth Leaders*, London: HMSO.

53 See Fletcher (1984), *op. cit.*

54 The key agents in the dissemination of educational gymnastics from the specialist physical education colleges to the generalist infant teachers were the Inspectorate and LEA Advisors, may of whom were women.

55 Centre for Contemporary Cultural Studies (1981), *op. cit.*

56 See Jones (1983), *op. cit.*, for a discussion of this point.
57 D. Bennett (1982) 'Education: Back to the Drawing Board,' in R. Smith (1985) *The Inequalities Debate: An Interpretive Essay*, p. 95, Geelong: Deakin University Press.
58 See J. Hargreaves (1986) *Sport, Power and Culture*, Cambridge: Polity Press for a discussion of the ways in which the state in Britain has increasingly used sport as a vehicle for the development of national identity and culture since the end of the Second World War.
59 I. Thomson (1986) 'Professional Training in Physical Education and Sport within a Binary System of Higher and Further Education in England 1944–1985,' in *Trends and Developments in Physical Education*, Proceedings of the 8th Commonwealth and International Conference, pp. 61–74, London: E. and F.N. Spon.
60 Though as Fletcher (1984), *op. cit.*, p. 135 observes, women were not admitted to the advanced diploma course at Leeds University until 1966, eleven years after it began.
61 See Note 5.
62 Scratton (1986), *op. cit.*, p. 73.
63 Hargreaves (1985), *op. cit.*, pp. 47–8.

Acknowledgments

This paper draws on a research project which began in August 1987 during a study leave from the University of Queensland. I would like to thank the University for granting and funding the leave and Ian Jobling for his facilitation of it. I also want to thank a number of people for their very helpful and often challenging comments on earlier drafts of this paper, in particular Annette Corrigan, John Evans, Neil Kelly, Jane Kenway, Jim McKay, Tony Mangan, Gail Reekie and Ian Thomson, and Gordon Tait for his assistance in collecting some of the sources on which the paper is based. Needless to say, though, the shortcomings are all my own work.

Chapter 4

Oppression and Privilege in Physical Education: Struggles in the Negotiation of Gender in a University Programme

Alison Dewar

This chapter represents my concerns about the ways in which gender is constructed and represented in many teacher education programmes in physical education in North America. These concerns stem from my interests in the social construction of gender relations in and through physical education programmes that place a strong emphasis on individualistic, voluntarist analyses of the body, health and fitness, and human physical performance. Here I want to analyze how men and women students constructed their gender identities in a Canadian university physical education programme. The broad purpose is to locate this programme and these students within the context of the struggles and debates over the direction and content of physical education teacher education programmes in North American universities during the last twenty years.[1] The chapter is also intended to be a critique of what Kirk (1989) has called the 'orthodoxy' in research on physical education teacher education, which consists of a 'science of teaching' modelled on the epistemology and methodology of positivist science.[2] One need only look at the *Journal of Teaching in Physical Education* to understand the fervour with which many researchers are pursuing the promises of pedagogical science in physical education.[3] The almost unbridled enthusiasm for what this science will do for physical education teaching is worrying because of its apparent lack of reflectiveness and self-criticism. What I mean by this is that science seems to have taken on a life of its own for many of the protagonists of this science of pedagogy or 'sport pedagogy,'[4] and any criticism of this way of studying teaching is seen as heresy and unworthy of serious consideration.[5]

This chapter should not be read as another attempt to 'beat up' positivist science and orthodoxy in sport pedagogy, because it is not. It explores instead how students create space for themselves within this orthodoxy in physical education. It attempts to develop some understanding of the ways in which four distinctive groups of students define and create their gender identities within a curriculum that emphasizes and celebrates scientific knowledge and technical skill about human physical performance. A subtheme is to argue that the development of a science of teaching and coaching is not simply a matter of finding the best and most efficient ways of improving teaching and learning. The construction of a science of sport pedagogy involves much more than the development of 'better' teaching techniques. This construction involves decisions which have very real political, moral and social consequences. These decisions are ones that privilege fact over value, objectivity over criticism, and universality over historicity in the study of pedagogy. Alternative pedagogies, which are aimed at the development of educational practices that do not perpetuate the various oppressions that exist in capitalist patriarchal societies, are frequently discounted by teacher educators in physical education because they are assumed to be nothing more than the rantings of groups of self-interested, dissatisfied and disenchanted radicals bent on the destruction of liberal democracy. The power embedded in this kind of logic becomes evident when the perspectives of students in teacher education programmes are examined. These students, some of whom are discussed in this chapter, are not a carefully selected group of radicals, but see themselves as ordinary physical education students,[6] trying to make sense of their professional and personal identities. I intend to examine how students construct and negotiate their gender identities because gender is one way in which these relatively homogeneous students are differently privileged. Through an exploration of the ways in which they view gender relations in sport and physical education it may be possible to begin to make visible the connections between the technical, rational scientific knowledge they are taught about human physical performance in the programme and the realities of their lives as physical education students.

I begin by briefly examining the historical conditions that have enabled a scientistic and rationalized version of pedagogy to become hegemonic in physical education in the United States and Canada. The rise of a science of pedagogy in physical education needs to be located historically to underscore the point that its development arose out of a crisis in physical education in higher education, namely the disciplinary movement in the 1960s. Physical education changed significantly during this period and teacher educators were key protagonists in the process. To respond to widespread criticisms that physical education was not a legitimate area of study for higher education, teacher educators turned to the behavioural theories of psychology and methods of positivist science to establish a foundation for disciplinary status. The arguments embraced by the 'new'[7] pedagogues in physical education had at least as much to do with their concerns for legitimation and authority[8] as they did with the pursuit of knowledge about teaching and learning in physical education. What was at stake at this time was more than an appropriate paradigm for studying teaching. The very survival of teacher education in physical education in university programmes was being contested.

The results of this authorization of physical education teacher education through science are then explored in relation to the kinds of knowledge defined as important and 'really useful' for teacher education programmes. The focus of many programmes on technical skills required for successful teaching and learning and the reduction of knowledge about humans and their bodies to 'facts' about human physical performance that can be easily assimilated into models of good pedagogy is an indication of the importance accorded to science and the scientific method in sport pedagogy programmes.[9] The problem that needs to be discussed is the implications of defining teacher education in physical education this way. It is not simply a matter of articulating better ways to teach but involves the privileging of certain forms of knowledge, which in turn privilege only a few, already privileged people. The act of developing a science of pedagogy needs to be seen in the context of the messages it presents. Questions need to be asked about the ways in which knowledge about teaching and the body are implicated in the privileging of the already powerful in North America (white, middle-class, able-bodied, heterosexual men) and the continued oppression of others who do not fit into one or more of these categories of privilege. Data are then presented from an ethnographic study of one university physical education programme. The data illustrate the complex ways in which both women and men students struggle to articulate their gender identities within a programme that places a strong emphasis on the natural sciences and biological and behavioural knowledge. These data allow us to begin to see the ways in which particular kinds of knowledge become powerful tools in the oppression of a number of groups, and in this case in particular, of women.[10]

Sport Pedagogy: The Search for a New Science of Teaching

It is not uncommon for proponents of sport pedagogy to characterize this area of study as a young and newly developing science. The following statement by Metzler is relatively typical. In an article reviewing existing research on time in sport pedagogy, Metzler begins with the statement that 'however one might define it, and whether one might want to include or exclude certain parts of it, there is little doubt that a serious, contributing science of sport pedagogy has been around for only a few years' (Metzler, 1989, p. 87).

These claims are often used as a way of situating the progress being made by sport pedagogy researchers in a young, developing field. Although this may be seen as nothing more than an affirmation of the nascence of a developing discipline to those who work within its boundaries, it is suggestive of more than that. What is left unstated, but certainly implied in statements such as the one by Metzler, is that only certain kinds of scholarly activity are considered to be part of this serious and contributing science. It is the standards for judging what constitutes a science of sport pedagogy that are relatively new, not the existence of pedagogy in physical education. This distinction between the pedagogy of physical education programmes prior to the 1960s and the disciplinary movement in physical education in higher education in the United States and Canada and the 'new' science of pedagogy spawned from this movement is an important one. It allows for an analysis of the development of the terrain of the 'new' science of pedagogy, which is contextualized within the struggles for survival and legitimacy that have occurred in physical education in the last hundred years. It is clearly beyond the scope of this essay to develop an in-depth analysis of the struggles that have occurred over the appropriate subject matter for physical education in higher education in the United States and Canada.[11] What I will do in this section is argue, albeit briefly, that the disciplinary movement in physical education paved the way for the development of a science of sport pedagogy committed to the study of teaching and learning in ways that placed a premium on viewing individuals and their behaviours in technical, rationalized voluntarist models.

The history of physical education in higher education in the United States is characterized by struggles for professional legitimation and authority (Ingham and Lawson, 1986). These early struggles (from 1900 to 1960) were around both the subject material necessary for the development of a healthy, moral citizenry, and the best methods for delivering this subject matter to students in physical education programmes in schools. These debates focused primarily on method and content rather than purpose. Questions about *what* should be taught and *how* it should be taught were of concern to physical educators. Questions about *why* the content was being taught and *whose* interests it was serving did not appear to be an important part of the debate. As Ingham and Lawson (1986, p. 643) suggest, in this early stage 'physical education was a teaching-oriented field primarily geared to preparing teachers for the public schools.' They go on to state that:

> During these formative years, both physical educators and moral/social/political leaders had an 'elective affinity' for a residual Progressivist ideology. Central to this ideology was the conviction that reforming society involved reforming the manners, morals, and character of children and youth. This child saving enterprise led Physical Education to be conceptualized as both a functional-technical education and a moral education. (Ingham and Lawson, 1986, p. 643)

School physical education programmes became the tools for this moral reform and physical educators the agents. Sport and fitness became the focus of this movement and moral philosophers such as Clark Hetherington, Charles McLoy, Jay Nash and Jesse Williams were leading advocates for physical education that would develop healthy, moral and wholesome children and youth.

The definition of physical education as a moral activity and aimed at the development of healthy minds and healthy bodies is derived from the ideology of muscular Christianity popularized in the private boarding schools of Victorian England, while physical education in the form of both Swedish gymnastics and military drill was developed as a method for controlling the health and behaviour of under-class children in state schools in this period.[12] The celebration of this ideology and its translation into sport and fitness curricula may have provided physical educators with a *raison d'être* and *modus operandi*, but questions about whose interests were being served by this rationale and the methods for its delivery were not asked. The fact that an Americanized version of muscular Christianity was translated into physical education curricula that reflected and celebrated elitist, white, upper-middle-class, Anglo-Saxon, male values was never made explicit in these early debates. The translation of this gentlemanly code into a set of individualized moral imperatives by physical educators illustrates how successful the field was in defining health, fitness and morality as personal troubles for children rather than social issues in a capitalist patriarchal society. Urging children to reform themselves through the physical was the perfect slogan for physical educators in their attempts to gain control over children's bodies and souls.

Ingham and Lawson suggest that after securing an authorized foothold in higher education, physical educators turned their attentions to research. They argue that:

> the questions asked by researchers were predictably self-serving because scientific inquiry was 'added on' to firmly established frames of value reference. Self-legitimizing research would provide proof of the good or beneficial aspects of exercise and sport participation. Such research, then, was not *critical* and *evaluative* and its findings were weaved together to form elaborate, pluralistic justifications for programs already implemented in schools and colleges. Liberalism and practicality dictated the scholarly quest. Science was the veneer. (Ingham and Lawson, 1986, p. 644)

This activity of proving the value of physical education allowed researchers to turn their attention to questions of technique and method. The search was for the best and most efficient ways of teaching the contents of physical education curricula in schools. The 1960s marked a time of crisis and renewal in physical education in higher education. Questions were being asked both externally and internally about the future prospects for university physical education programmes. The result of this reassessment was a move away from the professional-vocational orientation of the field towards the development of physical education as an academic discipline, and this was also a movement away from the physical education of the past. The hegemony of teacher education was being challenged by emerging disciplinarians who were eager to move outside the narrow realms of school physical education in their quest to develop a unique body of disciplinary knowledge and method for studying health, exercise, sport and leisure. It was during this time that the foundations for a science of sport pedagogy were laid.

The proponents of the new 'sport pedagogy' were highly sceptical of the moves to form a discipline that separated itself from school-based physical education. However, this group was also concerned about distancing itself from the earlier work of the moralists and missionaries (Williams, Nash, Hetherington) and their disciples so prevalent in physical education teacher education programmes.[13] The solution for these new sports pedagogues was to argue against a disciplinary emphasis that did not focus on pedagogy and argue instead for the development of a discipline of sport pedagogy. This enabled them to remain centred on pedagogy but to reshape this perspective. These new pedagogues used the basic tenets of positivist science to legitimate their claims for disciplinary status. What this enabled was the promise of a new pedagogy that 'answers the calls for better research and better practice for school physical education programs' (Lawson, 1984, p. 143). This promise of better research and practice is the promise of a more efficient, effective under-standing of teaching and learning behaviours in a variety of school gym-nasia. This, I believe, is what Metzler was referring to when he stated that 'a serious, contributing science of sport pedagogy has been around for only a few years.' In claiming that the new science of sport pedagogy makes a serious contribution to our understanding of teaching and learn-ing behaviours, protagonists effectively separate and distance themselves from pedagogical research prior to the development of the new discipline.

In this context it is more important to question the ways in which this new discipline has been defined, rather than to evaluate whether the promises of the new science of sport pedagogy have been realized. When the concerns of sport pedagogues are located within the debates of the disciplinary movement in the rest of the field, it is abundantly clear that the new sport pedagogy has been developed as a discipline which remains dedicated to changing individuals' attitudes and behaviours. I am hard pressed to believe that all that much has changed. What we seem to have in the new sport pedagogy is a different kind of reform presented, under the guise of scientific rationality or scientism, as neutral 'facts' describing good teaching and learning. Although Ingham it not writing specifically about sport pedagogy, his point is relevant in that context:

> In physical and health education, we are generally guilty of a kind of intellectual apartheid in which kinesiological and health science, and curriculum implementation, is undertaken without much re-gard of the changes in political economy. For kinesiological and health scientists the triple tendencies of behaviorism, empiricism, and voluntarism combine to produce discrete response to holistic problems. We tinker with the biological and psychodynamic in-dividual rather than the socioeconomic and political structures. (Ingham, 1985, p. 51)

Sport pedagogues are as guilty of this as kinesiological and health scien-tists. The point here is not a call for the abolition of research in sport pedagogy. Teachers need technical skills to teach well, and it would be foolish to suggest otherwise. But there is more to teaching than technical skills. Understanding *what* is being taught and *why* are as important as knowing *how* to teach it. Questions about whose interests are being served both by the sports we teach in physical education classes and the notions of health and wellness we advocate in our programmes and practices help to develop this understanding. They help to unpack the moral imperatives associated with scientistic, voluntarist interpretations of teaching and learning. If one does not ask these questions or attempt to gain an understanding of the social and historical contexts of teaching and learning, it is easy to define physical education as an apolitical, ahistorical subject aimed at the improvement of health, fitness and physical well-being for all. This is exactly what the new sport pedagogy would have us believe. Yet, if one looks a little closer at what goes on in school physical education programmes, it is easy to see that much of what is being taught in programmes emphasizing sport skills, health and fitness is just the opposite. Sport pedagogy may have changed *how* we teach but *what* is being taught remains essentially the same. Like it or not, most physical education programmes in schools still have a strong white, bourgeois male bias. When we add to this even more scientific knowledge about human physical performance, what we get is elitist, white, androcentric ideology presented as scientific 'fact', which is assumed to require no justification because it is portrayed as objective, technical information about performance.

It is possible that this critique may be seen as an attempt to undermine hardworking, committed physical educators in both universities and schools and to celebrate the work of those physical educators committed to 'critical' educational theories and practices. On the contrary, it is not to apportion blame but to understand *how* our practices within physical education have been constructed, *why* they have been constructed in certain ways, and *who* or *what categories* of individuals benefit from these decisions. This is a *relational* analysis that questions how practices are structured in physical education in ways that may help to legitimate, reproduce or challenge the social relations of power and privilege that exist in Western capitalist patriarchal societies. Relational analyses are sometimes seen as irrelevant to the actual practices that make up physical education programmes in schools because they appear to be abstract, impersonal and unable to offer practical guidelines for change. The problem we face in doing relational work is that it is necessary to understand the complex connections that exist between individual practices, programmes and the social relations of power and privilege before it is possible to develop alternative anti-oppressive practices. In essence, the challenge is to understand the relationships between teachers' practices and the larger social structures within which their actions are given meaning and authority.

An example might be useful to illustrate this point. Imagine a basketball lesson with a grade eight co-educational class. A typical scenario for such a lesson might be that there are thirty students in the class taught by a white male teacher. The lesson begins with warm-up exercises that are linked to the skills to be learned during the lesson. The warm-up is directed and paced for the students by the teacher. The teacher has designed the lesson to allow students to learn how to perform the lay up shot. The class is lively, interesting and constructed to have the students actively engaged in progressively learning and practising the skills required for the lay up. The teacher directs the lesson, is well organized and provides appropriate feedback to students about their performance of the skills being taught. The skills are presented clearly and lead up to mini two vs. two games, which are designed to allow students to use the shooting skills they learned in class. This is the kind of lesson that is often seen as an example of good teaching. The teacher has planned the content of the lesson to meet predefined objectives, the students are engaged in their learning and the teacher is able to maximize the time of the students' engagement by being well organized and a skilled manager. When presented in this manner, it is easy to see how it might be claimed that physical education is nothing more than the teaching of performance skills in well planned, effective ways. However, what is not said about this kind of lesson is of crucial importance. There are questions that could be asked, but typically are not, which would reveal the problematic nature of such a lesson and such an account of the lesson. For instance, we might ask what kinds of students are most likely to succeed in basketball? Or, what does a student have to be able to do to be successful in basketball? What kinds of students are privileged when basketball is taught in this way? What kinds of students are made invisible by this view and presentation of basketball? How do students who are not strong, coordinated, able-bodied, lean and muscular feel in a class such as this? What kinds of messages does such a class provide about what kinds of people and skills are devalued in physical education and sport? Who benefits most from learning these kinds of skills in this way? And why basketball anyway?

More questions could be asked which would attempt to understand how the teaching of apparently 'neutral' skills in fact privileges groups of persons in our culture who are already privileged. Asking these kinds of questions is one way to develop a sense of the connections between *what* we do as individuals and *how* this is structured and given meaning within North American culture. By addressing questions such as this it is possible to understand that the importance of strength, speed and power in most sports, and the emphasis on hard work, talent and competition is no accident. These help to make visible the ways in which the content of many physical education programmes has been developed to reward and celebrate white, heterosexual, bourgeois male privilege. When these questions are not asked and sport and physical education are seen as 'neutral', inherently 'good' activities for all, it is easy to understand why there is a large emphasis on the teaching of skills. The problem is if we choose to emphasize technical knowledge and skills, we are not making a neutral choice. We are making a political choice to continue to teach in ways that may ultimately serve the interests and needs of a minority of already privileged students. Thus, when we reduce the content of physical education teacher education programmes to 'facts' about performance and the teaching of performance, we effectively render them unproblematic and unrelated to social and political relations in capitalist patriarchal societies. This is what the new sport pedagogy does. It is able to present teaching and learning in this way because it has been successful in using science to universalize teaching and learning and separate it from the social and political contexts in which it occurs.

This move towards the development of a science of sport pedagogy has had implications for the kinds of knowledge taught in teacher education programmes in the United States and Canada. Biological and behavioural knowledge relating to both human performance and to teaching and learning are given centre stage in sport pedagogy programmes. Students are presented with the 'facts' and are given opportunities to learn and apply them to a variety of different teaching contexts. Opportunities for evaluation and reflection are also included in sport pedagogy programmes but they tend to be technical, focusing on what was done and how it could be improved. Critical, social, moral and political reflection is rare because it is deemed unnecessary in scientific analyses of teaching. The privileging of certain kinds of scientific knowledge in sport pedagogy is not a netural act. Science, as it is used in sport pedagogy, is a silent partner in the development of physical education programmes that privilege the young, the able-bodied, the lean and muscular, the middle classes, heterosexual men and white Christians. Physical education has the power to oppress because in its current form it uses science to blame its 'failures' or victims for their lack of success in programmes. Sport pedagogy extols the liberal democratic, individualist virtues of hard work and commitment, and advocates assume that it is possible to develop a fitter and more healthy nation by teaching students in physical education classes to work hard at and take responsibility for maintenance of healthy lifestyles.

Physical educators are the new moral philosophers who, armed with their scientific techniques and knowledge, are sent out to bring health, fitness and well-being to the nation's children. Unfortunately, in delivering this message they are presenting images of fitness, health and sport that reinforce the social relations of power and privilege in society. The failure of the new sport pedagogy to question the ideological basis of the content of physical education programmes means that students are sent strong messages that sporting and health practices in the United States and Canada have been developed for the greater good of all persons. The standards for measuring success in sport or in the achievement of wellness are assumed to be those toward which we should all be striving. Evidence suggesting that these standards are social and historical constructs, which privilege and celebrate the interests and needs of a powerful few, is masked in this new science of pedagogy. This new science works well in our capitalist patriarchal society because by focusing on technique and method it does not challenge the status quo. A kinder, gentler America may be the new rallying cry of George Bush and the Republican Party, but a kinder, gentler physical education is far from the reality created by the 'new' discipline of sport pedagogy.[14]

Negotiating Gender Identities within a Scientistic Physical Education University Programme

The argument presented in the first part of this chapter contends that many sport pedagogy programmes have become scientistic in their search for disciplinary status and prestige within physical education. One result of this authorization through science has been the creation and development of a number of physical education programmes in schools and universities that select and reward a relatively small number of individuals who tend to be privileged by, among other things, their bodies, gender, social class position, race and physical abilities. These processes of selection and the allocation of reward present physical educators with very real social, moral and political problems because they fly in the face of most of our claims that physical education can and will provide opportunities for health, fitness and well-being for *all* students. In the latter part of this chapter I will present data from a case study of one university physical education programme. These data allow us to examine how students who have been successful in sport and physical education programmes and are privileged by their bodies, physical abilities, race and social class positions negotiate their gender identities.

The decision to examine the social relations of gender in these relatively privileged students' lives was made because this is one important way in which these students are different. Consequently, these data allow an exploration of how the gender relations of power and privilege are negotiated in a scientistic physical education programme. This represents a first step in a critique of the orthodoxy in physical education and is limited because it can only discuss one form of oppression in physical education. The next step, which requires further research, is to investigate other forms of oppression and examine how teacher education students translate these struggles into actual teaching practices in schools. Once we have a better understanding of how privilege is negotiated and contested in physical education teacher education programmes and the contradictions that exist in these negotiations, it may be possible to make visible the very difficult, often obscure connections that exist between social structure, programme ideology and individual practices.

The data are primarily drawn from in-depth interviews with twenty-eight physical education students, thirteen males and fifteen females. The interviews took the form of conversations, and each interview was structured to allow the students to set the pace, direction and scope of topics discussed. Where appropriate, I introduced topics and, when necessary, probed for clarification and detail. During the interviews I responded to any questions about my experiences in the study or my opinions about any of the issues we were discussing.[15] The data were analyzed in two stages: first, as an ongoing process during the study, where emergent themes and ideas were tested, scrutinized and developed; second, after the completion of the fieldwork and the interviews the data were analyzed a number of times to synthesize, collate and develop themes, which were then checked and rechecked against data from other sources. This process of constant comparison of data (Glaser and Strauss, 1975) facilitated the reduction and organization of the data in ways that addressed the central theme of the study — an analysis of the social construction of gender within this physical education programme.

Before examining how students created and negotiated their gender identities it is important to examine how knowledge was constructed in this particular physical education programme. The first and most striking aspect was the strong emphasis on biobehavioural coursework in the curriculum. This emphasis on 'scientific' analyses of human physical performance in the curriculum is consistent with the basic tenets of 'orthodox' physical education programmes. The biobehavioural courses in the programme provided students with technologies and skills for analyzing and correcting human physical performance. These courses presented students with a scientistic framework to view physical education in schools. It was in these courses also that students were encouraged to adopt a perspective that fragmented the human body, exercise and sport into small parts that could be isolated and treated or 'tinkered with' to achieve maximal performance outcomes. Students were expected to develop technical, rational views of teaching, learning, health, sport and exercise in these courses. This meant that students were rewarded for developing professional identities and skills that isolated teaching practices from the social, political and cultural contexts in which they occur.

These biobehavioural courses used 'science' to provide students with technologies and skills for effectively and efficiently treating the human body. This particular construction of knowledge was one that clearly focused on questions of *what* to teach students and *how to* best teach it. This 'applied' orientation presented students with potentially 'useful' knowledge in the sense that it could be seen to have direct and immediate application to vocational practices like teaching, coaching and the health professions. At no time in any of these courses were students asked to develop the kinds of questions suggested at the end of the earlier example of a 'model' basketball lesson. In fact, the whole purpose of these courses was to help students develop the technical knowledge and skills to allow them to deliver rather than to question such a lesson.

There was a small number of courses in the programme — sociocultural courses — that challenged the scientistic view of physical education presented in the majority of biobehavioural courses. In these courses knowledge from the social sciences and humanities was used critically to analyze sport as an historically produced, socially constructed, set of cultural practices. Important knowledge was defined by the faculty who taught them as knowledge that helped students critically to analyze the dominant frameworks within which play, games and sport are understood, and policies governing their practices are constituted in North American culture. These courses were designed to challenge students to ask 'why?' They were also structured to present students with ways of seeing sport and physical education that allowed them to locate their practices as teachers and coaches within the structures of power and privilege that exist in North America. The basic premise of these courses was to challenge much of what the students took for granted in their worlds and to present them with a different way of defining 'relevance' and 'application' for teaching and learning.

When these differences in the construction of knowledge are examined in relation to how gender was presented in the programme, we are provided with an example of how science is used to define a social relation as an abstract category or 'neutral' fact about performance. When gender was mentioned in biobehavioural courses, it was presented as one variable that could affect performance. When it is defined in this way, gender is viewed as a discrete variable or personal attribute rather than as a social construct. The focus of attention in this kind of analysis is directed towards explaining how *differences* between males and females *explain* any gaps in their performance outcomes. The assumption underlying this presentation of gender is that once the 'performance gap' between men and women is explained, teachers can use this knowledge to develop 'realistic' expectations for the male and female students they teach and coach. At no time in these courses was this assumption questioned or were students asked to question how this kind of analysis may bolster stereotypical and patriarchal images of women.

When gender was taught in a small number of sociocultural courses, it was presented as a social issue. The analysis in these courses focused on inequality in sport and in some cases included discussion of the ways in which play, games and sport have been developed and structured to privilege white, bourgeois male interests and needs. This treatment of gender was antithetical to the construction of gender in the biobehavioural courses since it provided students with analyses that located gender inequality in the social relations of sport and society, rather than in biological and behavioural differences between the sexes and, as such, directly challenged scientistic views of gender.

Although students were presented with a few opportunities to challenge the dominant ways of thinking about teaching and learning in the curriculum, they tended to view important knowledge in ways that defined scientistic knowledge as 'really useful' and any knowledge that is critical of this as 'peripheral' and irrelevant. This had implications for how students viewed knowledge about gender in the programme. The dominant construction of gender was that presented in biobehavioural courses. In these courses patriarchal definitions of gender were presented as unproblematic and the primary focus was on teaching students 'objective facts' about sex differences in performance. An alternative was presented in sociocultural courses, where scientistic, voluntarist notions of inequality were challenged and (re)presented as social and historical constructions.[16] The students were not equally receptive to the different constructions of gender presented to them. They tended to give more credence and credibility to the 'scientific facts' presented to them in biobehavioural courses because these were seen as directly relevant and applicable to practice. Potentially emancipatory, critical knowledge about the social relations of power and privilege was defined as 'peripheral' because students had trouble seeing its relevance or applicability to physical education or sport. What this means is that for these students, 'scientific' frameworks were defined and accepted as 'useful' and applicable for teaching, coaching and work in the exercise and health professions. It is such constructions of knowledge that ensure that the links between teaching, learning and oppression of women in sport remain largely invisible to many students.

The discussion that follows illustrates the complex ways in which four groups of students negotiated and created their gender identities in a programme that placed a strong emphasis on individualistic, voluntarist, biological and behavioural analyses of the body, health, fitness and human physical performance. These negotiations and struggles are important because they illustrate the contradictions that occur for students as they attempt to create space for themselves in a programme that presents them with knowledge that both supports and challenges patriarchal power relations. The data help to make visible the differences that exist in these men's and women's lives simply as a result of how their abilities and skills are constructed and interpreted in a male defined subject in a patriarchal society. These data do not discuss how these students define good teaching practices. My position here is that it is important to understand how oppression, in this case sexism and heterosexism, impacts on the lives of these students before it is possible to explore the nature and consequences of any teaching practices they may develop. Therefore, the following discussion is limited to developing an understanding of how women and men understand and respond to the social relations of gender in a programme that tends to present gender as an 'objective', 'fact' of life rather than as socially constructed relations of power and privilege.

'Prissies, Jocks and Dykes': Students' Constructions and Reconstructions of Gender

The four groups of students to be discussed (super jocks, women jocks, ordinary jocks, and non-jocks) identified in varying degrees with the label 'jock'. This label was constructed in a number of ways by these four groups and was central in their negotiations over their identities as men and women in the programme. This label is often used to refer to physical education students. It is a label that has a gender of its own; for some it is a celebration and symbol of heterosexual masculinity; for others it means being a good athlete and being highly skilled in human movement. In this programme the term symbolized the possession of both constructions as highly valued attributes in physical education: enhanced heterosexual male sexuality and athletic prowess. The two groups I will discuss first developed and articulated the most clearly identifiable identities as 'jocks'. These groups, which I have called the 'super jocks' and 'women jocks', illustrate the complex ways in which women and men who identify as 'jocks' negotiate and define their gender identities.

The 'Super Jocks'

The 'super jocks' were a small group of men, usually football players, who were readily identifiable among the physical education students in the programme. The 'super jocks' represented an extreme. They were a group who were unashamedly masculine.[17] In order to describe this group, I will focus on one individual, Randy, a student who was an avowed member of this group.[18] The first thing that was noticeable about Randy was his hair, or lack of it. He had a very short crew cut, and it looked as if his head had been shaved. This seemed to exaggerate his build. The second thing that was noticeable was that he was about six feet tall and looked strong and powerful. He had the unmistakable look of a football player. Being a 'super jock' is unmistakably male. Randy was the archetypical macho, aggressive, athletic man. The way he dressed, his body, his walk, his hair, his friends, the wad of tobacco in his cheek were all worn as symbols of his masculinity and heterosexuality.

The 'super jocks' had a presence. They did not walk, they seemed to strut and exuded confidence by the way they moved. They commanded attention by their very presence. They were physically intimidating. The 'super jocks' were envied yet despised by other physical education students. They did not, however, go unnoticed. This group and their overt displays of their sexuality were viewed with disdain by many of the women. One women recounted an incident that typified the ability of Randy and his friends to use their bodies to intimidate: 'I remember we did a little project and all the guys in my group were football players and then this guy comes in...I didn't even notice him...right behind him was this huge guy, I mean huge, and all he was wearing were little shorts and couldn't he put something on? He looked...just on top of me and I thought oh my god.'[19]

There was also some folklore about the sexual exploits of the 'super jocks'. Whether real or imagined, these tales served to perpetuate the macho, aggressively masculine image of this group. For example, one women said of the 'super jocks', 'I've heard things about them I wouldn't repeat...this is with women...like one guy well he got a girl to agree to come home with him and she gets there and walks into the room and there were all these other football players and they had this massive bang. I've heard that.' For the other male physical education students in the programme the 'super jocks' were an irritant, yet at the same time they were viewed as enigmas. One male student said of them, 'You know there is no doubt about it. I mean those guys...if you let them bother you then they're really annoying...I know they're big and strong but I don't know how strong they are otherwise. I know they think they're great when they're with a bunch of guys...if you get them alone I don't know what they are like. I mean can they talk to you or are they still like...what are they?' Another male student said of the 'super jocks', 'I don't like the way they act...it's just the image...the football players for some reason think that they can't be nice guys...for some reason when they get together as a group they seem to think that they really have to get tough and be different.'

For Randy the criticisms of others were unimportant. He was confident about his athletic ability and comfortable with the ways in which he was expressing his sexuality. He did not care because he got a feeling of belonging and camaraderie from his associations with other 'super jocks'. He explained this sense of belonging in his comment, 'I don't know, I think guys have that mentality and just abuse their bodies. I think they all have the same type of mentality and they all group together. Everyone shows up in their team jackets and they're all together in a group...it's really like that.'

Randy's sense of himself and his views about women and their capabilities in sport were deeply rooted in biology. He believed that there are certain biological differences between the sexes that serve as legitimate reasons for the exclusion of women from certain sports. For example, he illustrated his position on sex differences in the following comment on the possibility of girls playing on boy's football or hockey teams: 'I'd feel fine, but I'd look at the maturation studies because at age 14 she's probably still on a par. The guys probably haven't hit adolescence yet. But as soon as they start sprouting and putting on the pounds...I wouldn't let her play, no. She's just going to get hurt.' Randy used biological and behavioural 'facts' as evidence to support his belief that women are 'naturally' weaker than men. This evidence was seen as legitimate grounds for excluding women from certain sports because he believed that women must be protected and saved from potential injury by men. Women who are big, strong and powerful and who contravene biological and behavioural evidence, which suggests that they are inferior to men, were not seen by Randy as examples of women who contradict 'the facts'. He had a hard time taking these women seriously and said, 'It's like the big, healthy girls who go out on the field and smash each other. Field hockey is a tough sport...I can't say I rib them...nobody ribs them face to face.' When pushed, Randy admitted that his description of these women was part of the repartee that goes on between different groups of male athletes. He admitted that he rarely thought about these women and if he did it was usually in ways that were 'playful' and 'in jest': 'We call the hockey players hockey pucks and they call us pigskins. I think that it just goes on between all teams. The ribbing about the women's field hockey team is not anything malicious.'

For Randy stereotypes of women in sport were nothing more than a bit of fun. Teasing other physical education students was just part of asserting himself as a 'super jock'. His ambivalence to the achievements of women athletes fitted with his beliefs in women's biological and behavioural limitations. The achievements of women athletes were easy for Randy to ignore. Women's achievements did not have to be taken seriously by the 'super jocks' because women do not generally participate in the sports played by Randy and his friends and therefore do not challenge or threaten their masculinity or images of their superiority over women.

Randy and the 'super jocks' were confident and aggressive in their displays of heterosexual masculinity. They were usually found in groups and were easily identifiable by their size, dress and behaviour. 'Super jocks' worked hard at their sport and expected kudos from their achievements on the field rather than in the classroom. Being successful in sport, being members of the 'team' and being big, strong and tough were symbols of this group's indisputable masculinity and sexuality. These symbols served as evidence for them of the close link that exists between sport and heterosexual masculinity. Women could not gain access to this group. They could not be 'super jocks' in the same ways as Randy and his friends. The 'super jocks'' exaggerated bodies, behaviour and overt displays of heterosexual masculinity made this an exclusively male group. These men give a material form to the belief that men are naturally stronger and more powerful than their female counterparts. They were celebrated as the pinnacle of male power and physical prowess and, as such, served as examples of what other men could achieve in and through sport and physical education. As a result of this construction of 'super jocks', there was little conflict for these men between the dominant, scientistic constructions of gender in the programme and the ways in which they had created their gender identities. The 'super jocks' reproduced in their everyday lives a set of gender relations that appeared to be unproblematic. They constructed themselves in ways that presented patriarchal explanations of men's superiority over women as natural and immutable, rather than as embedded in the social relations of sport and society.

The 'Women Jocks'

The 'women jocks' were another group who identified very strongly with the term 'jock'. This identification, however, took on very different forms and had quite different consequences than those developed and expressed by the 'super jocks'. As one 'woman jock' said of herself, 'Sometimes if I play sport I'd rather be considered not feminine because it doesn't have good connotations. I think of someone feminine as someone who can't shoot, can't dribble, can't do anything.'

'Women jocks' were not an easy group to locate. They were a minority group in this programme. They were the women who most closely resembled the male students, and they claimed the label 'jock' and were proud of their physical abilities. These women were positioned in this programme in contradictory ways. On the one hand they manifested many of the characteristics and behaviours of the male physical education students, so in some senses formed part of the dominant group. Yet by identifying as 'jocks' these women did not manifest traditionally feminine behaviours and were defined as marginal in relation to other women in the programme and women in society. The position of these women created tensions for them. These tensions are important if we are to understand how the 'women jocks' were located within a programme that was both enabling and constraining and that had the potential to reproduce and challenge male hegemony.

Chris, Ann and Jo were three 'women jocks' in the programme. They were clearly identifiable and usually wore the standard 'uniform' of the 'jock' — running or court shoes, white knee-length tube socks, sweat pants pulled up to the knees, and sweat shirts or t-shirts. Chris, Ann and Jo were close friends and spent a lot of time together. These 'women jocks' understood the tensions that existed for them in this programme. Such tensions are created within a scientistic programme that seems to foster the development of gender identities in which heterosexist stereotypes of women's abilities and skills are used as standard for judging all women's lives. In the following comments the 'women jocks' illustrate the contradictions that exist when women are described and defined in this physical education programme. Jo began by suggesting that: 'With all the courses that you're in, stereotyping happens all the time. I find that in my soccer and my football class there is the girl who is the feeb, then there's the jocks, then there's the girl we say is butchy.' All three women defined the majority of the women in the programme as 'feebs' or 'prissies'. Prissies are described in the following conversation between Chris and Ann.

Ann: The prissy girl with the dress and heels....
Chris: Which we assume is a motor moron....
Ann: Yes...they can't play sport they just want to fuck the guys.

They went on to describe prissies as women who 'play like girls'

> *Chris:* They, if you play like a girl you play wimpy.
> *Ann:* Also there's no aggression or anything put into it.

'Women jocks' on the other hand are viewed by these women as athletic, yet feminine women. Ann suggested that: 'If you're a jock...OK, well butch and dyke are so close to jock...I don't think skill level has anything to do with a butch but it has something to do with a jock.' Women who were defined as 'butch' represented an extreme for the 'women jocks'. 'Butch' was described by Jo as someone who 'goes out there, she doesn't care, she'll push the guys around. I'll play and I'll play to my ability but I don't seem to have the same attitude that she does...sport that's just what they do it's their life.' 'Butch' was also described by Chris and Ann.

> *Ann:* It depends...I think the way you dress has a lot to do with it.
> *Chris:* And the way you cut your hair, the way you look.
> *Ann:* The way you carry yourself, if you bump around like you know kind of flexing...
> *Chris:* Try to look like a guy severely then you're a butch. I think people with a butch attitude don't think they can succeed unless they are like a guy as aggressive and ugly [laughter] and dress the same the whole bit. Their image is masculine right to the end.

Chris, Ann and Jo defined themselves as jocks. They did, however, recognize that they may be defined by others as 'butch'. All three women were acutely aware of the contradictions that existed in the ways they were positioned in this programme, recognizing that in a heterosexist programme and culture they were marginalized. When the men in the programme accepted them as 'one of the guys', they did so in ways that devalued them as women. When the other women in the programme defined them as 'butch' or masculine, they also devalued them as women. Ann captured this best in her comment that: 'You're in a bit of a dilemma...you're right down the middle, the girls hate you because you're so butchy and you're so much better than them at all sports and the guys hate you because you are so threatening to their masculinity, so you ride down the middle road.' Riding down the middle road for the 'women jocks' meant creating an identity for themselves in which they could truly be what they were — strong, athletic women who loved sport. Yet in creating their identities as 'women jocks' they maintained the heterosexist categories they were trying to escape by vigorously denying that they were butch, and in so doing accepted and recreated the negative stereotype of 'butch' and 'prissy'.

Performance was central to Chris, Ann and Jo's perceptions of physical education and physical educators. Athletic ability was crucial for acceptance as a 'woman jock'. Without it, acceptance into this group was not possible. Chris, Ann and Jo were very unforgiving of women who failed to meet their performance standards. This is how they separated themselves from other women in the programme. The irony for the 'women jocks' was that the definitions of performance and the criteria they used to define success in relation to performance were those that emphasized and reinforced the scientistic images of gender presented to them in biobehavioural courses, rather than those presented in sociocultural courses that could have helped them to see sport as problematic instead of the individual women who choose to compete in it. By using knowledge about gender from biobehavioural courses the 'women jocks' were able to define themselves as different from or superior to other women who failed to meet their standards for excellence. These women were the ones the 'women jocks' wrote off as 'prissies and motor morons'.

Although competitiveness, aggression and athletic ability were valued by both men and women in this programme, this value was constructed in different ways. For men, particularly the 'super jocks', having an athletic body was enabling. It was celebrated and displayed as a symbol of their heterosexuality and privilege as, in the case of this programme, white, athletic men. For the 'women jocks' the possession of an athletic body was constructed in a different way. Their bodies were not celebrated as symbols of their heterosexual femininity. In fact, the opposite occurred, and placed the 'women jocks' in a difficult position. In their own small group having an athletic body was celebrated in ways that allowed these women to create space within this programme where strong, athletic women were able to express themselves in ways that took on traditional definitions of heterosexual femininity, but to do so with other supportive women. The ironies for Chris, Ann and Jo were that in order to create space for themselves in this heterosexist and lesbophobic programme they learned to live with and reconcile the contradictions between their experiences as athletes and strong women. They were acutely aware of how the boundaries for acceptable behaviour were constructed for women in both physical education and this programme. They understood the choices they had made in creating their identities as 'women jocks' and the consequences of these choices. They managed to survive and even thrive in physical education because they were gifted performers. Their very presence in this programme and the ways they chose to articulate their gender identities were potential challenges to patriarchal images of women as weak and inferior to men.

However, the challenge posed by athletic women like Chris, Ann and Jo did not really threaten male hegemony in this programme because they developed their identities in ways that ultimately accommodated patriarchal definitions of gender. All three women had experiences that led them to question biological and behavioural explanations of women's capabilities. Yet all three women seemed to accept biobehavioural explanations for the other women in the programme, who were seen as passive, weak and inferior to both themselves and the men. Ironically, in trying to separate themselves from the other women in the programme the 'women jocks' reproduced the very categories their sporting prowess challenged. The result was that they essentially defined themselves as 'exceptions' and, as such, their actions presented no real threat to male hegemony. At the same time, although the actions of the 'women jocks' were largely unsuccessful in challenging hegemonic masculinity, their very presence in the programme and their physical achievements at least redefined how women and their capabilities could be viewed. In a culture where physical ability was so highly valued it was difficult to ignore the achievements and skills of talented women, even if these were defined as exceptional or abnormal. The 'women jocks' performances 'spoke for themselves'. This is important because it points towards the possibilities for challenges to male hegemony.

The experiences of the 'women jocks' in the programme illustrated the problems and difficulties that women encounter when they try to challenge patriarchal definitions of gender. The resistance that the 'women jocks' expressed in relation to traditional definitions of gender allowed them to develop a strong sense of their own identities. However, this resistance was also accompanied by accommodation to and acceptance of the dominant structures and forms of knowledge that existed in the programme. The 'women jocks' had strong 'applied' performance orientations and viewed scientistic knowledge from biobehavioural courses as 'really useful'. The paradox for these women was that they developed challenges to hegemonic patriarchal gender relations without rejecting the forms of knowledge that helped to create them. The result was that in the short term the strategies employed by the 'women jocks' made the problems they faced more manageable and tolerable. They were able, despite their acceptance of traditional definitions of gender — 'prissies, jocks and dykes' — to extend the boundaries of these categories and find a place for themselves within the programme. However, in the long term this strategy was not one that effectively challenged the white, male, heterosexual hegemony that existed in the programme. Rather, the compromise for the 'women jocks' was to create space for themselves within existing structures and practices.

'Ordinary Jocks' and 'Non-Jocks'

There were two other groups of students in the programme who created their identities in ways that were quite different from the 'super jocks' and 'women jocks'. These students did not identify strongly with the label 'jock' and created space for themselves in this programme by distancing themselves from the stereotypes they believed to be associated with this label. The majority of the male students in this programme viewed themselves as 'ordinary physical education students'. I have labelled this group the 'ordinary jocks' because of the contradictions that existed for these men in both identifying with and distancing themselves from the label 'jock'. 'Ordinary jocks' were typically trim and well toned without having the bulk or size of the 'super jocks'. They wore their hair short but not cropped and dressed in what appeared to be the 'uniform' of this group: tennis shoes, blue jeans or sweat pants, and a t-shirt, sweatshirt or rain suit jacket. 'Ordinary jocks' had a sense of community. Being part of a group with common interests was important to them. The common bond for these men was sport. This, above all else, allowed them to identify with other physical education students. In the words of one 'ordinary jock', 'one thing you've got a lot in common with the other people in terms of sports, in terms that you are an athletic type...you get to know people.' It is tempting to describe the 'ordinary jocks' as a milder version of the more extreme 'super jocks'. But this was not the case. 'Ordinary jocks' presented themselves in ways that allowed a wider range of expressions of their masculinity than the narrowly defined heterosexual masculinity of the 'super jocks'. 'Ordinary jocks' played a number of different sports and were not expected to be as aggressively 'machismo' as the 'super jocks'.

There were, however, limits on what was taken to be acceptable behaviour for the 'ordinary jocks'. They understood very well the tensions that existed between being a good student and a good athlete. On the one hand they felt a need for balance between work and sport. Yet they were also acutely aware of the pressure that existed for them to be athletes first and academics second. For example, an 'ordinary jock' said, 'you learn to play a role out here...and personally if I can't do what I want to do then I just go nuts. So I think you can find the time to do sport you may suffer a bit as far as your marks go but personally I will sacrifice a bit of it for my own well being.'

There was a dilemma for the 'ordinary jocks' in this programme. If they became too anti-intellectual, they risked being labelled as 'dumb jocks'. Yet if they were seen to be too studious, they risked losing their credibility as athletes and being labelled as 'unmasculine' and 'wimps'.

'Ordinary jocks' were expected to be aggressive and competitive performers, which encouraged them to construct traditional heterosexual expressions of their masculinity. If they were not seen to be doing this, they risked having their sexuality and masculinity questioned. The following statement is an example of one way in which an 'ordinary jock' struggled with definitions of masculinity and how these related to sports performance:

> I work at a sports center at the same time as this guy and he is the third ranked baton twirler in the world...he looks really funny out there and it just doesn't fit. And figure skaters, male figure skaters are all considered gay...there is a continuum again between fags or someone who is feminine and someone who is gay...I think most people know when they say fag they don't mean gay they just mean he is feminine. He's just wimpy looking and likes girls' stuff.

This comment illustrates the powerful ways in which heterosexism and homophobia have become embedded in the lives of the men in this programme. The 'ordinary jocks' understood how their gender identities were bounded. They knew that they could be good students, sensitive and caring as long as they were also seen to be skilled, aggressive competitors in traditionally defined male sports. If they were not seen in this way, then they risked having their intellects and sensitivity used as evidence of a lack of heterosexual masculinity. 'Ordinary jocks' were also constrained by their bodies and physical abilities. If they were excellent performers, the boundaries for expressions of alternative expressions of heterosexual masculinity appeared to be possible. If not, the options were much more limited and there was pressure for them to construct very traditional, heterosexist definitions of their gender. The following comment illustrates this contradiction simply and clearly. 'I'm sure girls are more receptive to a guy who can cook or who is interested in what is going on with women and stuff and still be able to look good in a muscle shirt. You know it's like that Billy Joel song 'Keeping the Faith', it's great. He says, I learned how to dance and still look tough.'

In their discussions of women's capabilities in sport 'ordinary jocks' moved beyond scientistic explanations of sex differences. They appeared to recognize that women's participation in sport has been limited both by biology and by social expectations of the limits of biology. An example of their perspectives on gender issues is provided in the following comments by an 'ordinary jock' about his girlfriend.

AD: Say you get a woman who for example is good at football
       and she hangs around in her sweats and cleats, do people say
       'what a butch?'
OJ: They survive it because they're feminine enough looking,
       like my girlfriend Jan is always thought of as cute.
AD: And people know she's your girlfriend too.
OJ: But even beyond that she's got a tiny voice, she's cute and
       she's always been like that. She's had both sides. But if she
       happened to be. . . .

These comments illustrate this man's awareness of the ways in which
women were also constrained by heterosexism and lesbophobia in this
programme. However, his position was hardly sympathetic, which is
reflected in his statement that:

> there are girls who have a very hard time trying to figure out if
> they are girls or guys. . .they're not worried, they just don't try
> to be feminine. Most of them have devoted their lives to playing
> and they're so into it that it becomes central in their lives. Some
> of them are big they lift weights, they're muscular, they're heavy
> . . .it's just a girl who has masculine features she's big maybe
> not attractive. . .the ones who couldn't care less how they look.

This comment shows clearly how this 'ordinary jock' viewed women
who challenged hegemonic definitions of heterosexual femininity. When
pushed, he came down on the side of voluntarist, scientistic definitions of
gender relations. He suggested in the final analysis that women should be
like women and not like men, which meant that they should conform to
patriarchal, heterosexist definitions of their gender. He said, 'I think that
there are certain biological differences between men and women and
rather than try to erase them to work at equalizing the opportunities that
they each have and work together to improve them. . .not be afraid to do
the very best they can do but not go out and be like men.' This comment
illustrates the contradictions that existed in the lives and beliefs of the
'ordinary jocks'. They wanted space within the programme to express
themselves but did not want to challenge the ways in which sport and
physical education have been created to make this extremely difficult.
They wanted to be allowed to be sensitive, intellectual and slight but also
felt compelled to demonstrate their athletic prowess. Their expectations
of women in the programme had the same pattern. They would tolerate
women who were aggressive, competitive and who 'played like men' as
long as they displayed traditional forms of heterosexual femininity when
they were not playing.

The 'ordinary jocks' developed their gender identities in ways that accommodated to and reproduced traditional, hegemonic notions of heterosexual masculinity and femininity. They did so because they developed overt expressions and symbols of their heterosexuality, such as the possession of an athletic body and the use of this in aggressive and competitive ways in any sporting practices in which they were involved. Although these expressions of their sexuality and masculinity allowed these men to choose to be sensitive and intellectual, this did not serve to challenge the ways in which patriarchy defines gender relations as natural and immutable. They accepted these definitions and felt comfortable within a programme that celebrated and privileged the white, middle-class, heterosexual views of both their lives and the place of sport and physical education in them.

The 'non-jocks' were women in the programme who wanted to distance themselves as far as possible from the term and label 'jock'. These were the women referred to by 'women jocks' as 'prissies' and whom the 'ordinary jocks' celebrated as 'ideal' women who seemed to have the best of both worlds. They held the 'women jocks' in contempt and, in part, agreed with the 'ordinary jocks'' views of their lives. Mary, a 'non-jock', described her positioning in the programme in the following way:

> I think because we don't have our whole identity in what we're doing. You know, we have a lot more other interests. And too it's that whole thing of masculinity and femininity I think. For me I'm not going to go around hanging on to my hockey stick wearing sweats all the time because it's not me. That's not what people's conceptions of what a girl is supposed to be and I don't feel good being that. I don't want to be considered a jock or a dumb jock or anything like that so I'm not going to adopt that kind of thing.

This statement illustrates the ways in which the 'non-jocks' have developed their athletic identities in ways that complemented patriarchal definitions of their heterosexuality and femininity. Being recognized as heterosexual, feminine and attractive was vitally important to the 'non-jocks'. It is in this respect that these women differed most dramatically from the 'women jocks' in the programme.

Dawn, a friend of Mary's, was another 'non-jock'. She and Mary looked very similar to the majority of women in the programme. Both wore street clothes to go to class. Unlike the 'women jocks' they did not wear sports clothes as symbols of their athleticism. For Mary and Dawn being in physical education meant that they could have the best of both worlds. They could be athletic and still be seen as heterosexual, attractive women. They took their sport and their heterosexuality seriously. In this brief extract from a conversation, Mary and Dawn characterized how they saw themselves in the programme.

Mary: I see myself as a typical physical education student.
AD: What does that mean?
Mary: I go to my classes, do my work and most of my friends are from phys.ed.
AD: So would you describe yourselves as hard workers who also work out at sport and that's a typical physical education student?
Mary and *Dawn:* Yeah.

Mary and Dawn were typical of 'non-jocks' in the programme. They did, however, share one major thing in common with all the other students: they loved sport. At the same time the sports they participated in were the ones they viewed as suitable for women, or activities that did not tend to be seen as tough, aggressive or 'masculine'. Both women were conscious of ensuring that they participated in activities that would not be viewed as compromising their femininity or heterosexuality. It was important for them to be seen as feminine and athletic. This contrasts with the 'women jocks' who despised women like Mary and Dawn because of their overt celebrations of their heterosexuality. A good example of this contrast is illustrated in the following conversations both groups of women had about the same women tennis players.

Chris: I wish I played tennis like Martina (Navratilova).
Ann: She's my idol she's awesome...I know people call her a butch because she's awesome...they assume she was a dyke because she was such a good tennis player, because she has such good muscles and has low body fat.
AD: No one would say that about Chris Evert.
Chris: She doesn't look like Martina at all. I would think I could walk on to the court and drill her into the ground. She looks like a prissie.

Mary and Dawn took the opposite view:

Mary: Well Martina and Billie Jean King you can easily point a finger at them...they don't look feminine.
AD: No one would say that about Chris Evert.
Mary: Because of her looks, she looks feminine, I like Chrissie as a tennis player she does have the feminine part about her.

> *Dawn:* And I identify more with her than Martina...I'd like to play like Martina and look like Chris.

Mary and Dawn created an identity for themselves that allowed them to feel comfortable in this heterosexist, lesbophobic programme. However, in so doing they accepted these contraints in their lives as natural and used them to separate themselves from women who did not conform to their standards of heterosexual femininity. This construction of their gender identities enabled them to be more than simply feminine women. It allowed them to be athletic too. But the price they paid was that in order to do this they accepted limited and limiting biological definitions of women's capabilities in sport. Both women viewed issues concerning women's participation in physical education and sport in contradictory ways. They recognized that inequality is a problem for women in sport and physical education and understood that this is socially constructed rather than biologically determined. However, they also believed that things are improving for women and the achievement of full equality is only a matter of time and, as such, not an issue of any great importance in their lives. Despite their willingness to accept that inequality is a social issue, Mary and Dawn took a different view of women's performance capabilites in sport. They came down heavily on the side of biological determinism on this issue and at times saw this as a justification for some of the inequality in sport. For example, Dawn suggested, 'when you put two people out there, they put you out there and a guy, the guy is going to beat you and that's just the way it is.' Biobehavioural, scientistic explanations for sex differences in performance were acceptable for both women because they had no desire to compete against men or to participate in what they defined as 'male' sports. They used the knowledge they were taught about gender in biobehavioural courses as evidence that their views of gender were 'the ways it is'. They were able to do this because they viewed women who wanted to compete against men as lesbians, or 'butch'. This construction of their lives was very comfortable for Mary and Dawn, and they found support for their views in both the knowledge that was taught in this scientistic programme and the realities of their daily lives. This 'comfort' existed because in supporting heterosexist views of gender they were able to point to other women as 'unfeminine' and establish themselves as standards for heterosexuality and femininity in the programme.

The 'non-jocks' in this programme accepted patriarchal definitions of women as natural and inevitable. Their views were confirmed in biobehavioural courses in the programme and these 'facts of life' were used to construct their images as athletic, yet heterosexually feminine, women.

This construction of their gender identities was seen as comfortable for the 'non-jocks'. The fact that they were contributing to women's oppression more broadly was not an issue for them. They did not see themselves as oppressed and to continue to do so they positioned themselves in juxtaposition to the 'women jocks' whom they defined as 'butch women who want to be like men'. These women represented the 'non-jocks'' worst fears and to neutralize their impact on their lives they simply and effectively marginalized and trivialized them. This is yet another way that patriarchal hegemony remained secure in this programme.

Taking on the Orthodoxy: What Can Be Done in Physical Education Teacher Education?

It is difficult, if not impossible, and certainly in this case undesirable, to provide a definitive set of policies and practices for challenging the orthodoxy in physical education teacher education programmes. The data presented here illustrate that there is no one best way to challenge hegemony; it is always a struggle, a contested process, and one that has to be contested in multiple ways in multiple sites. My purpose in writing this chapter is to recognize the need for initiating and continuing challenges to what seem to be taken for granted as 'good educational' practices in physical education. My focus was on gender, but our challenges need to go much beyond this. We need to begin to think about how our programmes and practices are oppressive to many categories of people. It seems clear from the data reported in this chapter that the messages presented to students in most mainstream 'scientific' courses, whether these be about pedagogy or biological and behavioural determinants of performance, encourage students to accept and celebrate oppressive forms of physical education and sport as unproblematic. Challenging these views of physical education, health and fitness which, in the minds of many, are designed to liberate us from the evils of unhealthy, sedentary, destructive lifestyles is no simple task. Adding in a course or two that challenge anesthetized, scientistic models of teaching and learning does not appear to be enough. Students may simply disregard this knowledge as peripheral and irrelevant to the real task of teaching students sports skills in effective and efficient ways.

The real challenge for physical education is to develop alternative anti-oppressive pedagogical practices in all the courses that comprise teacher education programmes. Merely tinkering with various parts of the curriculum will not work. We need to view all the knowledge and skills that we teach in ways that allow them to be developed with multiple possibilities. Future physical educators need to be given opportunities to understand how they have been both privileged and oppressed by the nature of the content that makes up physical education programmes. This kind of personal understanding might allow for a greater sensitivity to the oppression of others who have found their physical education experiences to be conducted in what felt to be very hostile and unsafe spaces. Knowing where to begin or exactly how to begin is probably less important than recognizing that we need to put into practice some of our theories and understandings about oppression in physical education. Making visible the facade of the 'kinder, gentler, physical education' promoted by many sport pedagogues and sport pedagogy programmes is only part of what needs to be done. The real challenge is to develop in ourselves, our programmes and our students opportunities to rethink and re-evaluate our own lives as physical educators in order that we can move on to understand that we are implicated in the creation of the conditions for liberation or oppression in all of our lives.

Notes

1 The last twenty years represent an important period in the history of teacher education in physical education in North America. During this time there have been struggles over the disciplinary status and focus of physical education programmes in universities. These struggles are important in understanding the social construction of knowledge in physical education, which in turn influences the ways in which gender is constructed and represented.
2 Sandra Harding (1986) provides an excellent discussion and critique of positivist science.
3 This is not to say that all of this journal is dedicated to the advancement of the orthodoxy in sport pedagogy. There are examples of critiques (see Kirk, 1986, 1989; Schempp, 1987; Sparkes, 1989; Tinning, 1988) of this orthodoxy but these articles represent a minority of the work published in this journal.
4 The selection of the term '*sport* pedagogy' is significant because in this use of the term sport is seen as unproblematic and 'good'. This view of sport is in direct contrast to the 'critical' analyses presented by sport sociologists like John Hargreaves, Jim McKay, Richard Gruneau, Alan Ingham, Susan Birrell, Lois Bryson and others.
5 See the debate between Siedentop (1987) and Schempp (1987, 1988) for an example of the ways in which a leading protagonist of a science of pedagogy responds to criticisms about this kind of teacher education in physical education.
6 Although this group of students define themselves as 'ordinary', they are a fairly homogeneous group of relatively privileged able-bodied, physically gifted, white, middle-class men and women. This homogeneity may in fact represent the norm and define 'ordinary' in teacher education in physical education in North America, which in turn may make it difficult for students

to see the ways in which the physical education and sport systems tend to select and reward people like themselves, who tend to be privileged in important ways.

7 I am calling the disciplinary movement in teacher education in physical education the 'new' pedagogy because of its attempts to separate and distance itself from teacher education in physical education prior to the 1960s.

8 I am using 'authority' here in the same way as Ingham and Lawson (1986) who suggest that the struggles for authority or authorization involve 'securing the legitimacy to exclusively define and perform work; a process involving social negotiations between aspirant professionals and persons holding power in social structure' (p. 643).

9 See Dewar (1987a; 1987b) for a discussion of the social construction of knowledge in physical education.

10 I focus on the oppression of women in this chapter because this was the most obvious and visible form of oppression in this programme. Unfortunately, the processes involved in socialization into physical education (see Templin and Schempp, 1989) encourage the selection of students who are predominantly white, middle-class, able-bodied, physically gifted, lean and muscular, heterosexual men and women. This selection process meant that in this particular programme, as in many others, women's oppression is apparent simply because other forms of oppression, while present, appear invisible because they have been successful in selecting out individuals who do not fit into the categories of persons selected for physical education teacher education programmes.

11 See Ingham and Lawson (1986) and Lawson (1984) for a more detailed discussion of the struggles over the subject matter of physical education.

12 See Mangan (1981) and Dunning and Sheard (1979) for detailed analyses of athleticism and muscular Christianity in Victorian and Edwardian public schools in England, and MacIntosh (1968) for a discussion of the role of Swedish gymnastics and military drill in physical education in state schools during this time.

13 This is not to suggest that the 'new' sport pedagogues were unconcerned with moral issues but simply to stress that their concerns were different than those of their predecessors.

14 I am indebted to Alan Ingham for helping me see this link and phrasing it in this way.

15 This kind of in-depth interview is based on a commitment to the development of a non-hierarchical relationship between the researchers and the individuals in the study (see Eichler, 1988; Oakley, 1981; Stanley and Wise, 1983). Feminist research methodology assumes the development of cooperative, non-hierarchical relationships between the researcher and participants in the study, enabling them to talk about and analyze their own lives. This kind of work aims at allowing men and women to describe and re-create reality in their own terms and in relation to their own histories, biographies and the structures they live and work within.

16 It is important to note that the courses that gender is taught in are not as important as the way in which it is constructed. In this particular programme scientistic constructions happened to occur in biobehavioural courses and challenges to this in sociocultural courses. This is not always the case as it is

possible to present scientistic or critical constructions of knowledge in both biobehavioural and sociocultural courses.

17 My use of the term 'masculine' here refers to the stereotypical construction of masculinity in which men present themselves as aggressive, competitive, strong, powerful beings in the world. This use of masculine is different from the term 'male', in that 'male' simply refers to the biological sex of the individual, whereas 'masculine' refers to a set of socially constructed, culturally developed ways of being in the world.

18 The names used in this study are pseudonyms to protect the confidentiality of the subject in the study.

19 The quotes are taken from in-depth interviews and field notes. They represent how students talked about their experiences and have largely been left unedited. The only editing that has occurred is to remove idiosyncratic expressions of speech such as 'um', 'er', and 'you know'.

References

DEWAR, A. (1987a) 'The Social Construction of Gender in Physical Education.' *Women's Studies International Forum*, 10, 4, 453–65.

DEWAR, A. (1987b) 'Knowledge and Gender in Physical Education,' GASKELL, JANE AND McLAREN, ARLENE (Eds), *Women and Education: A Canadian Perspective*, Calgary, Alberta: Detselig Enterprises

DUNNING, E. and SHEARD, K. (1979) *Barbarians, Gentlemen and Players*. New York: New York University Press.

EICHLER, M. (1988) *Nonsexist Research Methods*. Boston, Mass.: Allen and Unwin.

GLASER, B. and STRAUSS, A. (1975) *The Discovery of Grounded Theory: Strategies for Qualitative Research*. Chicago, Ill.: Aldine.

HARDING, S. (1986) *The Science Question in Feminism*. Ithaca, N.Y.: Cornell University Press.

INGHAM, A. (1985) 'From Public Issue to Personal Trouble: Well Being and the Fiscal Crisis of the State.' *Sociology of Sport Journal*, 2, 43–55.

INGHAM, A. and LAWSON, H. (1986) 'Preparation for Research in Physical Education: A Biographical Perspective.' *Proceedings of the International Committee of Sports and Physical Education*. Yokohama: Yushido Press.

KIRK, D. (1986) 'A Critical Pedagogy for Teacher Education: Toward an Inquiry Oriented Approach.' *Journal of Teaching in Physical Education*, 5, 230–46.

KIRK, D. (1989) 'The Orthodoxy in RT-PE and the Research/Practice Gap: A Critique and Alternative View.' *Journal of Teaching in Physical Education*, 8 (2), 123–30.

LAWSON, H. (1984) *Invitation to Physical Education*. Champaign, Ill.: Human Kinetics Publishers.

McINTOSH, P. (1986) *Physical Education in England Since 1800*. London: G. Bell and Sons.

MANGAN, J.A. (1981) *Athleticism in the Victorian and Edwardian Public School*. Cambridge: Cambridge University Press.

METZLER, M. (1989) 'A Review of Research on Time in Sport Pedagogy.' *Journal of Teaching in Physical Education*, 8 (2), 87–103.

OAKLEY, A. (1981) 'Interviewing Women: A Contradiction in Terms?' in Roberts, Helen (Ed.), *Doing Feminist Research*. London: Routledge and Kegan Paul.

SCHEMPP, P. (1987) 'Research on Teaching in Physical Education: Beyond the Limits of Natural Science.' *Journal of Teaching in Physical Education*, 6, 111–21.

SCHEMPP, P. (1988) 'Exorcist II: A Reply to Siedentop.' *Journal of Teaching in Physical Education*, 7 (2), 79–81.

SIEDENTOP, D. (1987) 'Dialogue or Exorcism? A Rejoinder to Schempp.' *Journal of Teaching in Physical Education*, 6, 373–6.

SPARKES, A. (1989) 'Paradigmatic Confusions and the Evasion of Critical Issues in Naturalistic Research.' *Journal of Teaching in Physical Education*, 8 (2), 131–51.

STANLEY, L. and WISE, S. (1983) *Breaking Out: Feminist Consciousness and Feminist Research*. London: Routledge and Kegan Paul.

TEMPLIN, T.J. and SCHEMPS, P.G. (Eds) (1989) *Socialization into Physical Education: Learning to Teach*. Indianapolis, Ind.: Benchmark Press.

TINNING, R. (1988) 'Student Teaching and the Pedagogy of Necessity.' *Journal of Teaching in Physical Education*, 7 (2), 82–9.

Chapter 5

Pedagogy as Text in Physical Education Teacher Education: Beyond the Preferred Reading

Jennifer M. Gore

A Scenario

The class about to begin is a 'methods' class in volleyball. It is a weekly event this semester as is a similar class most semesters of the undergraduate programme. Some students have gathered early and are shooting baskets with whatever projectiles they can find (the 'proper' equipment is still locked in the storeroom). 'The boys' tend to dominate this activity. The lecturer arrives slightly before class is due to commence. He instructs the students to set up the volleyball nets and get enough balls from the storeroom so that each student can have his or her own. The students, all in 'appropriate' athletic attire, comply. Some students try to slip unnoticed into the gym while this activity is in progress. They have learned to avoid the chores of the class.

The students are called together and a warm-up commences. The lecturer outlines the plan for the day while the warm-up is in progress; some of the students are leading the stretching activities today, by prior arrangement. The lecturer then takes over. Students are instructed to take a ball each and practice the digging and setting activities that were taught during the past couple of lessons. The gym is filled with purposeful activity. 'Time on task' could hardly be higher except when a couple of students get too close to each other and decide to switch balls with every dig and another student, bored with this repetition, decides to see how high she can dig the ball without hitting the lights. These 'deviant' activities are noticed by the lecturer and students are reminded of the set task.

Students are called back to a central spot with their backs to the door of the gym, so as to avoid distractions from passers by, and with the balls

placed on the ground and out of the way. The lecturer begins an explanation and demonstration of the spike. Students walk through the movements en masse and have the opportunity to ask questions of clarification
— hardly any do — before moving with a partner to an area where they
can practise. Spare balls are safely returned to the bins before this activity
commences. The lecturer walks around giving feedback to the students as
they practise. Occasionally he calls the activity to a halt in order to give
feedback to the whole group or to introduce a variation in the skill
practice. After a time students are called back together and the next
activity explained. The skill is to be put into a game-like situation with
students working in groups of four across the volleyball nets. One person
throws the ball across the net for another to dig to a setter who in turn
sets the ball for the spiker. The ball is retrieved by the 'server', the
process repeated five times, and then positions rotated. The last ten
minutes of the period are reserved for game play with an emphasis on
using the skills as they have been taught in these lessons. The students are
called back in and the lecturer reviews the lesson, also explaining how he
might have taught it differently with a school class. All students are then
required to help with the packing up, although a couple sneak away and a
couple of others explain to the lecturer that they have urgent commitments elsewhere. The students have enjoyed this opportunity to be physically active and feel they have learned some helpful ways for introducing
these activities to school students. Unless it is a course requirement, only
a couple of students write notes on this lesson.

This scenario is one representation of both the dominant approach to
physical education teacher education and, according to many, a model of
good pedagogy (e.g. clear instructions, plenty of practice, efficient use of
time, space and equipment). The lecturer has modelled skills of good
('effective') teaching, as well as teaching these pre-service teachers both
how to perform and how to teach certain volleyball skills. These explicit
aims of the lesson can be referred to as the 'formal curriculum'. It is now
widely accepted that much more is taught and learned than the formal
curriculum (Bain, Chapter 2 in this volume; Dodds, 1985; Jackson, 1968).
Thus questions can be asked about the 'hidden', the 'null' and the 'functional' curricula (Dodds, 1985) such as: What else has been learned from
this experience? What is learned from the fact that this experience is
repeated in slightly different form throughout students' undergraduate
education? What has been left out? Who benefits? While I would agree
that such questions are important, and perhaps even essential for the
development of alternative practices, I consider problematic the usual

assumption that the different curricula (hidden, null, functional) *can* be identified and named in much the same way as the formal curriculum. The formal curriculum is usually available as a written document, while the hidden, null and functional curricula must be identified through observation and interpretation. These latter types of curricula are, after all, analytical constructs and not physical objects in the world. This view does not deny their existence but rather insists that it is inaccurate to talk of *the* hidden curriculum or *the* null curriculum in the same way that we can talk of *the* formal curriculum. The characterization of hidden, null, or functional curricula will depend not only on what is observed but on who does the observing. I well elaborate this argument by drawing on the notion of 'text'.

I use 'text' here to refer to social signs which can be read, signs which indicate to us that a number of things are happening in any given social situation; which we use, for example, in our identification of the hidden curriculum. This notion of text is different from our usual ways of using the term. Lundgren (1983), for example, distinguished between 'texts *for* pedagogy' (texts from which teachers could teach, or the formal curriculum) and 'texts *about* pedagogy' (texts that describe and theorize about pedagogy and curriculum for teachers and others). Although this text, this chapter, is about pedagogy and for pedagogy (directed mainly at teacher educators), its focus is neither. I want to emphasize a third type of text: that is, texts *of* pedagogy or *pedagogy as text*.

While texts *for* pedagogy are largely *pre*scriptive, and texts *about* pedagogy are largely *de*scriptive, it is my contention that the notion of pedagogy *as* text facilitate prescription, description *and* reflexivity. Pedagogy as text does not itself prescribe and so escapes the dogmatism of many texts *for* pedagogy. As I will elaborate later, the prescription relies on the audience. The description from pedagogy as text acknowledges multiple readings, multiple realities, and so provides a much fuller portrayal of pedagogy or curriculum than many texts *about* pedagogy. Because pedagogy as text insists that meaning is negotiated, found partly in the text and partly in the relation of the 'reader' to the text, there inheres a strong reflexivity, a sense of its own history. As such, pedagogy as text can be taken as part of a critical theory: it can enable full critique (description), it can assist with the naming of alternatives for social transformation (prescription), and it has an immanent sense of its own history, its own limits (reflexivity). I shall return to these ideas in the concluding section of the chapter.

One of my central purposes, along with introducing the notion of pedagogy as text, is to demonstrate a critical approach to physical education teacher education. Unlike some critical work in teacher education, drawing on notions of text and the related concept of discourse enables me to avoid suggesting that I have *the* answer, to avoid polemical paradigmatic arguments. 'Text' and 'discourse' enable me to remain reflexive and so to acknowledge that, in turn, the position I am taking in this chapter is also open to a multitude of readings or interpretations. A danger with this kind of argument, however, is the possible charge of relativism, and the subsequent conclusion that we all construct unique and equally valid readings. However, in my own reticence to blame individuals for the positions they hold, I am not suggesting that all positions have equal merit, validity or legitimacy for the conduct of physical education teacher education. On the contrary, I am arguing for pedagogical practices which are reflexive (aware of the contradictions between their own form and their espoused aims), morally and politically defensible, and therefore educative. That physical education is a negative and destructive experience for a significant (*practically* significant) number of students is itself condemnation of some practices we carry out in the name of physical *education*. From the critical perspective I am presenting in this chapter, deciding on appropriate practices requires that we look closely at the contexts in which those practices are carried out and examine the morality of the practices in those contexts. For example, what is it about physical education and its conduct that attracts a rather homogeneous population of white, middle-class, ectomesomorphic young men and women to becomes its next generation of teachers? Moreover, can we justify the relative exclusion of Aborigines in Australia, the poor, the fat? What have we, in physical education, done to the body images and self-images of those who deviate from our 'athletic' norm? My point is that we must be reflexive; we should examine the forces in the formation of our own positions on teacher education and consider the implications of those positions for prospective teachers and students in physical education.

Having laid out some of the arguments on which this chapter is based, I turn next to a clarification of what it means to talk of pedagogy as text. I will then return to the opening scenario and demonstrate some of the possible readings of that pedagogy as text. Then I will outline an alternative text of pedagogy, drawing from my own work as a teacher educator in physical education. Students' responses to that pedagogy, their readings of that text, will be presented and discussed. It is important to make clear that I conducted this study prior to considering pedagogy as text, and so I will initially leave aside the concept in presenting that study's findings. I will then bring together the earlier sections of the chapter by performing a reading of both my pedagogy and my initial analysis of students' responses; that is, I will apply the concept of pedagogy as text to the text of my prior study. In conclusion, I will outline advantages (and limitations) of thinking of pedagogy as text over other ways of thinking about pedagogy in physical education teacher education.

Pedagogy as Text

If the scenario presented above is treated as a pedagogical text, it is possible to 'read' it in a number of ways. Although our common-sense understanding of text extends only as far as written documents like textbooks, curriculum guides and report cards (which of course are open to multiple interpretations), the term has long been used in critical cultural studies to refer to other phenomena such as films and television programmes and, through its focus on discourse, to be likened to social experience. Said (1983, p. 4) helps us understand the links between texts and social experience, commenting that 'texts are worldly, to some degree they are events, and even when they appear to deny it they are nevertheless part of the social world, human life, and of course the historical moments in which they are located and interpreted.' All texts are social and all social experiences provide texts. It is also helpful to locate this notion of text in relation to notions of language and discourse. Weedon (1987, p. 41) says text or 'meanings do not exist prior to their articulation in language and language is not an abstract system, but is always socially and historically located in discourses.' The meanings we give to these terms — text, language, discourse — are themselves situated in particular discourses. The discourse on 'discourse' I find most helpful is illustrated in the following statement.

> In any society, there are manifold relations of power which permeate, characterize and constitute the social body, and these relations of power cannot themselves be established, consolidated nor implemented without the production, accumulation, circulation and functioning of a discourse. There can be no possible exercise of power without a certain economy of discourses of truth which operates through and on the basis of this association. We are subjected to the production of truth through power and we cannot exercise power except through the production of truth. This is the case for every society. (Foucault, 1980, p. 93)

It is certainly the case for pedagogy which relies on particular relations of power (for example, between teacher and learner) and is intimately connected with knowledge or truth production. According to Lusted, pedagogy, as a concept

> draws attention to the *process* through which knowledge is pro-
> duced. Pedagogy addresses the 'how' questions involved not only
> in the transmission or reproduction of knowledge but also in its
> production. Indeed, it enables us to question the validity of separ-
> ating these activities so easily by asking under what conditions
> and through what means we 'come to know'. How one teaches
> ...becomes inseparable from what is being taught and, crucially,
> how one learns. (Lusted, 1986, pp. 2–3)

The 'how' of pedagogy is often associated with 'methods' courses in
teacher education programmes. Instead, linking Lusted and Foucault, we
can argue that focusing on the process of teaching necessitates attention to
the politics of those processes and to the broader political context in
which they are situated.

In thinking of pedagogical practices as texts in this way, we acknowledge that, like other texts (books, television programmes) they 'do not
have a single meaning, but are relatively open texts, capable of being read
in different ways by different people' (Fiske, 1987b, p. 260). The way that
pedagogy is received becomes a process of negotiation, a struggle over
meaning. Fiske (1987a, p. 14) says, a television programme (we could
substitute pedagogy) 'becomes a text at the moment of reading.... Texts
are the site of conflict between their forces of production and modes of
reception.' This sense of negotiation is in keeping with most recent
accounts of student teacher socialization (see Zeichner and Gore, in
press), whereby the student is considered to be an active maker of
meanings from the experience and not simply a passive recipient of
already allegedly constructed ones. Furthermore 'negotiation' implies
'that there is a conflict of interests that needs to be reconciled in some
way' (Fiske, 1987b, p. 260). 'Negotiation' thus acknowledges the relations of power which are an integral part of any teacher education (or
other social) situation and which, in the end, construct the boundaries
within which any text of pedagogy is enacted/produced or read.

Given this notion of pedagogy as text, it no longer makes sense to
talk of being able to locate hidden, null or functional curricula *except from
a particular position as reader*, except from a particular subjectivity. What *I*
read into a particular situation, what I consider to be happening at overt
and covert levels, will differ from others' interpretations depending on
our social positions: 'depending on', not in a mechanistic, singular, causal
way, but in terms of delimiting boundaries (Fiske, 1987a). Thus conceptions of hidden, null or functional curriculum cannot be *de*scribed without
also being *in*scribed from particular social positions. It is, therefore,
problematic to speak of *the* hidden curriculum in a universalistic way

which suggests that it operates for everyone in the same way. On the other hand, even though others' readings of the hidden curriculum in a given context will be, most likely, different from mine, there are certain commonalities, or 'partial equivalences' (Bourdieu, 1984) in the way we will read a particular text. The possible meanings in a given context are not infinite. 'The text does not determine its meaning so much as delimit the arena of the struggle for that meaning by marking the terrain within which its variety of readings can be negotiated' (Fiske, 1987b, p. 269) As an illustration, my representation of the traditional 'methods' class in physical education teacher education (the opening scenario) is quite different from how others would represent the same event: for example, mine includes a particular sensitivity to gender relations which might be missing from other accounts. But that sensitivity or awareness is not simply an individualistic claim. Rather, it is testimony to the structured gender oppression of the society in which that gymnasium and that lesson were (and still are) situated.

Theories of reading in cultural studies have shifted from Hall's (1980) account of three broad reading strategies — the dominant, the negotiated, and the oppositional — which are produced out of the social class positions that people occupy, to accounts which consider viewers or readers to be in positions that conform to the dominant ideology in some ways but not in others and which consider a variety of determinants of readings rather than emphasizing social class (Fiske, 1987a, 1987b). The notion of *preferred* reading proposes that programmes (television, teacher education) generally favour a particular set of meanings that work to maintain the dominant ideologies, but that these meanings cannot be imposed, only preferred (Fiske, 1987b). Fiske (1987a, p. 65) argues that 'it is more productive to think not so much of a singular preferred meaning, but of structures of preference in the text that seek to prefer some meanings and to close off others.' The extension of this notion to educational contexts seems appropriate in that there are certain meanings teacher educators prefer students to glean from teacher education programmes, meanings which support the dominant ideologies of the institution, programme and faculty, but these cannot be imposed. Texts of pedagogy can no longer be seen as self-sufficient entities with their own meanings that exert a similar influence on all readers. Rather, these texts 'must be seen as having a potential of meanings that can be activated in a number of ways' (Fiske, 1987b, p. 269).

From this perspective a pedagogical practice is seen to have no particular meaning in and of itself. The meaning can only be determined in context. For example, the practice of separating boys and girls for a particular physical activity is not, in itself, an instance of the reproduction of gender differences. We would have to consider whose decision it was to make the separation, the purpose of the separation, the nature of the particular activity, the specific techniques of the separation, the teacher(s), and student-teacher relations, the historical, cultural and institutional location of the practice, and the discursive fields within which the practice can be read. This is not to say that we can simply explain away accusations of, for example, sexist pedagogy, by claiming that it is just a radical's reading. Rather, cultural studies in its current state of development argues that 'the distribution of power in society is paralleled by the distribution of meanings in texts, and that struggles for social power are paralleled by semiotic struggles for meanings. Every text and every reading has a social and therefore political dimension, which is to be found partly in the structure of the text itself and partly in the relation of the reading subject to that text' (Fiske, 1987b, p. 272).

The term 'subject' is important here. 'Theories of the individual concentrate on differences between people and explain these differences as natural. Theories of the subject, on the other hand, concentrate on people's common experiences in a society as being the most productive way of explaining who (we think) we are' (Fiske, 1987a, p. 258). Foucault (1983) has written at length about how human beings are objectified in ways which make us subject to particular discourses and which make us view ourselves as subjects. It is possible to identify a number of subjectivities which construct, and are constructed by, the scenario with which I opened this chapter. Among them are the subjectivities of student and teacher/expert (which sets up particular power relations between the students and the instructor); learner and prospective teacher within each student (which might create tensions if being treated as a learner while becoming a teacher); woman and 'PE woman' (e.g. often seen as 'butch'), or man and 'PE man' (e.g. often seen as 'macho').[1]

The social subject has a history, lives in a particular social formation (a mix of class, gender, age, ethnicity, etc.) and is constituted by a complex cultural history that is both social and textual (Fiske, 1987a). 'The subjectivity results from "real" social experience and from mediated or textual experience' (Fiske, 1987a, p. 62). For each person subjectivities are always multiple, often contradictory, and shift according to the particular historical moment. At this historical moment subjectivities are largely influenced by struggles for power around issues of gender, race, class, religion, sexual orientation, ability, size and no doubt other oppressive formations of which I am currently unaware or which I am currently unable to name. Pedagogy as text, with its acknowledgment of multiplicity, draws our attention to these often neglected issues of power.

Reading the Scenario as a Text of Pedagogy

Consider possible readings of my opening scenario. If we consider the preferred reading, or structures of preference, of that text within the context of a fairly traditional teacher education programme, we can point to a range of possible readings which can be characterized as extending from acceptance to opposition. One's reading of the scenario will depend on one's subjectivity/subjectivities. A feminist might support the pedagogical practice but abhor the gender relations being played out from the moment students entered the gym, whereby 'the boys' monopolized the space. A student who, in an instrumental way, wants to learn how to teach volleyball might think it was wonderful. Another student might find its rigidity, in terms of the 'uniform' she is required to wear and the direct style of instruction, to remind her of her own school experiences and of all that she hoped to change by becoming a physical education teacher. An exercise scientist from the same department might consider it to be a waste of university resources and something s/he would never want to teach. Another faculty member with a background in pedagogy might see it as a model lesson. A third faculty member, also with a background in pedagogy but who takes a critical position, might read the scenario as ideologically conservative and even dangerous. Thus our position as subjects in terms of gender, class, race, intellectual background and so on will influence our readings. Although all readings of the scenario can be characterized as somewhere along the continuum from acceptance to opposition, it is not difficult to construct two main intellectual responses within existing teacher education discourse. The preferred reading fits within the perspective from which the scenario was constructed, that is, one which has its roots in positivism, emphasizes a science of teaching and stresses technical skills, and treats the relationship between schooling and society as relatively unproblematic. The oppositional reading emerges from a critical' perspective which has its roots in critical theory, emphasizes political and ethical issues in teaching, and treats the relationship between schooling and society as problematic (Kemmis and Fitzclarence, 1986).

These two positions can be likened to the 'behaviouristic' and 'inquiry-oriented paradigms' of teacher education which Zeichner (1983) has elaborated.[2] Although it is possible to identify elements of what Zeichner calls the 'personalistic paradigm', whereby there is an attempt to be responsive to the self-perceived needs and concerns of students (in physical education see, for example, McBride, 1984a, 1984b), and elements of the 'traditional-craft paradigm', which views teacher education primarily as a process of apprenticeship (consider our continued faith in traditional field experiences), most physical education teacher education programmes fit clearly within the behaviouristic orientation in which the emphasis is on the skilled performance of predetermined teaching tasks. The critical paradigm which I am presenting as oppositional to the dominant approach is gaining increasing momentum in mainstream teacher education (see, for example, Apple, 1979; Giroux, 1980; Popkewitz, 1987; Zeichner and Liston, 1986; Zeichner and Teitelbaum, 1982) but is in its infancy in physical education teacher education (see Gore, 1988; Gore and Bartlett, 1987; Kirk, 1986, 1989; McKay, Gore and Kirk, in press; Tinning, 1987). In writing this chapter I am attempting to extend the critical work in physical education teacher education by posing a critique to those approaches which link themselves to critical theory and by offering additional political and analytical tools which emerge from post-structuralism and contemporary critical cultural studies. In particular, through the notion of pedagogy as text, I want to emphasize the multiplicity of meaning, attention to specific contexts and reflexivity, all of which minimize the dogmatism of critical work.

Beyond the Preferred Reading

Rather than present in detail a variety of possible readings of the scenario, I will focus on *my* reading with the aim of going beyond the preferred, or dominant, reading. This focus on my own reading enables me to keep central my aim of demonstrating, and advocating, a particular critical perspective. Moreover, the focus on my own reading acknowledges that I cannot assume to speak for others, nor even in their langauge, that there will always be gaps in my ability to know (Narayan, 1988) your 'text' since it is a product of collective and individual social experience. Before launching into an elaboration of my 'critical' concerns with the scenario, I hasten to add that there is much I support about the conduct of that volleyball lesson: technical skills of teaching seemed to be employed competently and appropriately; the progression of learning activities seemed well planned and executed; there seemed to be plenty of activity and plenty of opportunities for practice. Taking a critical perspective does not mean that technical skills are not valued in teaching. Rather, technical skills are seen as simply a means to an end. Besides, my own background in teacher effectiveness research continues to influence the value I place on technical skills, despite the fact that I now consider the emphases of the teacher effectiveness approach to be misplaced. Moreover, my commitment to practice, to getting things done, means that technical skills have a place; but, again, not for their own sake. From my critical perspective I have two major sets of concerns with the scenario; these centre on issues of knowledge and issues of power relations. I separate these issues for purposes of analysis only and acknowledge their dialectical relation. Given that all texts exist in context, and have meaning through their interaction with particular subjectivities, my reading of the scenario necessarily draws on experiences and knowledge, both in and outside physical education, and so shifts constantly between the particular event depicted in the scenario and other contexts.

Issues of Knowledge

Perhaps, unwittingly, teacher education in physical education of the type outlined in the scenario implies, among other things, that knowledge is unproblematic and uncontestable and that technical knowledge is of para-mount importance in learning to teach. In the presentation of the lesson as a model for students' own practice, the message might be that this is *the* way to teach, and perform, the spike in volleyball. Students were not encouraged to ask questions about the process of the lesson, nor about what counts as knowledge in physical education, who benefits from the current form and content of physical education, are there other ways of doing this, or how will this activity apply to other contexts in which physical education will be conducted. The de facto effect of these omis-sions is the privileging of technical knowledge. Belka's (1988) research demonstrated that pre-service physical education students value what is taught in their programmes. Of the three categories he used, the focus of students was most often on teacher behaviour, then on content of lessons, and least on pupil behaviour. Through such teacher education program-mes, technical skills of teaching can become understood as the focus and the main purpose of teaching. While many teacher educators would point out that of course they realize that teaching is more than a number of specific technical skills, their programmes actually create and reinforce such a view as much by their omissions as by their content (Tinning, 1987).

As Smith (1988) argues, we have also lost sight of the child in this 'scientistic' and behaviouristic approach to physical education.[3] In work-ing out what is best for a particular child, Smith (1988, p. 10) asks, 'what can be better than attempting to define [the] present activity as the stuff of good memories?' Smith's argument raises questions about the types of knowledge which are considered legitimate within traditional physical education teacher education programmes, and highlights the extent to which we have relied on science and have neglected to draw on our own feelings and experiences. With this reliance on science we have portrayed sport in work-like terms when we could have chosen instead to associate it with 'recreation, freedom of movement, freedom of expression, and intrinsic qualitative enjoyment' (Beamish, 1982, p. 11).

If we consider the historical development of physical education as a university programme and its links to both science and professionalism, it is not difficult to understand why knowledge in physical education has been constructed in these ways. With the progressive introduction of training programmes for physical educators into the universities came a tendency to 'scientize' the occupation. Demers (1988) claims that the dominant model of science was attractive because these new university faculty were seeking academic and professional status both within the university and with outside funding organizations and because they were also trying to improve the image of physical education within society. Given the prestige of science in our society, it imparted legitimacy to their work and offered them power. Thus it is not surprising that university physical education programmes have focused on a science of teaching and have emphasized teacher behaviour, while humanities courses are undervalued (Ross, 1987) and sociological and philosophical questions tend to be tacked on to the end of courses, almost as an afterthought, if they are raised at all.

Issues of Power Relations

The scenario also suggests that teachers should be expert 'knowers' rather than 'expert learners' and that teachers are the only participants in a lesson who are capable of instructing or providing feedback. The type of class depicted in the scenario is often considered to be *prerequisite* to any opportunities for students to teach, and so in the volleyball lesson the lecturer taught all the 'really useful knowledge' while students were permitted only to conduct the warm-up. Students' own knowledge was devalued and learning to teach was separated from actually teaching. Clearly the lecturer was in a position of power through which he was able to define important knowledge for the class. He took control of all aspects of the lesson: students did not have access to the equipment until the lecturer arrived and gave instructions; even when the students led the warm-up it was under the surveillance of the lecturer; the students had learned to comply, or at least give the impression of complying, with the lecturer's instructions.

Partly because of the power exercised by the lecturer, the relation set up between teacher and students was, at moments, antagonistic. Consider the students who sneaked in and out of the gym, and the hierarchical discipline methods employed when students attempted to push the boundaries of what was acceptable behaviour. Consider also the eyeball rolling and the sniggering which might have accompanied the step-by-step massed practice of the moments of the spike. The claims to truth, to certainty, to 'what is', which accompany the 'scientized' and 'professionalized' approach to teaching physical education are part of the construction of the subjectivities 'teacher' and 'student'. This particular construction of power relations is no doubt a factor in the negative experiences many people carry away from physical education classes. We have to question whose interests are served by the practices which maintain the authority of the lecturer. Would these pre-service students have benefited from leading more of the lesson themselves, or having opportunities to ask different kinds of questions? To what extent does the kind of lesson depicted in the scenario simply serve the ego of the lecturer and his or her desire to impress the students with knowledge and skill? I am not suggesting that the authority of the teacher should be eradicated; given the institutional location of these practices, that is highly unlikely anyway. Rather, I am pointing out that the lesson could have been conducted differently.

Issues of power relevant to the scenario are much wider than those of teacher-student relations. The domination of space by the male students before the lesson began points to relations of power around gender. Despite the fact that these young men and women plan to become physical educators, they still have much to learn about playing together. How much of their own insensitivity to, or inability to confront, gender issues will be carried into the schools in which they teach? Issues of race, class, size, sexual orientation, ability, religion were not articulated in my representation of the lesson, but even in their absence, in the unspoken, power circulates. In the conduct of the lesson none of these issues was raised; my point is that they could have been. This is not an argument to turn 'methods' classes into sessions on moral deliberation. Rather, I argue that the decontextualized (in terms of the social, political, historical context) emphasis exclusively on technical skills (of teaching or volleyball) is indefensible.

Beyond Reading: A Case Study of a Reflective Teaching Course

The scenario is not fictitious, but was typical of the conduct of a class I had the opportunity to restructure and teach. Given my concerns about knowledge and power relations in teacher education, I set out to replace that course with one which might alter dominant patterns. I wanted to move beyond the preferred reading, not only in my critique but in my practice. Drawing on existing literature in teacher education, the notion of 'reflective teaching' was attractive given its potential to challenge conventional conceptions of knowledge and teacher-student relations. This section of the chapter centres on the course I constructed in the hope of facilitating reflective teaching. I will leave aside the notion of pedagogy as text for the moment, as it was not part of my earlier conception of the study. However, I will return to pedagogy as text at the end of the chapter to demonstrate how helpful it has been in rethinking both my pedagogy and my earlier analysis. I hope this 'laying out' of the process will add clarity to the argument I am making for an expansion of critical approaches to teacher education to include notions of discourse, subjectivity and historical specificity.

'Reflective teaching' has become part of the discourse of contemporary teacher education, but takes a variety of forms depending largely on the intellectual ideological backgrounds of its advocates. For example, the work of Cruickshank and his colleagues can be situated within a behaviouristic paradigm with its separation of content from process and ends from means,[4] whereas the work of Zeichner and colleagues, with its attention to moral and political contexts of teaching and to issues of knowledge and power, can be located within a critical paradigm. Zeichner (1981–82) actually disassociated himself from Cruickshank *et al.*'s (1981) packaged form of reflective teaching. Nevertheless, the Cruickshank approach offered several pragmatic advantages for the context in which I was working, and so, in developing the course, I used some of its procedures in conjunction with the substantive ideas of more critical approaches to reflective teaching. In the next section I provide a detailed account of the specific context in which my study was conducted, details which we often fail to provide in accounts of teacher education. As already stated, however, all texts exist, and must be read, within context.

The Context of the Study

'Introduction to Movement Education' (course code HM115) was the first course in the Bachelor of Human Movement Studies (Education) degree program in the Department of Human Movement Studies at the University of Queensland, Australia, which directly addressed physical education. Class meetings were scheduled four days per week (for a two-hour lecture and three hour-long practical sessions) for one semester (fourteen weeks). The central purposes of the course were to introduce students to the core activity areas of physical education curricula (i.e. dance, aquatics, gymnastics, athletics, games) and to introduce them to education, teaching and schooling. In 1986 I modified the course from a form which matched the scenario with which I opened the chapter, that is, learning the subject matter from the 'master teacher', to include peer teaching and other group activities in an attempt to facilitate reflectivity among participants through shared experiences of the teaching act. Given the constraints on time and financial resources, peer teaching seemed to be the only way of providing experiences of the teaching act within this course.

The 1986 experience of teaching HM115 led to further changes in 1987, with the major features of the course being:

1 *Peer teaching sessions.* Students taught fifteen- to twenty-minute lessons to a group of six or seven peers. The remainder of the fifty-minute class period was spent reflecting on the experience, first within the small group and then within the larger group (twenty-two to twenty-four) students. The subject matter of lessons was specified by the lecturer (e.g. the concept of rhythm in hurdles, creative dance using poetry as a stimulus, games making, timing in breaststroke, springing and landing) but student teachers were left with all the decisions regarding specific content, teaching strategy and so on. Students also wrote critiques of all peer teaching sessions. In addition, one member of each group took photographs of each peer teaching lesson as a way of encouraging students to focus on all that was happening in a given lesson, including how participants appeared to be feeling/reacting. Students later examined the photographs and selected two or three for the photographer and teacher to comment upon. Thus within each group one student was the teacher, one was the photographer and the remaining participants were the students. They were asked to act naturally rather than to pretend that they were school children as is sometimes the case in peer teaching. I anticipated that these peer teaching sessions would carry messages such as: students' own knowledge is to be valued, collaboration and collegiality are important components of teaching, and students can learn to teach by experiencing the teaching act. In addition, I believed that the peer teaching experience might be helpful in minimizing the typical focus on issues of management and discipline which accompany students' earliest experiences in schools and that this would free students to move beyond a concern with technical skills at the expense of other issues.

2 *A personal journal.*   Some guidelines were provided to assist students in the keeping of a journal (Holly, 1984; Walker, 1985) but they were encouraged to approach it in a manner which suited their own style, needs and interests. During the semester, four specific journal tasks were set:

1   Week 1: 'My career in teaching'. Students were asked to discuss their motives for wanting to become a physical education teacher, any alternative careers they were considering and their aims as a physical education teacher. They were also asked to describe the characteristics of teachers who were and were not 'the sort of teacher you would like to be'. Finally, they were encouraged to explore the meaning of the terms 'physical education', 'human movement studies', 'sport', 'play', 'recreation', 'coaching' and 'teaching'.

2   Week 7: Students were asked to identify a crucial incident in their development as a teacher and person. They were encouraged to identify incidents which occurred within the course but were free to discuss extraneous incidents.

3   Week 9: Students were asked to use the photographs of the lessons for which they were the teacher as a starting point in addressing the following questions:
Is the teacher I am in these photos the person I am?
Is the person I am the teacher I hope to be?
Is the teacher I am/hope to be the person society wants?

4   Week 13: Students were asked to explore the following question: What is a good teacher of physical education?

No specific requirements or constraints were imposed on students' use of the journal for the remainder of the programme. The journals was essentially a means by which students could explore their private thoughts and personal development. However, to facilitate the sharing of thoughts and experiences, selections from individual journals were typed to ensure anonymity and then distributed to all participants. Three such collections were printed during the semester.

3 *A series of lectures, seminars, videos and readings.*   These were structured around the central purposes of the course, however questions were raised and contradictions highlighted throughout, in an attempt to facilitate reflection and present knowledge as problematic. A series of three videos was shown of 'model' teachers:

1 *From Mao to Mozart* — Isaac Stern, the violinist, touring China and teaching young violinists to play with feeling and not just technical expertise;

2 *The Karate Kid* — Mr Miyagi teaching Daniel karate via seemingly unrelated tasks; authoritarianism was a focal point of discussion;

3 *The Devil's Playground* — a *60 Minutes* segment where the teacher Frank Dando uses (abuses?) physical activity to improve the self-concept and academic performance of 'delinquent' boys.

Readings were also selected to encourage students to think more broadly about teaching: for example, Eisner's *The Art and Craft of Teaching*, Kemmis' *Three Views of Education*, Locke's *Ecology of the Gymnasium*, Hoffman's *Traditional Methodology: Prospects for Change* and Giroux's *Teachers as Transformative Intellectuals*.

In summary, the course provided a variety of experiences in which students were required to think, to talk and to write. Students' experiences as school students and as 'teachers' in the peer teaching context were taken as the starting point for the development of reflective teaching. Wherever possible, I participated in these activities with the students; for example, I taught two lessons which I opened to their critique, and I kept, and shared selections from, a personal journal.

Students generally took HM115 in the first semester of their second year at the university. Forty-six students (twenty-three male, twenty-three female) enrolled in and completed the subject in 1987. A survey conducted during the first week of the semester provided some biographical information about each student. Analysis of that information revealed that the group was quite homogeneous in terms of *age* (approximately 75 per cent of students were either 18 or 19 years of age, the oldest student was 24), *career choice* (over 90 per cent of them were enrolled in the BHMS (Ed.) degree, a degree which qualifies students to teach physical education at the primary or secondary level), involvement and *prowess in sport* (over 90 per cent played sport at, at least, club level with 50 per cent of the group playing or having played sport at state or national level) and estimated *social class* (using parents' occupation, 55 per cent of working fathers and 50 per cent of working mothers held professional or administrative positions, while technical and clerical positions accounted for a further 12 per cent of working fathers and 46 per cent of working mothers; of the non-working parents, two were pensioners, and the remainder were mothers who were housewives). A large percentage of students (46 per cent) came from private school backgrounds (30 per cent were from Catholic private schools) with the remainder (54 per cent) having completed their education within the state system. The university entrance score of these students was above 930 (the highest possible score is 990) which ranked high in the university, behind only those students entering medicine, law, dental science, veterinary science, pharmacy and the therapies.[5]

As a group these students could be seen as successful both academically and athletically, young and of at least middle-class origin. Although the BHMS (Ed.) enrolment would suggest an aspiration to become physical education teachers, only 60 per cent of students came into the subject with an expressed interest in *teaching*, with others more interested in sport, physiotherapy, sports journalism and the recreation and tourist industries.

The Conduct of the Study

In carrying out a study of students' responses to the course I worked with a colleague.[6] He acted as a 'critical friend' to the study and restricted his involvement to discussions with me about the project and limited contact with the students. To understand students' experiences of the course and to monitor their development as reflective teachers, qualitative research methods were used to provide most of the data. Field notes were generated as a result of observations, although it was later decided to cease writing them because they were not proving to be a rich source of data. Semi-structured interviews were conducted with twelve of the students who were selected because they appeared to be representative of certain subgroups within the class, or because they stood out as different in some way.[7] Interviews were taped, transcribed and then returned to interviewees for editing or comment. A large quantity of data was also generated by way of the students' written work: journal entries, lesson critiques, photograph comments. Three questionnaires were also used in association with the course. One questionnaire was used to collect demographic/biographic information at the beginning of the semester. Two questionnaires were administered at the end of the semester. The first of these was designed to allow students to evaluate all aspects of the course. The second questionnaire was administered as a routine end-of-semester teaching evaluation.

Questionnaire data were collated and frequencies and percentages calculated for the numerical response items. Descriptive statistics were provided for the teaching evaluation questionnaire. Most of the data generated by other sources, that is, student journals and critiques, personal field notes, photography comments and interview transcripts, required document analysis. The major purpose of the study was to begin to understand the varied responses that students made to the programme intent on helping them to become critically reflective teachers and thus focused on student journals and interview transcripts.

Findings

Any attempt to promote reflective teaching is likely to meet with a heterogeneity of responses. Students could be expected to, and in fact did, differ in terms of their general orientation to course-related reflection and the focus of that reflection. In other words, they differed in terms of *how* they reflected and *on what* they reflected. Although each student's experience of, and commitment to, the programme was unique, three broad groups were identified through the analysis of data. In the following discussion of these groups reference will be made to individuals in an attempt to retain the richness of their personal experience.

The three responses identified have been labelled 'recalcitrance', 'acquiescence' and 'commitment'. Such responses are not particularly surprising and can be found in most classes at any level of schooling. However, students' responses to reflective teaching courses (or other teacher education programmes) have not been well documented even though they are important in understanding the impact of those courses. Although presented here as ideal types, the shifting membership of each group and the dynamic nature of each student's experience should not be forgotten.

The *recalcitrant* students rejected the need to reflect on teaching and failed to see the relevance of keeping a journal. Reflecting was seen as at best peripheral, and at worst irrelevant, to the task of teaching. Rosemary commented, for example, that 'marks should be on teaching, not reflecting' (Week 5).[8] Students in this group consequently used their journals infrequently throughout the semester. In some cases when the journal was used it was not used as a forum for discussion of teaching and course experiences but was instead used solely as a personal diary. Other characteristics of the recalcitrant group were that most of them were male and for most of them teaching was not their major career aspiration.

Although several students demonstrated a resistance to reflecting on the course at various points during the semester, only one student really forcefully articulated this position. Scott's early definition of teaching as simply 'conveying knowledge' (Week 1) and his description of himself as 'result-oriented' partially explained his reluctance to use his journal regularly. In Week 4 he stated, in a rare journal entry, that unless each aspect of the course 'does something for one's teaching' it is 'worthless'. He described other students' journal entries as 'crap' which was 'written purely for the sake of writing' and stated that he was 'not into this regimented reflective stuff (Week 5). (I will return to these comments at various points in this discussion.) Scott seemed typical of students who enter a professional programme interested only in those things which they perceive to be directly related to practising in the profession. Perhaps this attitude intensifies when teaching is not the first career choice, as was the case for Scott and most other recalcitrant students. The attitude indicates an instrumentality whereby questions of efficiency and effectiveness dominate over concerns with purposes or with the moral or political implications of one's practice.

Although Scott was the only student bluntly and openly to make his position known to the lecturer, approximately two-thirds of the class indicated by raising their hands that they agreed, in part at least, with Scott's criticisms. Also some students commented in their journals later that they supported his statements and admired his courage in speaking his mind. 'The person who wrote this is being extremely critical, although I praise him/her for being honest. I agree to a certain extent, with some of what this person has had the courage to say. I agree that some people only write in their journal because if they don't they are afraid they will lose marks' (Janet, Week 10). The issues of assessment will be raised again later. It is clear, however, that many students believed that such an honest criticism of the programme might affect the grade they received and so opted instead to comply with what they understood as the reflective requirements.

The *acquiescent* response was by far the most common of the three identified and the students in this group were the least homogeneous. The group's character is perhaps best summarized by a student from the 'committed' group who said, 'not many people are willing to take the hard road if an easy road is made an option to them' (Richard, Week 14). This description applies to the various subgroups identifiable within this 'acquiescent' category, that is, to those students who would prefer to resist but were afraid that it might mean their failure in the course, and to those students like Bruce who commented that 'being reflective takes effort, it's much easier to simply cruise along and do the minimum' (Week 5) and Tom who said 'it hurts to think' (Week 11). Acquiescent students used their journals sporadically, mainly when they thought that the journals had to be submitted. They were more likely to back-date entries to give the appearance of regular use than were students from the other two groups. They were also far more concerned about assessment and, as Gordon said, 'the journal suffered on [their] list of priorities because of its 5 per cent weighting' (Week 14). University work was done by most of these students for the extrinsic rewards it offered such as receiving a particular grade and getting along with the lecturer.

Students in this group were also likely to 'stir' their more committed peers about their conscientious approach to the course, and to accuse them of 'crawling'. Such an attitude is consistent with the 'anti-academic perspective' of physical education students reported by Helen Schembri (1976) in her case study of undergraduates. As with the recalcitrant students, instrumentality tended to dominate among these students with a 'how to get through this course' concern being paramount. Thinking about teaching and schooling was essentially a means to that end. Likewise, teaching had been selected as a career possibility largely for reasons such as the holidays, hours and opportunity to work outdoors in a sports-related occupation. Sandra's description of these students as just drifting along in their own comfortable worlds is quite insightful, although a generalization and perhaps a bit harsh.

> They just don't see the flaws in their own thinking, their own outlooks. It seems like they've rarely argued with themselves because they've never felt the need. Everything is rosy for them because (particularly in first year) they've been inflicted with this 'I'm a big uni. student now' syndrome and that's all that matters. They can just flow along day after day without realizing the sources of influences on why they think the way they do. There *is* life beyond HM. (Sandra, Week 9)

The students in the *committed* group were quite different from their recalcitrant and acquiescent peers. They enjoyed writing in their journals regularly, commented on their love of thinking and learning and, like Peter, 'stuff my marks, I'm doing what I want to do' (Week 3), tended to de-emphasize assessment. Instead they focused on the *process* of learning and reflecting. Stephen articulates this position.

> This subject has made me realize as a student that there is more to education than just assessment. Writing journal entries and lesson critiques on myself and my peers, contributing to group discussions, and teaching prac lessons to my peers, just doesn't occur to me as assessment. All of it is a learning experience and I treat it as such. I want to learn more and more this way because it's interesting and stimulating. My development as a teacher also stems from these new types of learning experiences. I find myself continually reflecting on all that I have learnt in the past. (Stephen, Week 8)

All the students in this group felt sure about teaching as their chosen career, a decision which may well have contributed to their commitment to the course and their success in it. Generally speaking, these students were better teachers and better scholars than students in the other two groups. (This statement is based on students' assessment of their peers by way of their critiques, as well as my own assessment.) 'Committed' students were generally more willing to express their views in front of their peers and to face the brunt of gibes about 'crawling', 'brown-nosing' and writing 'flowery crap'. Furthermore, the attitudes which Dewey (1933) claimed were necessary for reflective thought — open-mindedness, responsibility and wholeheartedness — were certainly evident in these students. The focus of their reflection was also different from that of their peers, as shall be discussed in the next section.

The Focus of Students' Reflection

It is clear from analysis of students' journals that the focus of students' reflection differed among individuals, and indeed between the various groups (as previously identified) within the class. Van Manen's (1977) levels of reflectivity as modified and presented to the students in Week 10 of the subject: (1) reflection on *technical skills*, (2) reflection on *educational purposes*, and (3) reflection on *critical goals*, provide the basis for the following discussion. Given that the majority of students were engaging in their first formal act of teaching and that all the students were engaging in their first formal act of peer teaching, it is not surprising that reflection on technical skills, questions of 'how to teach' dominated during the early weeks of the course. Discussions following peer teaching lessons and written critiques of those lessons were almost exclusively focused on such teaching skills as positioning, pacing, feedback, instruction, demonstration, distribution of equipment, voice projection and timing. Within *two or three weeks* all students seemed to have understood the need for those technical skills and were able to identify them in their own and their peers' lessons.

Several students commented that discussions and critiques were becoming boring and they were ready to extend their focus to other areas.

> These critiques are getting mighty monotonous. Three in just two days. It's a bit of strain on the old vocabulary. How many times can you rearrange the same sentence appears to be the major task at the moment. Perhaps I should start looking from a different angle, but what is the angle? What else is there besides

looking on it as either a student or a teacher? Wait on. There has to be some in-betweens somewhere. There's got to be a little tangent waiting for me to jump on. Hmm. Maybe if I looked at ways of improving activities in each lesson. Or perhaps, how you could extend those activities into a full forty minute lesson. Or perhaps still, ways of bending the activities, adding here, taking there, to cover the full range of abilities you're likely to encounter in a school. But these approaches all seem too narrow. They seem to disregard the person actually teaching. It's hard to see at the moment a new way of looking at it. Damn it! I hate being stuck like this. (Sandra, Week 4)

It was at this point that the attitude students had toward the subject and its reflective components became important. The recalcitrant students were reluctant to extend the focus of their reflection except in rhetorical or flippant ways. Gerry, for example, commented that he wanted 'to revolutionize PE to get a spot on Page 1 of the Courier Mail' (Week 12). Students in this group were more likely than others to believe that the most important aspect of teaching was that 'kids were learning' (Graham, Week 11). *What* they were learning and what methods were employed were largely irrelevant. Thus it was students in the recalcitrant and some in the acquiescent group who argued that the militaristic approach of Frank Dando in 'educating' alienated 10-year-old boys (videotape 3) was appropriate. For example, 'Whilst some people would be critical of his militaristic approach to teaching, it is hard to knock the success he attained. He turned problem kids, who no-one could deal with, into responsible fun-loving kids who could take some pride in themselves, and taught them the necessary skills (the 3 R's) to prepare them for further education' (Gordon, Week 11). The outcome was all that mattered. Moral and political issues were just not important and in some cases seen as inappropriate. Wendy, for example, was critical of her peers for raising moral issues: 'I loved [the] bikie dance lesson despite the fact that most people spoilt the discussion of it by pointing out the negative aspects of the dance...perhaps they are fanatics...it did not enter my head that the lesson would be misleading or harmful in any way' (Wendy, Week 7).

In general, the acquiescent students *were* concerned about *what* and *how* kids were learning as well as being concerned with technical skills. They supported the need to be able to justify one's teaching and to ask questions like 'why am I teaching this?' However, students in this group tended to restrict their reflection to the school level. Occasionally reference was made to 'the system' but their belief was essentially that

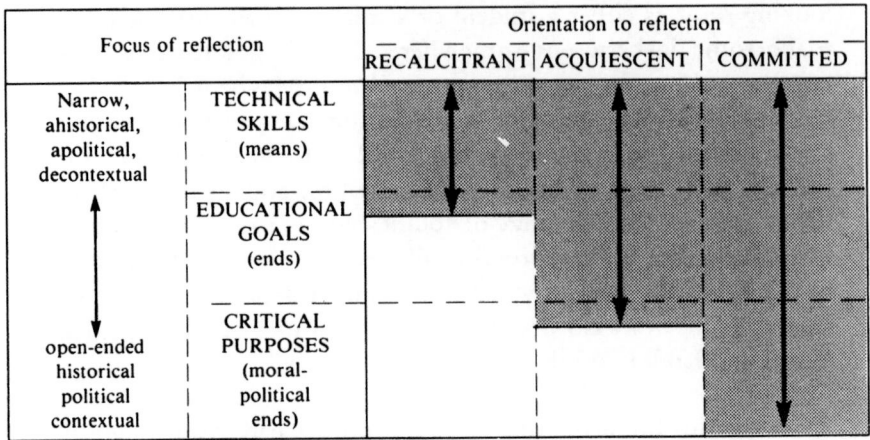

Focus of reflection		Orientation to reflection		
		RECALCITRANT	ACQUIESCENT	COMMITTED
Narrow, ahistorical, apolitical, decontextual	TECHNICAL SKILLS (means)			
	EDUCATIONAL GOALS (ends)			
open-ended historical political contextual	CRITICAL PURPOSES (moral-political ends)			

Figure 1. The Relationship between Orientation to, and Focus of, Reflection

teachers' major concerns must remain at the level of their own classrooms and schools. Committed students valued the technical skills of teaching, but tended to be more concerned about their role as teachers in the broader context of society. They acknowledged the role of schools in reproducing the status quo and believed in the need for change and that they could make a contribution towards that end. Andrea articulated this position well.

> Good teachers must firstly recognize that schools are inherently political. They must recognize the hegemonic values that pervade schools and society, then actively work towards their exposure to help in the quest for equality. . . . Optimistically, I believe that I can hold on to my beliefs and attempt to put them into practice within the confinements of the present system. After all, it is only from within that the beginnings of resistance and change can emerge. (Andrea, Journal Task 4, Week 14)

Although the relationship between approach to reflection and the focus of reflection was not direct or consistent for *all* students within each of the identified groups, a definite trend was evident, as is represented in Figure 1.

Broken lines are used deliberately to indicate the shifting membership of groups and to indicate the interrelatedness of the various reflective foci. For example, moral-political ends were unlikely to be considered without reflecting on educational purposes and the technical skills involved. The heavy arrows are used to indicate the shifting focus of individual students. Committed students, for example, might be located at any point along the line at a given time. The difference between them and their peers was that for a good deal of the time their focus was on critical purposes.

Reflecting on the Course

My experience of attempting to facilitate critical reflectivity brought some satisfaction. Some students appeared to be reflecting critically (although it is impossible to establish the extent to which the course was responsible for that) and I was pleased with the process and particularly the group reflecting which was a part of the process. However, many students were not committed to the goals and processes of the course as I presented them. In this section of the chapter I want to reflect on the course in order to highlight central issues which may be relevant to others who conduct, participate in or may be thinking of conducting courses which aim to facilitate critical reflectivity.

Time was certainly a major barrier in the development of critical reflectivity. As was mentioned earlier, reflective teaching was not one of the *central* purposes of HM115 and although many opportunities were used or created for reflecting, time was limited. I felt constrained by time particularly when it came to working with the photographs. Each photograph taken by students in the peer teaching lessons captured only an instant of the lesson. As a result, the photographs tended to draw students' attention toward the minutiae of the experience, toward the visible features of the lesson, such as the teacher's positioning/stance, the apparent attention of the students and so on and did not really promote critical reflectivity as I have defined it thus far — reflection on moral and political purposes as well as technical and educational concerns. The exception to this was when the photos were used in Journal Task 3 whereby questions were asked which encouraged students to use the pictures as a starting point for discussion of themselves and their future role as teachers in society.

Time constraints aside, I wonder if I should have pushed the students more by introducing concepts like 'the transformative intellectual' (Giroux, 1985) sooner. I wanted to proceed gently but am still unsure of the decisions I made. Scott's comments which were critical of 'this regimented reflective stuff' pointed to a possible contradiction between my objectives and my method. As Brian Fay says, 'One cannot impose on another person a new attitude of belief, or create a situation in which the person has no choice but to accept this new belief, and at the same time claim that his [sic] acceptance is due to critical reflection. This is just a straightforward contradiction between objective and method' (Fay, 1977, p. 227). Although the potential for such a contradiction exists, we need to see what the evidence from this study suggests. Did I act as an ideologue trying to force critical reflectivity on this cohort of students? Was I raising their consciousness? Indoctrinating? Educating?

The extent to which I was perceived to be an exemplar of reflective teaching is important in answering this question. Sarah's evaluation of my decision to involve a second investigator in the study illustrates one perception:

> I think it's a good idea because I see it as you wanting to improve yourself. I mean, it shows that you don't think 'Well, I'm Jenny Gore and I know it all because I teach HM115.' And I think a lot of lecturers sort of get this high and mighty opinion of themselves that they, you know, *do* know everything and that they couldn't possibly improve on what they're doing. So I think it's — I think it's really honest in a way. (Sarah, interview transcript, Week 6)

Her statement appears to be representative of the students given that in a questionnaire completed at the end of the course, 81 per cent of students disagreed with the statement 'the lecturer does not practise what she preaches' (16 per cent were unsure and only one student agreed). The question remains, however, as to the extent to which I *was* 'preaching'. In response to a follow-up question about my influence on the course (October, 1988), Sandra (who was nearing the end of her third year in the programme) wrote:

> While political beliefs influence, consciously or unconsciously, the content of every lecturer's course, how they organize it, etc., it was the *nature* or the direction of your beliefs (or more accurately I guess, how I perceived them) that influenced what happened most. This stands out because most of the subjects I had done up 'till [then] were just concerned with passing on lumps of information with which to pass an exam, rather than critically reflecting on anything broader. I guess the slant that you gave to 115 made me feel 'at home' at uni for the first time. Besides your political beliefs, I think your personality, too, influenced what happened. You were tolerant, patient and gentle which helps in a subject where people are teaching for the first time and where perhaps the nature of the content (political) can grate on some. I think if you had been overbearing or aggressive towards students' ex-

isting beliefs (which you weren't), introducing political reflection
may have been a lot harder. You kind of eased the blow.

Sandra's comments suggest that I might not have imposed my perspective on the students. Too few responses to this question were received to
know if her view is representative, but I certainly value the opinion
Sandra expressed.

Sensitivity to the students' biographies was a factor in not pushing
the 'political' aspects too heavily. Given the vocational orientation, the
success in sport, physical education and school generally, and the background in science as opposed to the arts and humanities, which characterized the students entering the programme, it is hardly surprising that
many students expected to learn techniques and technical skills and saw
no need for changes to existing arrangements or practices in schools. As
Ann Berlak (1988) identified the issue in another teacher education context, these relatively privileged students did not feel much 'empathy' or
'outrage'. Many of them enter the course having never been unsuccessful
in learning a new physical skill, not knowing what it's like to be chosen
last for basketball, unable to imagine what it's like to be fat and in any
case having little sympathy for fat people, unable to comprehend how
it happened that many girls are socialized *out* of physical activity, and
conceiving of sport and politics as autonomous. It would be interesting to
compare the biographies of the committed students with those of their
acquiescent and recalcitrant peers, especially in the light of the emphasis I
am now placing on the link between subject position and the reading of
texts. Given another opportunity to conduct this study, I would certainly
place greater emphasis on collecting biographical data.

I also wonder if I could have created more authentic opportunities
for action. Peer teaching was not 'real' teaching as it would be experienced in schools. But my feeling is that the peer teaching context may
have actually enhanced critical reflectivity, as opposed to a school teaching experience, because management, discipline and survival concerns
were minor. Such concerns can still be expected to arise when students
enter the schools as student teachers. However, I believe the timing of the
course at the beginning of students' teacher education programme, and its
peer teaching context, may be crucial in breaking with students' experience of what schools and teaching are about and, as a result, creating
possibilities for change.

Given the successful and highly competitive (by virtue of the nature
of schooling itself) backgrounds of these students, peer pressure was
influential. This was perhaps more obvious because of the peer teaching

context. Some students lacked confidence to voice their opinions in public, as is vividly illustrated in a journal entry by Kate, following the class discussion of Scott's criticisms of the course.

> Some students regard this journal-keeping task as 'crap'...I'm scared now that I'm the only one (or one of a few) who is taking this reasonably seriously.... Can you believe this, I said 'reasonably' because I was scared that if I said *very* seriously...you would think I was a 'conch' [conscientious]...I'm actually *scared* to admit to the majority that I like doing this stuff!!!.... I can, at least, write down how I feel. (Kate, Week 10)

The journal consequently became very important to some students as a place for articulating thoughts and ideas which their shyness, lack of confidence or desire for peer approval prevented in class. Kate, for example, wrote:

> God, I'm so shy. I want to say so much, and just when I'm about to spill my knowledge (or lack of it) on to the rest of the world, someone else regurgitates it, or some loudmouth confidently exclaims it with no qualms about shyness at all!!! I know, as I get to know everyone better and better, things will change — but for now, I hope people realize I'm a 'WORTHWHILE' person!!! Just give me a little time — I'll show them....(Kate, Week 2)

Similarly, Gordon stated that:

> For me the journal was the best part of this, or any other, course...I like sharing my feelings and don't like bottling up emotions, but my experiences in the past have made it difficult to know who to trust. I found the journal as an opportunity to express feelings and thoughts that might not otherwise have been aired. I have to admit there were some very personal articles I wanted to include in my journal which did not make it. This was not due to a lack of trust (I would love to have poured out my emotions), but rather a fear that it was becoming too much of a personal diary, and a feeling that it wasn't fair to burden you with my personal problems. (Gordon, Week 14)

The competitiveness which underwrote peer pressure was partly a result of the assessment and credentialling function of university life. Most students, naturally enough, develop a list of priorities using criteria such as the weighting of each component of assessment and the perceived difficulty of the work involved.

> In the long run whether a 115 student is awarded a 4 or 7 is really not the important outcome of this subject, 115 is encouraging us to 'think' and to 'reflect'. I think that if we develop this type of approach/attitude now then we will benefit in the long term when we are actually teaching.... I think that long after we've forgotten our 115 rating, those fortunate enough to have gained something more than just a 'mark' will realize the value of self-examination or 'reflection' or whatever term is used. The thing is, by looking at ourselves 'critically'...as a person/teacher, at individual lessons etc. we can't help but 'but learn'— and that is worthwhile. (Sam, Week 10)

Some students, like Sam, were able to see beyond assessment, a factor which seemed to facilitate their commitment to the process of reflecting. Others, like Bob, who thought I was brave to have 'the test' when there were still four weeks of lectures to go (Week 13), remained trapped within the instrumentality which seems to be reinforced by the exigencies of university study.

The organization of the Bachelor of Human Movement Studies (Education) degree with its strong emphasis on scientific study, moderate emphasis on professional preparation and almost perfunctory approach to the social sciences and humanities (for example, there is no philosophy component to the programme) can be seen to reinforce the entering orientations of the students and the disdain for reflection which some demonstrated. Some students enjoyed and valued this 'new' approach to university teaching like Annette, who 'came to lectures because I wanted to, not because there was an exam to sit' (Week 14) (there was a test worth 10 per cent in Week 10) and like Peter, 'it gives me a buzz to write freely and uninhibited like this' (Week 10). For some, HM115 clearly resonated with their own uneasiness about certain features of school life. 'I never liked the "marks oriented" nature of school' (Peter, Week 10). Other students would clearly have preferred simply to be given a 'recipe' for good teaching, opportunities to practise those skills and experience in the 'real world' of teaching. Rather than make summary comments about the facilitation of reflective teaching among pre-service physical education teachers at this point, I want to return to the notion of pedagogy as text and do a 'reading' of the pedagogy and analysis I have presented above. This next section of the chapter should demonstrate clearly the ways in which we get trapped within the discourses available to us.

Reading My Own Pedagogy and Analysis

Although my aim was to go beyond 'the preferred reading' (the dominant approach to physical education teacher education) in both my reading and my practice, it is clear that I had my own 'structures of preference' in the teaching of HM115. I have already listed the types of messages I hoped students would glean from the course such as valuing their own knowledge and collegiality, reflecting on all aspects of teaching, and experiencing teaching within a peer teaching context. I still believe that these were important messages and that they successfully subverted some conventional attitudes toward knowledge and power relations within teaching. I have also alluded to some of the difficulties of facilitating such changes within the university context such as the requirement to grade students; for example, whether or not desirable, the hierarchical relation of teacher to students cannot be eradicated but only modified, given the institutional authority vested in the position 'teacher'. Moreover, in seeking to present knowledge as problematic, I had to counter years of school socialization which had led many students to want answers rather than questions, recipes rather than a few ingredients.

I expect readers of this chapter will read my pedagogy differently because of our different subjectivities and because of the impossibility, at any particular moment, of stepping outside the discourses which are available to us and which construct us. Another reason for our different readings might be my incapacity to convey on paper all that happened in 115 classes. Creating a written text out of a social text literally and metaphorically flattens it. The suggestion that we are trapped within our discourses *at any particular moment* does not imply that there can be no movement. As an example, within physical education teacher education I have shifted from a discourse of teacher effectiveness, to a discourse of ideology-critique at the time of the study and analysis, to my current affiliation with a discourse of critical cultural studies, a discourse on discourse. Of course, these shifts are partial and overlapping; as I said earlier, I still draw on my knowledge of teacher effectiveness research and, as I hope is clear in both my reading of the opening scenario and my advocacy of a critical perspective, I am trying to move beyond dominant ideologies of teacher education.

The shift to cultural studies occurred as I became increasingly dissatisfied with the capacity of the 'reflective teaching' literature (including that based in ideology-critique) to help me in understanding the HM115 experience. That is, the discourses of reflective teaching were inconsistent with the lived experience of teaching HM115. To illustrate this point, I wish to return to Figure 1. Although the categories emerged from the data as I thought about the ways in which students differed in their responses to the course, I now realize that, in using the categories, I was attempting to be more precise than reality. Analytical distinctions are separate from reality, resting with the researcher; in this case, with my view(s) of the world. Furthermore, the construction of such distinctions necessarily leads to both abstraction and simplification. There is a tendency to view the world in dualisms such as good/bad, political/apolitical. As an example, if we consider my use of the *categories of focus* (technical, educational, critical), we can see the limitations, the forced tidiness, of using those categories. Tom wrote:

> I think that despite wanting to be as open-minded as I possibly can, the teacher I want to be is one who will essentially 'go with the flow' or reserve the status quo, or produce little capitalists, whatever the case may be. As bad as that sounds to me, I think to deny it to myself would be naive. As much as anyone would like to produce open-minded, liberated and free students, we're inadvertently going to continue the traditions of society, if not by just the Departmental directives or whatever, through our own subconscious habits. No-one could realistically be 'value-free', so the whole matter is not really worth worrying about. (Tom, Week 8)

Reflecting on his comments, my tendency was to categorize this statement as not quite critical because he wasn't determined to combine his reflection with *action* for social change. Furthermore, in suggesting the goal was to be 'value-free', he had not understood my position. On the other hand, this comment from Peter was categorized as critical. 'Teachers have a responsibility to help kids develop in the face of the demands of society, not to make them into jigsaw pieces that neatly fit into the puzzle. The only way we can make society better is to teach our children how to make it better, not how to make themselves better for society' (Peter, Week 5). However, *both* students address the status quo and ask moral and political questions. The major difference lies in their resolution, with Tom lacking Peter's optimism. Thus within the distinction between the categories of 'critical' and 'educational' I was making another distinction about commitment to action, something I value/d in teachers. I maintain that there is value in this distinction but am able also to see the limits of my analysis as researcher. At least I needed to change my explicit definition of 'critical'.

Even before the act of reading, my tendency was to attempt to separate out critical, educational and technical concerns. But as I indicated in my description of Figure 1, most moral-political issues demand 'how' questions and, as Noffke and Brennan (1988, p. 9) point out, 'technical skills are not merely valuable, they are *essential* to getting things done' and they necessarily are the focus of much teacher reflection. Teachers in their daily practice are confronted with decisions of *what* to do and, for example, in deciding how to deal with a sexist comment by a student, confront both moral and technical issues and, whatever their decision, take a political stance. Another concern I have with the categorization is the implication that critical purposes are 'good' and a 'better' focus than technical skills or educational goals. But even if we call for political transformation, there is a danger in advocating transformation for its own sake. Transformation of what? Transformation towards what? In the reflective teaching literature the rhetoric of transformation derives from critical theory which privileges, in rather abstract ways, justice and equality. However, other values such as caring and nurturing may be just as valid, perhaps more central, and certainly related, in the ethical choices teachers make (Noddings, 1984; Noffke and Brennan, 1988).

As another example of the limitations of categorization, let us consider the *categories of students' responses* which I identified through my analysis of data. These responses can be seen to fit neatly with the reading strategies I outlined earlier: dominant, negotiated, oppositional. That is, in relation to my preferred reading of the pedagogy, students either agreed, acquiesced, or resisted. But the use of the categories suggests more stability and less contradiction for individuals than exists in reality. My attempt to indicate the lack of stability with the broken lines of the diagram in Figure 1 does not overcome the simplification. There were, no doubt, moments of acceptance and opposition for each of the students and varying degrees of negotiation with the text. For instance, Scott's moment of overt resistance should not have labelled him a 'recalcitrant' student. His initiation of a two-hour discussion of the course with me on one occasion is hardly the behaviour of a student who resisted everything about the course. If only because of the legitimacy I was granted *as teacher*, Scott was prepared to engage in dialogue about the course with me.

None of us should need reminding of the bias or subjectivity of all research which limits us to seeing only that which we are looking for. Our categories start to take on a life of their own and we find it increasingly difficult to separate our analytical distinctions and reality. As an example, if we return to Sandra's comments about the extent to which I was 'preaching', my initial analysis was to claim that I had support for my hope that I had not imposed my perspective on the students. A cynical reading might be that Sandra was taken in by my preferred reading, or at least able to understand my mission, and simply told me what I wanted to hear. A major purpose of this section of the chapter has been to demonstrate the reflexivity which the notion of pedagogy as text can promote. With this reflexivity we begin to acknowledge the sources of our thought, of our categorizations, and to be more humble about our abilities to define what is true and what is good. The notion of pedagogy as text enables us to see positivistic research and ideological analyses, indeed all inquiry, as incomplete.

Concluding Comments

Reflexivity naturally also applies to the concept of pedagogy as text. What is gained through its use? What is lost? As I argued in the introduction to this chapter, pedagogy as text enables fuller, more complex descriptions than other approaches to pedagogy. For example, teacher effectiveness research tends to describe only that which is easily measured and to describe only from the perspective of the researcher; ideology-critique might describe pedagogy in terms of its class, race or gender formations (and often only one of these), providing a rather singular account of the pedagogy (for example, *the* hidden curriculum). I have illustrated above some of the multiplicity of meaning that seems almost impossible to grasp with such forms of observation and description, particularly if they are unreflexive. For example, with the concept of pedagogy as text I have shown that students in HM115 were not *simply* recalcitrant, acquiescent, or committed. That description drew on the language of a particular discourse which sought monolithic explanation. Pedagogy as text enabled a more complex understanding.

It is in the realm of prescription that pedagogy as text might be considered weakest. The notion allows multiple meanings and the 'deconstruction' of almost everything, but in so doing it provides no guidelines for judging whose position should be taken, whose interests should be served. As stated earlier, the prescriptive moment is left to the audience. Hence some readers might use my reading of the opening scenario to insist that 'things' are as they should be: teachers *should* maintain their hierarchical, institutional authority over students. Physical education *is* the domain of the thin, muscular, white and middle-class. Other readers, and I would like to believe many, would agree with me that we cannot and should not continue practices which are destructive to the self and body images of physical education students; nor should we continue practices which are uneducative. While 'pedagogy as text' does not itself prescribe, it certainly can promote prescription. In the acknowledgment that there are multiple realities, multiple meanings, partial subjectivities and so on, and in the reflexivity which acknowledges the social construction of any discourse or practice, pedagogy as text points to overlooked or marginalized meanings. As such, it points to inequities and injustices, the acknowledgment and correction of which depend on the audience, on its moral and political commitments. Thus the full description facilitated by pedagogy as text should not be seen as an end in itself. It is against arguments about the political weakness of notions like pedagogy as text (which can be limited to description and deconstruction) that other post-structural concepts become helpful. In particular, Michel Foucault's (1980) notion of 'regime of truth' adds an emphasis on power relations and their effects on people's lives to the full description and reflexivity provided by 'pedagogy as text'. It is not within the scope of this chapter to elaborate on the concept of regime of truth, but interested readers may want to refer to Gore (forthcoming). Nevertheless, I maintain, and believe I have demonstrated, that the notion of pedagogy as text is helpful to the research and practice of physical education teacher education.

In this chapter I have demonstrated both an alternative pedagogy of physical education teacher education and an alternative way of thinking about that pedagogy; namely, pedagogy as text. The chapter is complex and multilayered but a major point I have tried to make is that so is reality. The notion of pedagogy as text helps us to capture some of that complexity. We avoid portraying knowledge as uncontestable and pedagogy as the automatic transmission of knowledge or skills. Meaning is always a site of struggle and students are far from passive in their own construction of meaning. Likewise, we acknowledge the limitations of dualisms and vitriolic ideology-critique by recognizing that all meanings are formed out of the intersections of discourses and subjectivities and that meanings are specific to the historical moment. In either case we give up a search for *the way* to conduct physical education teacher education and own up to the uncertainty with which we approach both our pedagogical and research work. This is not to suggest that we should give up the search for *better* ways; indeed, I have introduced and explored the notion of pedagogy as text as part of that search.

Notes

1 See Dewar (1987) and Chapter 4 in this volume and Woods (1989) for an elaboration of tensions for athletes and physical educators around issues of sexuality and gender.
2 See Tinning (1988) for a discussion of these paradigms in physical education.
3 By 'scientistic' I mean a dogmatic belief in the value of scientific knowledge.

4 See Gore (1987) for a detailed critique.
5 The TE score ranks year 12 students in Queensland in a particular year, according to their achievement in senior secondary school studies. The highest TE score in any year is 990, and this is assigned to a number of students roughly equivalent to 1 per cent of the 17-year-old population in Queensland in that particular year. In 1987, for example, 460 students were assigned TE scores of 990. TE scores then range down in bands of five (985, 980, 975, etc.), which represents 0.5 per cent of the population, until all eligible students have been assigned a score.
6 This study was supported by grants from the Board of Teacher Education (Queensland) and the Universities Research Grants Commission. See Gore and Bartlett (1987) for the original report of this study.
7 For example, Stephen and Kate were selected because they expressed strong desires to teach, James and Brett were repeating the subject, Sam and Andrea were slightly older, Joanne and Brian dressed differently from the majority of the class and Joanne was extremely quiet. Elizabeth appeared a bit 'suspicious' of the programme. Graham was quite forward and appeared very frank. Pseudonyms are used throughout to preserve anonymity.
8 Unless indicated otherwise, all citations of students' statements are of entries made in their personal journals.

References

APPLE, M. (1979) *Ideology and Curriculum*. London: Routledge and Kegan Paul.
BEAMISH, R. (1982) 'Some Neglected Political Scenes in Sport Study.' Paper presented at the 77th meeting of the American Sociological Association, San Francisco.
BELKA, D. (1988) 'What Preservice Physical Educators Observe about Lessons in Progressive Field Experiences.' *Journal of Teaching in Physical Education*, 7 (4), 311–26.
BERLAK, A. (1988) 'Teaching for Outrage and Empathy in a Post-secondary Classroom.' Paper presented at the Annual Meeting of the Americal Educational Research Association, New Orleans.
BOURDIEU, P. (1984) *Distinction*, Trans. E. NICE. Boston, Mass. Harvard University Press.
CRUICKSHANK, D.R., HOLTON, J., FAY, D., WILLIAMS, J., KENNEDY, J., MYERS, B. and HOUGH, J. (1981) *Reflective Teaching*. Bloomington, Ill.: Phi Delta Kappa.
DEMERS, P.J. (1988) 'University Training of Physical Educators' in HARVEY, J. and CANTELON, H. (Eds), *Not Just a Game: Essays in Canadian Sport Sociology*, pp. 159–72. Ottawa: University of Ottawa Press.
DEWAR, A.M. (1987) 'Knowledge and Gender in Physical Education,' in GASKELL, J. and McLAREN, A. (Eds), *Women and Education: A Canadian Perspective*, pp. 265–88. Calgary: Detselig.
DEWEY, J. (1933) *How We Think: A Restatement of the Relation of Reflective Thinking to the Educative Process*. Chicago, Ill.: Henry Regnery Co.
DODDS, P. (1985) 'Are Hunters of the Functional Curriculum Seeking Quarks or Snarks?' *Journal of Teaching in Physical Education*, 4 (2), 91–9.

EISNER, E.W. (1983) 'The Art and Craft of Teaching.' *Educational Leadership*, 40 (3), 4–13.

FAY, B. (1977) 'How People Change Themselves,' in BALL, T. (Ed.), *Political Theory and Praxis: New Perspectives*, pp. 200–37. Minneapolis, Minn.: University of Minnesota Press.

FISKE, J. (1987a) *Television Culture*. London: Methuen.

FISKE, J. (1987b) 'British Cultural Studies and Television' in ALLEN, R.C. (Ed.), *Channels of Discourse: Television and Contemporary Criticism*, pp. 254–89. Chapel Hill and London: University of North Carolina Press.

FOUCAULT, M. (1980) 'Truth and Power,' in GORDON, C. (Ed.), *Power/Knowledge: Selected Interviews and Other Writings 1972–1977*, pp. 109–33. New York: Pantheon Books.

FOUCAULT, M. (1983) 'The Subject and Power,' in DREYFUS, H.L. and RAINBOW, P. (Eds), *Michel Foucault: Beyond Structuralism and Hermeneutics*, 2nd ed., pp. 208–28. Chicago, Ill.: University of Chicago Press.

GIROUX, H.A. (1980) 'Teacher Education and the Ideology of Social Control.' *Journal of Education*, 162, 5–27.

GIROUX, H.A. (1985) 'Teachers as Transformative Intellectuals.' *Social Education*, 49 (5), 376–9.

GORE, J. (1987) 'Reflecting on Reflective Teaching.' *Journal of Teacher Education*, 38 (2), 33–9.

GORE, J. (1988) 'Reflective Teaching and Preservice Teacher Education: A Relationship Worth Pursuing.' Paper presented at the Tenth Annual Conference on Curriculum Theorizing and Classroom Practice, Bergamo Conference Center, Dayton, Ohio, October.

GORE, J.M. (forthcoming) Discourses of Feminist and Critical Pedagogy: Regimes of Truth and Repressive Moments (tentative title). PhD dissertation, University of Wisconsin-Madison.

GORE, J.M. and BARTLETT, V.L. (1987) 'Pathways and Barriers to Reflective Teaching in an Initial Teacher Education Program.' Paper presented at the Australian Curriculum Studies Association National Conference, Sydney, July.

HALL, S. (1980) 'Encoding/Decoding,' in HALL, S., HOBSON, D., LOWE, A. and WILLIS, P. (Eds), *Culture, Media, Language*, pp. 128–39. London: Hutchinson.

HOFFMANN, S.J. (1969) 'Traditional Methodology: Prospects for Change.' Paper presented at the Nebraska Education Association Conference.

HOLLY, M.L. (1984) *Keeping a Personal-Professional Journal*. Geelong: Deakin University Press.

JACKSON, P. (1968) *Life in Classrooms*. New York: Holt, Rinehart and Winston.

KEMMIS, S. (1983) 'Getting Our Thinking Straight: Three Views of Education.' *Advise*, 3 (7), 1–3.

KEMMIS, S. (1985) 'Action Research and the Politics of reflection,' in BOUD, D., KEOGH, R. and WALKER, D. (Eds), *Reflection: Turning Experience into Learning*, pp. 139–63. London: Kogan Page.

KEMMIS, S. and FITZCLARENCE, L. (1986) *Curriculum Theory, Curriculum Theorizing: Beyond Reproduction Theory*. Geelong: Deakin University.

KIRK, D. (1986) 'A Critical Pedagogy for Teacher Education: Toward an

Inquiry-oriented Approach.' *Journal of Teaching in Physical Education*, 5 (4), 230–46.

KIRK, D. (1989) 'The Orthodoxy in RT-PE and the Research-Practice Gap: A Critique and Alternate View.' *Journal of Teaching in Physical Education*, 8 (2), 123–30.

LOCKE, L.F. (1974) 'The Ecology of the Gymnasium: What the Tourists Never See.' Paper presented at the SAPECW Fall Workshop, Gatlinburg, Tennessee.

LUNDGREN, U. (1983) *Curriculum Theory, between Hope and Happening: Text and Context in Curriculum.* Geelong: Deakin University.

LUSTED, D. (1986) 'Introduction: Why Pedagogy.' *Screen*, 27 (5), 2–14.

McBRIDE, R.E. (1984a) 'Perceived Teaching and Program Concerns among Preservice Teachers, University Supervisors, and Cooperating Teachers. *Journal of Teaching in Physical Education*, 3 (3), 36–43.

McBRIDE, R.E. (1984b) 'An Intensive Study of a Systematic Teacher Training Model in Physical Education.' *Journal of Teaching in Physical Education*, 4 (1), 3–16.

McKAY, J., GORE, J.M. and KIRK, D. (in press) 'Beyond the limits of Technocratic Physical Education.' *Quest*.

NARAYAN, U. (1988) 'Working Together across Difference: Some Considerations on Emotions and Political Practice.' *Hypatia*, 3 (2), 31–47.

NODDINGS, N. (1984) *Caring.* Berkeley, Calif.: University of California Press.

NOFFKE, S. and BRENNAN, M. (1988) 'The Dimensions of Reflection: A Conceptual and Contextual Analysis.' Paper presented at the Annual Meeting of the American Educational Research Association, New Orleans, March.

POPKEWITZ, T.S. (1987) *Critical Studies in Teacher Education: Its Folklore, Theory and Practice.* Lewes, New York and Philadelphia: Falmer Press.

ROSS, (1987) 'Humanizing the Undergraduate Physical Education Curriculum.' *Journal of Teaching in Physical Education*, 7 (1), 46–60.

SAID, E. (1983) *The World, the Text and the Critic.* Cambridge, Mass.: Harvard University Press.

SCHEMBRI, H. (1976) The Anti-academic Perspective of Physical Education Students. Unpublished honours thesis, Macquarie University.

SMITH, S.J. (1988) 'Where Is the Child in Physical Education Research?' Paper presented at the CAHPER/HPEC '88 Conference, University of Alberta, 5–8 May.

TINNING, R.I. (1987) *Improving Teaching in Physical Education.* Geelong: Deakin University.

TINNING, R.I. (1988) 'Student Teaching and the Pedagogy of Necessity.' *Journal of Teaching in Physical Education*, 7 (2), 82–9.

VAN MANEN, M. (1977) 'Linking Ways of Knowing with Ways of Being Practical.' *Curriculum Inquiry*, 6, 205–28.

WALKER, D. (1985) 'Writing and Reflection,' in BOUD, D., KEOGH, R. and WALKER, D. (Eds), *Reflection: Turning Experience into Learning*, pp. 552–68. London: Kogan Page.

WEEDON, C. (1987) *Feminist Practice and Poststructuralist Theory.* Oxford and New York: Basil Blackwell.

WOODS, S.E. (1989) 'Describing the Experience of Lesbian Physical Education

Teachers: A Phenomenological Study.' Paper presented at the Annual Meeting of the American Educational Research Association, San Francisco, March.

ZEICHNER, K.M. (1981–82) 'Reflective Teaching and Field-based Experience in Teacher Education.' *Interchange*, 12 (4), 1–22.

ZEICHNER, K.M. (1983) 'Alternative Paradigms for Teacher Education.' *Journal of Teacher Education*, 34 (3), 3–9.

ZEICHNER, K.M. and GORE, J.M. (in press) 'Teacher Socialization,' in HOUSTON, W.R. (Ed.), *Handbook of Research on Teacher Education*. New York: Macmillan.

ZEICHNER, K.M. and LISTON, D.P. (1986) 'An Inquiry-oriented Approach to Student Teaching.' *Journal of Teaching Practice*, 6 (1), 5–24.

ZEICHNER, K.M. and LISTON, D.P. (1987) 'Teaching Student Teachers to Reflect.' *Harvard Educational Review*, 57 (1), 23–48.

ZEICHNER, K.M. and TEITELBAUM, K. (1982) 'Personalized and Inquiry-oriented Teacher Education: An Analysis of Two Approaches to the Development of Curriculum for Filed-based Experiences.' *Journal of Education for Teaching*, 8 (2), 95–117.

Acknowledgment

The friends, colleagues and students whose comments on earlier drafts of this paper have been helpful are too numerous to name but I want to express my sincere gratitude to them all. For their particular contributions, I want to thank Bernadette Baker, Alison Dewar, Elizabeth Ellsworth, James Ladwig, James McKay, Stephen Smith, Jim Walker, Ken Zeichner and the editors.

Chapter 6

Ability, Position and Privilege in School Physical Education

John Evans

In the ordinary routines of our everyday professional lives, where time-tables and habit rule and the school bell tolls with a remorseless predictability, cohorts of children can pass through a teacher's consciousness with an alarming unfamiliarity, especially in the highly regulated systems of secondary schooling. Within such institutional conditions of work, pressured and demanding as they are, teachers could be forgiven for thinking that their impact on what children think about themselves, their bodies and each other is at best minimal or at worst of no significance at all. Rarely does mundane teaching work receive much attention, whether praiseworthy or malicious, other than at times of educational crisis or curriculum reform. Giroux, though perhaps underestimating the capacities of teachers, is not far off the mark when he states:

> Various dimensions of the schooling process are viewed by teachers as apolitical and ahistorical in nature; and, in the final analysis, schooling itself is perceived as an instrumental process governed by technical problems and answerable by 'common sense solutions'. This perspective flattens reality and effectively removes the dynamics of schooling from the realm of ethical and political debate. Educators, in this case tend to view themselves as impartial facilitators who operate in a value free and uncontaminated setting. (Giroux, 1981, p. 80)

It is my contention in this chapter that what goes on inside physical education classrooms, through both the organization and social relations of knowledge production (or the form) and the curriculum content of schooling, does matter greatly. It has an important bearing on the identities, abilities and opportunities of teachers and pupils and therefore on the kind of society in which we live. I will also claim that understanding what teachers do to children, how and why, for example, they typify, differentiate and label them as they do, sometimes to the detriment of many, may be inseparable from first knowing better how the lives of *teachers* themselves are shaped, created and constrained in the contemporary conditions of schooling and historically over time. Indeed, it might reasonably be argued that to date in sociological and educational debate issues of social control have been considered and discussed largely in terms of the control of children. Obviously, knowing how pupils are socially controlled is vitally important in any quest to understand how schools and physical education within them sponsor and develop particular sorts of attitudes and identities among children and so help position class and cultural relationships. But the point I will stress is that teachers in common with other workers are also subject to systems of supervision and control. Indeed, never has this been more evidently the case than in Thatcher's Britain (Evans and Davies, 1988a). They too are labelled and differentiated, typified and evaluated and have to work hard to protect their sometimes fragile educational identities and social positions. Teachers not only control pupils, they too are controlled by pupils, as well as being manipulated and processed by their peers and others outside the educational workplace in ways which we only sketchily understand.

In the first part of this chapter I will focus upon the way in which the abilities and opportunities of physical education teachers have been shaped in the educational processes of comprehensive secondary schooling in post-war Britain and illustrate how these processes are related to educational and political discourses in wider cultural contexts. It is claimed (Whitehead and Hendry, 1976) that the identities and consequently the career opportunities of physical education teachers are badly constrained not only by the powerful influences of the academic curriculum, an influence which reaches out to wider cultural evaluations of the status of practical and physical work in British society, and the ideology of patriarchy as it pervades the school system, but also by a particular version of equal opportunities which physical education teachers, like others, have long adopted. The latter has helped mask, legitimate and sustain the differential distribution of status, reward and opportunity afforded to individuals both inside and outside schools.

In the second part, however, I shall examine recent curriculum developments in physical education, with the question in mind of whether these initiatives help redefine, recondition or reposition the identities, abilities and opportunities of teachers in the educational process of secondary schooling. Here it is claimed that the 'new physical education' in Britain,[1] far from heralding a radical departure from the established tradition in physical education as the noise surrounding these innovations would sometimes have us believe, constitutes *a process of accommodation* in which the profession has understandably endeavoured to protect its interests and status within the curriculum in the light of recent changes in the discourse of wider educational and political debate which is redefining how education ought to be. This process involves neither a shake up of how teachers think about their own or others' 'abilities', nor a challenge to the status afforded to different sorts of knowledge in the school curriculum. The 'new physical education' does involve the emergence of new forms of practice but these contain a reformulation of old themes in which deep and principled commitments to the ideologies of equal opportunities and individualism remain soundly intact. As such, I will suggest, the new physical education does not presage the arrival of a form of practice which helps challenge either hierarchies of knowledge or the social hierarchies which prevail inside the subject, within the broader work context and outside school.

The analysis draws on the work of a number of critical social theorists, especially that of Michael F.D. Young (1971) and Basil Bernstein (1971, 1986). The detail of their work need not be documented here. But briefly it can be stated that the discussion takes up issues about the 'social construction of ability' which were challengingly introduced in Young's (1971) work but which since have rarely found expression in empirical research on the physical education curriculum. Young points out that knowledge, especially in the British educational system, has long been 'highly stratified'. By this he means that there is a clear differentiation between what is taken to count as valid and worthwhile educational knowledge and what is not. This type of curriculum organization legitimates not only a rigid hierarchy between teachers and taught but also, as I want to point out, between teachers too. In Britain 'academic knowledge' has been 'privileged' to achieve this status and this has implications for the ways in which physical education teachers' competencies and abilities are defined in the institutional workplace and for the business and nature of curriculum reform in the subject (cf. Sparkes, 1988; Kirk, 1988).

Both Young and Bernstein make the claim that there is nothing accidental or arbitrary about the way in which knowledge is defined or evaluated in the educational process and they enjoin us to explore how educational practice, in this case in physical education, helps sustain, contest or challenge social and cultural hierarchies in school and society. In Bernstein's provocative view 'how a society classifies, distributes, transmits and evaluates the educational knowledge it considers to be public, reflects both the distribution of power and the principles of social control' (Bernstein, 1977, p. 85). It is claimed that what is taught in schools, along with the value weighting given to different subjects and concomitantly to teachers within them, is neither arbitrary nor immutable, but in part reflects the power of some interest groups to define what is to count as valid knowledge and its proper form of organization. Following this line of thought, we have to consider that what passes for physical education in schools is also a social construction, and as such is inevitably a site of struggle over values and different conceptions of how the body, the individual and society ought to be, a contest in which individuals and interest groups may not all have the same opportunities or power to make their voices heard.

For Bernstein, the political nature of knowledge is expressed in the principles that structure the message systems (curriculum, pedagogy and evaluation) inherent in the process of schooling and he, like Young, stresses that in the process of schooling both form and content matter greatly. In his more recent work (Bernstein, 1986), which has a special bearing on the analysis in this paper, he reiterates this concern for both the medium and the message and claims that an interest in the latter has properly led sociologists of education to investigate the 'talk, the values, the codes of conduct' which underpin educational discourse and how these are 'biased in favour of a dominating group'. These values and codes 'privilege a dominating group, so such codes of communication are distorted in favour of one group, the dominating group. But there is another distortion at the same time; the culture, the practice and consciousness of the dominated group is distorted. It is recontextualized as having less value. Thus there is a double distortion' (Bernstein, 1986, p. 5, mimeo version).

Following this line of analysis, we have to consider that not only are there 'privileging texts' in physical education and the broader school curriculum but also that pupils (Evans and Clarke, 1988) *and* teachers may be differently positioned in '*relation to*' them. Elsewhere, using Bernstein's conceptual framework, I have attempted to illustrate *how* knowledge, defined as the 'new physical education', has been produced in the primary context (colleges of higher education and professional journals), recontextualized (by the 'popular media' and other political voices), then reproduced in very conservative form and content inside schools (Evans, 1988a). But that limited analysis hardly begins to explore how, and even less so *why*, the work of social and cultural reproduction seems to get done and is adopted so readily by physical education teachers inside schools, perhaps against their best or better intentions. This chapter tries to redress this imbalance by asking what and how knowledge has been and is valued within the comprehensive school system, how this relates to the professional interests of physical education teachers and to influences in wider social, cultural and political fields.

Comprehensive Schooling and the Construction of Teacher Abilities

The advent and expansion of a system of comprehensive schooling in post-war Britain, though an important and major change in the organization of secondary schooling, did not herald the arrival of either a widespread egalitarianism within the system or a curriculum capable of providing a 'physical education for all'. Indeed, it would have been more surprising if it had achieved such practices given the nature of the political origins and motivations which sponsored comprehensive reform (see, CCCS, 1981; Ball, 1984; Chitty, 1987). As Ball (1984) points out, the Labour Government, which in 1965 introduced Circular 10/65 *requesting* local authorities to submit plans for comprehensive reorganization, made no attempt to define or lay down guidelines about what should be the content or internal organizational form of such schools. So, although within the optimism of the early 1960s it is possible to find examples of innovation and curriculum change within comprehensive schools, and indeed within physical education during this time (a point to which I will later return), it is hardly surprising that some considerable time after the arrival of the system some of its advocates could sadly and angrily lament, 'it was impossible to ensure equality of opportunity without a definition of those minimum opportunities which should be available to all boys and girls in any school called comprehensive' (Benn, 1979, quoted in Ball, 1984, p. 2). Even more recently, Gregory could report:

> Twenty years of officially recognized comprehensive education have failed to produce strong definitive statements about the criteria and values upon which the genuinely comprehensive school should be based. HMI reports do not include any attempt to evaluate the extent to which secondary schools may be genuinely comprehensive. This makes it difficult to reply to those whose constant preoccupation is the perpetuation of myths about the alleged lack of competence of our comprehensive schools. (Gregory, quoted in Chitty, 1987, p. 7)

But the expansion of the comprehensive system, while principally unguided by policies relating to the internal organization and content of schools, was *not* without ideological or political foundations. There is insufficient space here to detail these or describe the social and political context of the 1960s which circumscribed the development of the comprehensive system; (that has been very well done elsewhere by, for example, CCCS, 1981). But for the purposes of this paper, it does need to be noted that two powerful ideologies, those of human capital theory and a particular version of equal opportunities, helped guide both the development of the system and form the actions of a good many teachers, including physical educationalists, within it.

In the economic expansion and social optimism of the early 1960s it was widely believed that the educational system could be changed in such a way as to produce both greater equality in society *and* economic efficiency (Chitty, 1987; CCCS, 1981). The ideological bases of this outlook in Britain, in the USA as elsewhere (Lauder, 1988) lay in 'human capital theory' and the view that 'investing in human capital not only increased individual productivity, but in so doing, also lays as the technical base of the type of labour force necessary for rapid economic growth' (Chitty, 1987, p. 9). As Chitty goes on to point out, at least a version of this philosophy proved highly attractive to a Labour Government which, in the 1960s, for a variety of political and ideological reasons (CCCS, 1981), was more committed to reform than to radical social and educational change, and for which the twin watchwords were social equality and economic progress (Chitty, 1987, p. 9). To the powerful Fabians who achieved dominance within the Labour Party, bringing children of different abilities and social sorts together within the comprehensive organizational form represented a means not only of moving the educational system in the direction of greater equality of opportunity and social justice, but also of securing economic efficiency. It would help avoid the un- or under-skilling of children which was contingent upon the selective system and putatively disastrous for an expanding and changing high-tech economy. It would also subtly confront the unfairness of a system which denied to all children *equality* of *access* to a high status (grammar school) education. The debates of the day thus centred on issues of wastage of talent and equality of access to education. Matters relating to what should be taught inside school were of comparatively little concern.

The point to be stressed is that the development of a comprehensive system was not grounded in anything approximating radical or indeed even democratic socialist principles, but in what Lauder (1988) has termed an 'enlightened liberal individualism', which warmly embraced a commitment to a discourse which emphasized both the skilling of more children and a version of equal opportunities which, with its emphasis mainly on issues of *access*, had very little to do with egalitarian concerns with social justice, or the structure or structuring of opportunities both inside and outside schools. As Wilby remarks:

Educational equality was an attempt to achieve social change by proxy. More and better education was more palatable and less socially disruptive than direct measures of tackling inequality. So was economic growth. Even the most complacently privileged could hardly object to children attending better schools and to the nation producing more wealth. Equality of educational opportunity had an altogether more agreeable ring to it than any other form of equality, such as equality of income or equality of property. With its overtones of self improvement, it could even appeal to the more conservative elements in society. Ugly words such as redistribution and expropriation did not apply to education — or nobody thought they applied. Education was a cornucopia, so prolific of good things that nobody would need any longer to ask awkward questions about who got what. (Wilby, in Chitty, 1987, p. 10)

In short, 'the reforms of the 1960s were seen as a means of ameliorating the more brutal inequalities in society, or at least producing a greater degree of social harmony without in any way disturbing the basic class structure of the capitalist system' (Chitty, 1987, p. 10). They were not concerned with issues of social class and on matters of gender there was a resounding silence.[2] The problem of achieving greater equality and social justice both inside and outside school was not a policy concern. It is thus hardly surprising that after twenty years of 'comprehensive schooling' in Britain the findings of educational research should consistently point out that processes of selection, differentiation and labelling are as evident within the comprehensive system, in physical education and in other subjects, as ever they were in the selective bipartite system of secondary modern and grammar schools. The expansion of the comprehensive system had effectively undercut the more obvious forms of physical separation, but it had not counselled teachers either to appraise or to reconsider their thinking about knowledge, the nature of ability, or for that matter the nature and purpose of secondary education.

As others have pointed out (CCCS, 1981), there was no break with the paradigm of measurable abilities. Though the qualities to be measured now tended to be more varied and inclusive, there were still differences in achievement by which children would be 'produced by schools and equipped for different places in the general division of labour' (CCCS, 1981). Nor were the place, status and position of 'academic knowledge' in the school curriculum called into question. In his powerful critique of comprehensive schooling, David Hargreaves (1982) has argued that the continued dominance of the examination system has ensured that the intellectual cognitive subjects have continued to occupy the heart of the comprehensive school curriculum (cf. Connell *et al.*, 1982, for a similar comment on the Australian scene). While lip service is paid to other kinds of knowledge, for example, the aesthetic, the practical or physical, the hidden curriculum of schooling informs pupils that only knowledge, skills and abilities that can be readily measured, especially in written tests, are to be treated as really worthwhile and valuable. Other forms of knowledge are relegated to a secondary position. Hargreaves goes on to lament, 'the more profound and disturbing message is that the very concept of ability becomes closely tied to the intellectual cognitive domain' (Hargreaves, 1982, p. 60).

There is little doubt that the development of a comprehensive system in the manner and form described above had an important bearing on the development of physical education programmes, on power relations within them and on the career opportunities of physical education teachers. It is this last consequence which is examined in some detail here. In passing, however, we might, with David Kirk in Chapter 3, note the implications of comprehensivization for the positioning and privileging of males and females within the subject. Secondary school reorganization did little to encourage teachers to call into question the content and organization of physical education or make problematic either its long established gender differentiated and differentiating practices, or the value and status distributed and imputed to different sorts of knowledge and pupils *within* the subject. On the contrary, the cultural climate inside schools, fed by the political and educational discourses described above, exacerbated rather than dissipated processes of gender differentiation within the subject, helped to *announce* the divide and the differences between male and female 'traditions' of physical education, privileging the form and sustaining its position of dominance within the subject.

As Kirk points out, the functional, scientific and competitive discourse of 'male physical education', with its emphasis very obviously on competition, the identification, development and measurement of performance skills and the utility of physical education for post-school leisure life, connected very well with the powerful trends and discourses in the broader political and educational context. By contrast, developments in 'female physical education', such as educational gymnastics and dance, which had gained some foothold in comprehensive schools, and which laid stress on creativity, expression and personal fulfilment through movement, could appear especially to the male observer to have little functional utility.

Debate within the profession between males and females over how and what physical education ought to be was very noisily expressed between the 1950s and early 1970s. A cursory glance at this debate does suggest that it involved a battle between two diametrically opposed versions of the purpose and practice of physical education, the one conservative, the other liberal, even radical, in design and intent. There is little doubt that the 'child-centred' discourse of women's physical education did explicitly and importantly challenge the emphasis given in 'male discourse' to competitiveness, aggression and skill training. But these differences tend to obfuscate the similarities and the deep conservatism which is evident both between and within these male and female traditions. Indeed, that both versions of physical education have been able to co-exist comfortably in secondary schools without too much tension or friction for so many years is some measure of this compatibility. For example, in the works of Munrow (1972) and Morrison (1969), two leading proponents of what might be termed the male and female traditions, we can very easily find similar commitments to individualism and the view that physical education should be capable of realizing every child's potential. Both lay stress on self-discovery, on the development of a knowledge of the body, and on a notion, most strongly expressed in Morrison's book, that physical education could offer some degree of compensation for the ills and limitations of modern urban living. Admittedly, in the discourse of the male tradition we find heavy emphasis upon the skilling of children for post-school organized sport, but there is a functionalism in the female discourse too. It received somewhat less emphasis than it does in the male discourse, but it is not disregarded.

Munrow, writing from a male perspective, assumed that the future of individuals is one of work and involvement in organized leisure, especially team sports. By contrast, implicit in Morrison's work is the conception that women's lives are likely to be structured by the demands of unpaid work, employment and unorganized leisure. Morrison's version of physical education, in this way, is no less functional than the male version, it simply has different ends in view. Its functional utility disappears only when assessed from the position of a male perspective, according to male criteria of success. In this respect the debate between these traditions is perhaps more properly read as a battle over means and methods, and the scientific veracity of the claims made (Munrow, 1972). As such, it would be quite inaccurate to suggest that women's physical education represented anything approximating a 'radical' discourse. While it may have presented a degree of challenge to the methods of male physical education, it did little to confront or challenge the processes of social and cultural production in schools. It was a functional preparation for women's work and leisure.

The point is that the instrumentality of comprehensive education, increasingly stressed, as we will see, through the 1970s and 1980s, helped both define the nature of social relations within physical education departments, privilege a particular version of physical education, and differently position men and women within the subject and in the perspective of others in the educational workplace. Men's physical education work remained more important and valued than women's. As such, it also had an important bearing on the career opportunities of women physical education teachers. Defining women's abilities and competencies in relation to men's, and according to 'male criteria', can hardly have helped ease the difficulties which women, then as now, experience when trying to develop a teaching career (Sykes, 1988).

The Career Opportunities of Physical Education Teachers[3]

In recent years the findings of research have consistently revealed that there are very clear patterns of advantage and disadvantage in the career opportunities of teachers, and physical educationalists do not feature well within them (Evans and Davies, 1988b; Williams, 1988; Evans and Williams, 1989). Despite comprehensive reorganization, these patterns remain deeply ingrained in our educational system and extend across schools to provide structural advantages for certain groups and disadvantages for others. The most significant of these is the organization of and status given to subject departments. This pattern, in large part contingent upon 'the hegemony of the academic curriculum', clearly benefits and privileges some teachers and disadvantages others. As has been argued elsewhere, 'if a headship is the target, then for teachers of equal experience the best chances of achieving this goal lie with history, physics, French and maths' (Hilsum and Start, 1974, p. 82). It seems that some subjects and the teachers that staff them lack credibility in the eyes of others, the gatekeepers to career opportunities. This status is reflected in the type of subject teachers who achieve positions in the senior hierarchy of schools and inside subjects, in the distribution of salary scale points and senior positions between and within subjects. But subject status alone does not entirely account for the difficulties which some teachers experience when seeking promotion. Women teachers are often profoundly disadvantaged in career terms by male dominance in schools. They are constrained not only by the value and status imputed to the knowledge they teach, but also by the language and structure of schools which are often shaped profoundly by patriarchy. The gatekeepers to jobs are predominantly men and they do not always believe that women are capable or suitable because of their competing family/work roles for advancement to senior positions.

For example, in a recent study of the career opportunities of physical education teachers in seventy-two English comprehensive schools (Williams, 1988; Evans and Williams, 1989), there was a great deal of evidence to support the view that men tend to occupy senior positions in physical education departments and receive higher pay scales (cf. Burgess, 1986; Scraton, 1989). When we examined the distribution of responsibilities, reward and status between men and women, a rather striking pattern emerged. Although most of the schools in the sample operated with a male and a female in charge of boys and girls in physical education, in 84 per cent of these schools it was a male teacher who held responsibility as overall head of the physical education department.[4] The notion that pupils and teachers have 'equal opportunities', the same chance to advance to the top, experience success and satisfaction in the workplace pervades the comprehensive system in Britain. Individual attainment is seen largely as a function of how hard an individual works and their inherent 'ability' or 'talent'. This view takes very little cognizance of the way in which individual abilities, identities and opportunities are structured and constrained by institutional arrangements and ideologies which pervade the educational workplace and other areas of social life, and which together ensure that often beneath the rhetoric of meritocracy or equal opportunities a system of sponsorship successfully but implicitly prevails (Evans and Williams, 1989).

Ball (1987) has made the point that women teachers may validly be regarded as a distinct interest group within the school if only because the overall pattern of their career development is so different from that of men. Many women have to manage two careers, one in the paid educational workplace, the other in the unpaid context of family life. This dual role often has important implications for how women are perceived in schools and concomitantly for their occupational careers. Over 40 per cent of the women in our study, for example, had taken a break from teaching to meet 'family responsibilities'. Only 8 per cent of the men had had a break from teaching and none of them for this reason. Even though the break in most cases seems to have been of a very short duration, many of the women felt that it had severely disadvantaged them in the career stakes, because in their view senior management regarded them with suspicion and now doubted their commitment to a career in teaching. As one teacher put it, 'once you start a family you are regarded almost as a part-time teacher as far as career prospects are concerned.' Others mentioned the hostility they had faced on returning to school, particularly from older colleagues, who made it plain that they felt women should be at home with the children rather than teaching. One female teacher summed up this particular problem: 'many of my older male colleagues don't disguise the fact that they think it almost immoral of me to return to school as soon after the baby. Mind you many of these still believe that women teach for 'pin' money. Equal opportunity? Sexual equality? — that really is a myth!' Another female teacher stressed that 'there is virtually no chance of a woman becoming head of department in this school. The head would never contemplate a female head of department and my only chance of promotion is in pastoral care or a move to an all girls' school.'

What we find is a situation in which the ideology of familism — that 'exaggerated identification with the myth that the family is the only place where a woman may experience self-fulfilment', firmly established in the thinking of powerful males in the educational workplace, operates as a substantial constraint on the opportunities of women to develop their careers within and outside the subject. But this process of disempowerment is not always obvious. What we have is a situation in which, within the organizational culture of comprehensive schools, ability is defined not only as a particular set of attitudes (an expertise at skilling pupils, for example) and a form of behaviour (expressed as a continuous unbroken involvement in teaching), but also as an attitude of mind towards the place and positon of paid work in the lifestyle of the individual (Evans and Williams, 1989). The upshot of this is that within the career stakes commitment is defined as an indissoluble component of teaching or teacher 'ability'. Clearly it is men, not women, whose lives are structured by the dual responsibilities of family and paid work, who are much more likely to have the capacity and the opportunity to display such 'talents' (Williams, 1988; Evans and Williams, 1989).

It is perhaps unsurprising, given the nature of the discourse which has sponsored the development of the comprehensive system, that we should find physical education teachers continuing to enjoy (sic) far less status in the institutional workplace than their academic counterparts, or that physical education teachers should routinely be faced with the problem of demonstrating their professional competence to their colleagues and the school hierarchy in order to gain acceptance and advance a career (Hargreaves, 1986; Whitehead and Hendry, 1976). But it is men rather than women who have been better placed to do this, to show both their commitment to their subject and their competence as 'good' teachers. In this respect women are profoundly disadvantaged. They are constrained not only by the hegemony of the academic curriculum which adversely defines their status in relation to other teachers outside *and* within the subject, but also by patriarchy as it pervades the school system and plays itself out sometimes less than subtly in the attitudes of men, the gate-keepers to promotion and career development.

The problems of developing a career in physical education, however, have not eased in recent years. On the contrary, the business of sustaining the position of the subject in the school curriculum and that of display-ing competence to significant others in the workplace, has become in-creasingly difficult. Crucially this process has become more problematic for both men and women in the subject. They have found it increasingly difficult to provide evidence of their success at both skilling pupils and imbuing them with attitudes which would secure their involvement in post-school leisure. Those difficulties have arisen at a time when signi-ficant others in the wider educational and political settings have called for greater accountability and an even more functionally-oriented form of schooling.

Many of the male physical education teachers in our study (Evans and Williams, 1989) felt that getting out of the subject depended upon their capacity either to achieve for themselves or their subject high public profile in and outside the school (through the production of successful sports teams, for example), or to display their academic credentials by teaching a second, non-physical education, academic subject. However, a long period of industrial action from 1984 to 1986 made it difficult for them to achieve this. Teachers were required by their unions to fulfil only their contractual duties. This meant that many physical education teachers and other subject teachers who provide voluntary help to the subject after school hours could not or would not continue to make available opport-unities or support for extra school sport. In effect, the industrial action severely constrained one of the most important means traditionally avail-able to physical education teachers in Britain to display their credentials, their commitment to teaching and coaching, the quality of their depart-ment and their competences as teachers. They were constrained in their endeavours to produce and publicly display their abilities at producing successful sports teams. The decision to support the union action put enormous strain on some teachers as they weighed up the consequences of their decisions for their careers. As one male teacher stressed, 'Since we stopped school matches I know the Head is far from happy with the physical education department. I'm sure he feels we should have con-tinued against our union's advice. My chances of a further promotion with this Head have disappeared' (in Evans and Williams, 1989, p. 244).

They were also subjected to pressure from senior management who, in a period of conflict between employer and employee, and often be-tween teachers in schools, were eager to maintain at least a public front of order, continuing commitment and productivity. Physical education staff have long acted as a point of contact between school and parents during the provision of extracurricular sporting activities, and when these activities stopped, members of senior management were often unhappy with physical education departments.

> We realized many parents would be unhappy [about the cessation of school matches, etc.] and the head and deputy I'm sure resented the physical education staff because of the conflict this caused with parents. At least it made them analyze the amount of hours physical education staff put in, which is very often taken for granted by parents and heads. (Male PE teacher, quoted in Evans and Williams, 1989, p. 244)

Furthermore, despite the cessation of teacher action, many teachers from other subject areas who had previously given to the teaching of physical education did not return to give this commitment. Contraction in the educational system resulting from a combination of falling rolls and government underresourcing had also meant that physical education teachers were either not being appointed or were taken on only as part-time or second subject teachers. This diminishing supply of trained physical education teachers and the 'helpers' from other academic areas had further limited physical education teachers' opportunities to develop their teaching in a second academic subject. Of the teachers in the study 67 per cent taught only physical education, and many felt that they were increasingly being 'locked in' to teaching more and more physical education (Williams, 1988; Evans and Williams, 1989). Facing these conditions of work, with few career opportunities and feeling that as a professional group they could expect to receive little support either from senior administrators inside the institution or from the public, parents and politicians outside it, it is perhaps hardly surprising that some should start looking to avenues outside teaching to find enjoyment and satisfaction in their lives or that the profession in general should begin to examine in earnest the purpose and future of the physical education curriculum and enter into the business of curriculum reform.

The New Right Critique of Education and the Reconstruction of Physical Education

The process of curriculum reappraisal had begun in earnest prior to the period of industrial action in the wake of a protracted critique of the educational system. Attacks on the teaching profession had begun in the late 1960s mainly through the voices of the Black Paper writers, especially politician educationalists such as Rhodes Boyson, then head of High-bury Grove school and subsequently junior minister in several depart-ments of state, now reconsigned to the Conservative backbenches, and Caroline Cox, now a leading educational figure in the House of Lords, who mounted organized attacks on policies of comprehensive schooling and other organizational and curriculum innovations. These, and others like them, claimed that in comprehensives there was widespread evidence of a rampant and insidious left-wing anti-professionalism damaging schools and the society of which they were part, 'that ideologically the comprehensive school represents a socialist society in miniature' and that reorganization was an expression of 'fanatical egalitarianism' (Ball, 1984, p. 5). The charge against the profession was that an incipient left-wing progressivism was responsible for falling educational standards and pupil underachievement. The acceptance or in some cases even the promotion by teachers of ill-discipline and poor pupil control was insinuated. There is little doubt that this attack upon comprehensive schooling and progres-sivism within it provided a source of further support for some males within the profession (see Munrow, 1972) to mount their attack on the putative excesses of child-centredness in physical education, state their definitions of what physical education ought to be, and in effect help elevate and sustain the position of males and the 'male tradition' within and outside the profession.

By the early 1970s, however, as Britain (for reasons which had very little to do with the state of schooling) slipped further into economic recession, the themes of school failure were taken up and aired even more noisily in 1976 by Labour Prime Minister James Callaghan in a speech at Ruskin College, clearly intended to receive wide circulation and gain his party more popular support. Taking for granted the problematic claim that standards were in jeopardy in the comprehensive system, Callaghan highlighted the relationships between schooling and work and chided the educational system for its irrelevance to working life. He claimed that schools were failing to prepare future generations for working life, and that new recruits did not have the basic skills to do the job required of them in work. The optimism which had sponsored the development of educational expansion and the comprehensive system had finally col-lapsed and given way to a deep pessimism.

Policy-makers of the 1960s had, after all, seen a direct link between educational reform and economic prosperity. A skilled and educated workforce would promote economic growth, ultimately full employ-ment. But as others now cuttingly point out, not only did the economy fail to grow, it fell into a second slump. Not only did young people not get jobs, there were very few jobs in some regions for them to get. But the cruellest cut of all was that education, once held as the agency for social and economic amelioration, was now purported to be significantly responsible for the decline of British capitalism (CCCS, 1981, p. 173). Voices of the political right and left now sadly converged to condemn schools and teachers in a cry for more relevance, greater efficiency and consumer accountability. Although at this time physical education was not subject to direct attack from central government, the shock waves from this discourse were evidently felt in the physical education profession. Only months after Callaghan's speech the main professional journal in Britain was challenging teachers with the question of whether they too were sufficiently efficient and effective in their practices and whether they could legitimately claim against mounting evidence to the contrary that they were skilling pupils for top level performances and laying the motivational bedrock for mass participation in post-school sport and leisure (Palmer, 1977; Wright, 1977a). But while the seeds of despair had been deeply sewn, they did not at this time bear immediate fruit in prescriptions for curriculum reappraisal or reform.

Attacks on the teaching professions did not reach their zenith or their most vehement until the arrival of Thatcher's government in 1979. Since then, the most right-wing government since the Second World War has ruthlessly exploited what it claims are the failings of the comprehensive system to produce among other things a disciplined workforce, sufficiently skilled to meet the demands of a technological society. At the heart of 'new right' discourse are two doctrines (Lauder, 1988), both attributable to the political theory of Hobbes, which have had a profound impact upon both educational and economic and social policy in Britain. The first stresses that human beings are *possessive individuals* who are 'essentially the proprietors of their own person and capacities, owing nothing to society for them' (Lauder, 1987, p. 2). The second is that the pursuit of *self-interest*, principally directed towards the acquisition of wealth, status and power, determines social arrangements. Within this perspective personal freedom is intimately linked to the operation of a 'free market' in which consumers have equal and sovereign rights to buy and sell their skills and other commodities how, when and where they choose. This view, like those which sponsored comprehensive reorganization, as Lauder goes on to point out, conveniently ignores the context in which exchange takes place. Essentially, the new right's is a model in which individuals are 'classless, ungendered, free of ethnic characteristics, and without limiting cultural assumptions'. People do not, however, enter or leave markets on equal terms, they are differently equipped to exploit them according to their class, their gender, colour and culture. Nonetheless, new right education policy in Britain has been founded upon this belief system. The public at large have been asked to perceive education as a private good to be bought and sold in the education market place (Wragg, 1988). The principal concern of teachers now is to school and skill children for their futures as consumers and to ensure that each individual is able to take responsibility for his or her future as a buyer and seller of work, leisure and health. Competition is to lie at the heart of this education process, as the spur to efficiency both within schools and the wider economic system.

Against the background of a sustained critique of the teaching profession (Ranson, 1988; Evans and Davies, 1988b), some of it now specifically directed at the physical education profession by politicians, media and other powerful figures (Evans, 1988a), it is perhaps hardly surprising that we should find physical educationalists beginning systematically to engage in the business of curriculum reappraisal both inside schools and through the 'official discourse' of the professional physical education journals, or that the 'solutions' found to the 'problems' facing physical education should be 'framed' by the ideologies featuring in the broader, extra-school political and cultural fields. By the mid-1980s the jitters of the 1970s had been replaced by a severe case of professional apoplexy, as critics of schools called into question the capacities and competence of physical education teachers effectively to skill pupils both for top level sports performance and for their futures in post-school organized leisure and sport, and as the very future of physical education in the school curriculum, especially for the upper school age range, seemed to be cast in doubt. It is in this material context, with its harsh and often unrewarding conditions of work and cultural climate, that two innovations, Health Related Fitness (HRF) and Teaching Games for Understanding (TGFU), emerged to feature prominently in the discourse of physical education, and the former in particular in the practices of teachers in comprehensive schools (Whitehead, 1987).

Noises about the place and importance of a health focus in physical education had appeared in the professional journal of physical education in the early 1970s. But it was not until the 1980s that debate about the relationship between health, fitness and physical education achieved a position of importance and legitimacy in the thinking of the profession. Its status was secured by a broader cultural climate, deeply influenced by new right thinking, which had already defined health and leisure as an individual rather than as a social responsibility and education as a process crucially involved in the skilling of children. The bare bones of both these innovations can be summarized as follows. In the case of TGFU it is argued (see BALPE, 1982; Bonniface, 1987) that it is not possible in traditional games for all pupils to be offered equality of experience, because poor physical skill acts as a barrier to further learning. Thus the emphasis instead is placed upon the cognitive rather than the technical aspects of the game. While learning the full adult version of a game may present a long-term goal, in the eyes of those advocating an 'understanding' approach it is not the main purpose of games teaching in schools. Mini-games with adapted rules and equipment are more likely to provide all pupils with opportunities to make decisions concerning their play and the game itself whatever their physical ability. In this context all pupils will be given the opportunity to take responsibility for their learning and to experience the satisfaction of achievement and success. It is these experiences, achievement, satisfaction, enjoyment which will form the motivational basis for a future of post-school involvement in physical recreation and sport. It is claimed, in contrast to traditional games, that success can be more easily achieved by the majority of pupils and that their aims are more relevant for children within today's society where it is desirable for all pupils to be offered equality in terms of experience. Here equality implies the provision of a curriculum content and pedagogical mode which not only permits equality of access to each and every individual irrespective of their levels of physical ability or skill, but also some measure of equality of outcome. Everyone should experience some but not necessarily the same level of success, achievement, satisfaction, enjoyment along with an understanding of the principles which underpin different game forms. The HRF literature (for example, see contributions in Biddle, 1987) also carries an image of educational practice in which organizational forms and curriculum content avoid the creation of losers and failures. But in this innovation the principle of equality of outcome is stressed even more strongly. The tone is against selection and the creation of ability hierarchies and for 'non-authoritarian', 'non-didactic' approaches to teaching. At the heart of this innovation is a concern for the development of each and every individual's 'health career', their positive 'self-esteem' and 'decision-making skills'. Both the TGFU and the HRF initiatives claim to be child- rather than subject-centred in philosophy. The focus is on 'individual needs rather than activities and on individual responses rather than marks of achievement' (Payne, 1985, p. 5). Both carry an image of practice in which relationships between teachers and pupils and between pupils and knowledge are significantly altered. Emphasis is upon a negotiated curriculum, on less didactic modes of teaching, upon pupils creating for themselves a curriculum (new game forms or personal HRF programmes) which is sensitive to individual interests, abilities and future lifestyles. Each individual is skilled and empowered to sustain their health and take responsibility for their own well-being and leisure in post-school life. In theory these initiatives seem to have the capacity radically to alter and challenge patterns of power and authority which have long featured in both the academic and physical curriculum of schooling. I now want to suggest that in practice they may do little to alter the social relations of physical education departments or the abilities and career opportunities of physical education teachers.

Redefining the Competencies and Abilities of Physical Education Teachers

Although the HRF literature is both weighty and wide-ranging, its theoretical emphasis remains predominantly physiological and psychological. It gives high profile to fitness testing, measurement, and the monitoring and assessment of each individual's 'health'. In this physiological discourse, as in the 'softer' social psychological elements of the literature, health is conceptualized in a particularly individualistic fashion. In it we see that HRF provides the means of physical or psychological *repair*, it is a way of helping children come to terms with the traumas of Western urban living, or a system of relief for stressed youngsters.

In this discourse we are offered what Doyal (1979) refers to as the view of the medical experts, a view that forms the dominant basis for the social definition of health and fitness throughout the developed world. In this perspective ill-health tends to be defined narrowly and primarily in terms of the malfunctioning of a mechanical, physical or psychological system. Consequently, treatment is considered in terms of some sort of medical intervention to repair or restore the body (the machine) to normal working order. Implicitly, this view carries an image of the individual as in some physical or psychological kind of pathological state. The functional element in this conception of health means, as Doyal points out, that in practice health is usually defined as fitness to undertake whatever would be expected of someone in a particular social position. This discourse, though critical of 'conventional' games-oriented physical education, still may be conservative and socially reproductive. As Doyal points out, 'The defining of health and illness in a functional way is an important example of how a capitalist system defines people primarily as producers — as forces of production. It is concerned with their fitness in an instrumental sense rather than with their own hopes, fears, anxieties, pain and suffering' (Doyal, 1979, p. 35). For example, in the HRF literature we find repeated reference to 'young people', the 'individual', the 'person', and, of course, the 'pupil' or the child. But this abstracted individual, this generalized 'youth', as Hargreaves and others have pointed out, seriously disguises a 'profound set of differences' (Clarke and

Willis, 1984) in the origins, the predispositions and the destinations of the children in our care.

This 'abstraction of youth' is especially evident in the use of the concept of 'health career' in the HRF literature. The transition into post-school leisure is presented as unproblematic once the school provision and the content of the curriculum have been sorted and put right. This conception creates the impression that progress along the 'health (or leisure) career path' towards a healthy lifestyle is both unproblematic and dependent only upon a positive interaction between the possession of a set of physical skills, a person's self-esteem, 'really useful' health knowledge and decision-making skills. This is an expression par excellence of the ideology of the possessive individual in which the person is thought 'free inasmuch as he is the proprietor of his person and capacities. The human essence is freedom from dependence on the will of others, and freedom is a function of possession. Society becomes a lot of free equal individuals related to each other as proprietors of their own capacities and what they have acquired by their exercise. Society consists of exchange between proprietors' (Macpherson, 1962, p. 3. quoted in Moore, 1987, p. 232).

As Moore (1987, p. 232) points out, this philosophy 'provides a rationale for an extreme delimitation of the political power of the individual restricting it to that of a consumer of work, and of leisure, whose purchasing power reflects the value of the skills owned.' It is a view in which skilling for work or leisure become the *raison d'être* of schooling. This view clearly has important implications for the physical education curriculum both in schools and teacher education. As Moore (1987, p. 232) goes on to say in his analysis of vocational education, 'curricular form and content and its pedagogy is derived from a behavioral specification of the needs of industry in terms of the requirements of the jobs.' In the same way we can see that the skills approach in physical education incorporates unproblematically the 'world of leisure' into the curriculum in the form of sets of behavioural objectives (individuals are underskilled; they should be 'skilled' for leisure; they should be measured, tested, trained to be 'fit for life'). In this sense (to paraphrase Moore) the representation of leisure or work is purely normative. The curriculum does not attempt to inform about post-school life of work, or leisure or family, or how these are crucially interconnected, but to prescribe behavioural criteria to which individuals must conform. Skills are treated as simply *given* by the nature of the tasks with which they are associated. They in themselves are not problematic. 'The only thing open to question is the competence of individuals to attain given levels of performance' (Moore, 1987, p. 233). In this now recontextualized 'new physical education' children will be provided not with a knowledge *about* health or leisure, how these are socially and culturally constructed by family life, patriarchy or how it is vested with political or economic interests. Rather, they will be presented with knowledge about themselves (Tinning, 1985) and how suitable they are individually for successful future health, sports and leisure careers.

It would be quite inaccurate to suggest, however, that the discourse of the 'new physical education' either simply or straightforwardly reproduces at the level of school practice or within the official discourse of the professional journals, the conservativism of new right thinking. Teachers are not cultural dopes nor are they always agents of reproduction and control. They too are controllers, consumers and producers of culture and their actions always and inevitably mediate the influence bearing upon them, sometimes in the form of direct policy prescriptions, from wider political and educational settings. But teachers and subject groups do not all have the same degree of power or the desire to resist or challenge the contemporary influences which bear upon the processes of comprehensive schooling.

In the language and vocabulary of the initiatives described above there are elements which seem to contest and challenge the discourses of the new right in Britain. In the discourse on games teaching, for example, we can find an important challenge to the emphasis given to competition and elite performance in physical education and this has often appeared substantially to contradict the educational intentions and philosophy of the new right in Britain, and the position and privilege of traditional male physical education. It is hardly surprising, therefore, that in recent years this innovation has been singled out and subjected to most vilification and criticism by the voices of the right, for its putative antagonism towards the development of a competitive individual and social order. As a result it may have very little future in the curriculum. The 'new physical education' is not then a homogeneous phenomenon. It contains within it both potentially liberal and conservative elements which need to be interrogated and 'named'. But the point to be stressed is that for very good reasons, which owe much to the material and ideological conditions of a teacher's work in the comprehensive system, it is the conservative elements in this discourse which are likely to achieve prominence and legitimacy in physical education. By adopting the discourse and practice of the 'new physical education', with their emphasis upon the 'intellectual' and the cognitive elements of physical activity, teachers may be able to move physical education 'up market' in the direction of the academic curriculum.[5]

However, although the 'new physical education' does not seem to offer a form and content which present a radical break with tradition in the subject, it does not free itself from either a version of equal opportunities, which leaves issues of class, gender and ability untouched, or a functionalism which lays stress on skilling, fitness and objective measurement. On the contrary, these commitments are recontextualized or reformulated and given expression in 'radically' new forms of curriculum and pedagogy. To claim this is not for a moment to deny or decry the liberal intentions or elements in these innovations. The discourse of the 'new physical education' does contain a genuine commitment to the business of opening up access to a physical education in which each and every child can experience success, satisfaction and enjoyment, in the hope that these experiences will secure not only involvement in school physical education but also participation in post-school sport and leisure. But the dominant concerns remain unquestionably ameliorative and hedonistic rather than socially transformative. There is a concern to alter the conditions of work for pupils to change the form and content of physical education towards goals of interest and enjoyment, the laying of a motivational bedrock upon which in later life to develop a sporting career. But it does not challenge conventional categories of ability or skill, conceptions of the body, or social and cultural hierarchies inside or outside school (Evans and Clarke, 1988). For example, while the 'new physical education' seems to pose a powerful challenge to elitism in physical education, it does not totally reject competition. Challenged, played down, it is recommended as a separate activity for the gifted or alternatively as a purely extra-curricular activity. The values of competition are questioned because it is this component of the curriculum which alienates pupils from physical education and sport, not because physical educationalists are critical of competitive individualism (Sherlock, 1987; Hargreaves, 1986; Evans, 1988b). The 'new physical education' thus refocuses the emphasis given to competition in physical education, but it does not problematize or challenge in any fundamental way either the categories of skill or ability or the social hierarchies to which they give rise, which have long prevailed in the subject. As such it does not represent a challenge to the hegemony of the academic curriculum or the stratification of knowledge which persists outside *and* within the subject. On the contrary, the discourse of the 'new physical education' celebrates a distinction between 'knowing how' and 'knowing that' and commits itself to the development of the latter, thus accepting a dichotomy, artificial in the eyes of many philosophers, which has long featured in the culture of comprehensive schooling to the detriment of the position of physical education teachers.[6]

Indeed, physical education enters the academic domain because 'the cognitive' is now defined increasingly in functional and technical ways. Contemporary educational debate tends to lay stress on the vocational utility of schooling and on the 'cognitive skilling' of pupils. Skill tends to be conceptualized as capacities which can be trained into people, that do not involve emotions, feelings, attitudes or any such degree of knowledge or understanding. As others have argued, to talk of skills in this way, as if they were isolated, discrete activities or performances which can be trained and perfected through practice, is badly misleading and ill-founded (Barrow, 1988). The concepts of ability and skill are, of course, both complex and problematic and it is not my intention to clarify their meaning here. But the 'new physical education', just as the old, does tend to reduce any thinking about 'ability' to concerns about skill and technique. If we minimally accept that 'skilling' is an element of ability and that the latter involves a power (not here meant as an inner essence) or capacity to perform in any relation, then we can hardly talk about, or enter into the practice of, 'skilling' pupils without at the same time treating seriously issues of class, gender or elitism, and providing children with a knowledge of how their skills might be exploited, constrained or developed by their gender, colour, class or the vested interests of powerful others.

In the recent condition of schooling, laying stress upon measurement and the skilling of children may seem strategically proper and firmly in the interest of all physical education teachers. But we do need to be aware of what this choice involves, and how it implicates, benefits and disadvantages those in the profession. Because the status of knowledge is taken as unproblematic in the discourse of the 'new physical education', its arrival in school may do very little either to help challenge or to restructure the power relationships between males and females in the subject or between physical educationalists and other subject teachers. For example, HRF and TGFU herald little that is new for teachers of 'girls' physical education'. The educational gymnastics and dance initiatives of the 1950s and 1960s were also explicitly child-centred in philosophy, content and pedagogical mode. But there is very little evidence to suggest that proponents of the 'new physical education' have made any endeavour to connect with these earlier 'progressive' initiatives. A language and vocabulary once rejected by males has now been appropriated but recycled and infused with a powerful and obvious functionalism, the traditional hallmark of male physical education. On the one hand, in speaking the language of child-centredness, the 'new physical education' may help to unite the profession or at least foster closer collaborative endeavour between men and women, boys and girls in the practice of physical education. But, on the other, as value and status are given to the functional elements in the discourse, it may succeed only in again reinforcing and emphasizing the position and status of men in the subject. We thus need to ask of the process of curriculum production and innovation in schools: who are the bearers of the 'new physical education', how are its innovations implemented in schools, with what values, emphasis and connection with extant curriculum practice, and who plays the role of primary producers and secondary support? In short, we need to ask again: how are women and men differently positioned and privileged in relation to the 'new physical education', who has the cultural competencies and resources to succeed and benefit from its development?

Ultimately, the 'new physical education' may do little to challenge or help reformulate the social hierarchies and power distribution in physical education departments, or for that matter those which prevail outside schools. In the present climate of comprehensive schooling, in conditions of work which are far from attractive for many teachers, it would be more than surprising to find the profession taking anything other than a route which is consonant with powerful trends in broader political and cultural fields. In these conditions the capacities of individual teachers or subject groups to resist such developments must be limited. But knowing better how we as teachers or as a subject group are implicated in their production and reproduction may at least be a first small step in the direction of securing their demise.

Effecting changes in physical education of a sort that would empower children and teachers irrespective of their social class, race or gender to experience and enjoy equality of opportunity in their work, health and physical education will not be an easy, a quick or a comfortable endeavour. Its achievement will much depend upon the profession's capacity and willingness to appraise, among other things, the way in which power, status and reward are distributed within departments, physical education and in the broader school and community contexts. It will mean examining how men's and women's and boys' and girls' careers in physical education are implicated by the way in which status is imputed to certain sorts of knowledge and the way individuals think about themselves and each other. In short, issues of power, authority, culture, patriarchy, sexuality and social class have to be placed high among our professional concerns. These are difficult and contentious matters, and to some they will seem threatening. They will, however, have to be addressed not just by teachers, but also crucially by teacher educators. The processes of teacher education and the occupational socialization of physical education teachers in Britain, as elsewhere, have long featured knowledge hierarchies in which the human and social sciences (and particularly certain sorts of social science; see Hargreaves,

1987) are less valued than the physical sciences (see Talbot, 1989; Dewar and Ingham, 1988). These hierarchies and the social ones which they generate and sustain may also be strongly gendered. This, as Talbot points out, may not only influence students' perceptions of what it is important to know and do in physical education, and their course choices, but also their future career possibilities as physical education teachers. If these knowledge hierarchies are widespread, then we really should not be surprised if we continue to find limitations in the official discourse of the 'new physical education', and also in the teachers purveying this discourse in schools. Both are ill-equipped to deal with the social, personal and ethical issues which affect their work, and unable to implement a pedagogy and curriculum capable of dealing with the social class, cultural and gender influences which are brought to physical education through the actions of the children in their care.

Detailing a curriculum framework which is capable of confronting and contesting the limits of liberal individualism and of achieving equality in physical education cannot be attempted here. Others have made valuable efforts to begin this difficult task (see Talbot, 1989; Scraton, 1989). To its credit, the 'new physical education' has helped to promote a critical appraisal of curriculum practices in physical education, it has challenged conventions and one can only hope that it will continue to provoke discussion and appraisal at every level of physical education. It would be a tragedy indeed if the discourse of the 'new physical education' became simply another orthodoxy, a new and immutable ideological carapace beneath which, but for a few additions to existing programmes or some surface changes in how physical education appears in schools, old habits, values, power structures and inequalities remain largely unchanged.

Notes

1 I use the term 'new physical education' to refer to a variety of curriculum initiatives, including Health Related Fitness, Teaching Games for Understanding, Creating Games and Co-educational physical education. The first two innovations in particular have achieved a position of importance in the discourse and increasingly in the practices of physical educationists in Britain in recent years.

2 One of the inspirational sources of comprehensive education in the late 1950s and early 1960s was a profoundly materialistic view of education as a commodity that simply required a more even distribution. This view has its roots in the relative affluence that followed post-war austerity and the explosion of consumerism. This view achieved a position of dominance in Labour Party policy, at the expense of a more radical and socialist perspective (CCCS, 1981).

3 This section of the paper draws heavily on extracts from J. Evans and T.

Williams (1989) 'Moving Up and Getting Out: The Classed and Gendered Career Opportunities of PE Teachers,' in P. Templin and P. Schempp (Eds), *Socialization into Physical Education: Learning to Teach*, Indianapolis, Ind.: Beechwood Press, 1988, pp. 235–51. I am grateful to T. Templin, P. Schempp and Benchmark Press for their permission to draw on material from that paper.

4 Although in recent years there has been some movement towards co-educational physical education in secondary schools in England and Wales, our evidence suggests that this organizational change is not yet widespread in physical education departments. In Scotland the movement to co-educational physical education has tended to result in the dissolution of separate, male and female departmental structures in schools. It would be important to discover who achieved the position of overall head when this occurs.

5 We provide some evidence of this in Evans and Clarke (1988). Some teachers certainly have seen HRF as a means of emphasizing the academic or educational qualities of physical education. In Australia examinations in physical education have been used to achieve this end (Kirk, 1988). In Britain, however, examinations have often been resisted, especially by progressive physical education teachers. HRF thus solves the problem of how to go up market and become academic without selling out the selectivism, competition and hierarchies which are inevitably a feature of examination systems.

6 There may be an important and interesting difference here between the content of HRF initiatives in the UK and those (the DPE project) in Australia. Colquhoun and Kirk (1987) point out that the latter lays stress on 'knowing how', on 'physicality' rather than 'knowing that'. The official discourse of the 'new physical education' in the UK by contrast emphasizes the cognitive, 'knowing that' (as well as the 'knowing how') elements in physical education. My point, however, is that because of the liberal individualism endemic in the profession, the knowledge base (the knowing that) of HRF and TGFU is incomplete. The silences in this 'new' discourse are likely to leave the individual child ill-informed about both how *and* why their opportunities for health and leisure are socially constrained or facilitated.

References

BALL, S. (1984) *Comprehensive Schooling: A Reader.* Lewes: Falmer Press.

BALL, S. (1987) *The Micro-Politics of the School.* London: Methuen.

BALPE (1982) 'Reflections on the Teaching of Games.' *Bulletin of Physical Education*, British Association of Advisers and Lecturers in Physical Education, University of Technology, Loughborough.

BARROW, R. (1988) 'Skill Talk.' *Journal of Philosophy of Education*, 21 (2), 187–97.

BENN, C. (1979) 'Elites versus Equals: The Political Background of Educational Reform,' in RUBENSTEIN, D. (Ed.), *Education and Equality.* Harmondsworth: Penguin.

BERNSTEIN, B. (1971) 'On the Classification of Educational Knowledge,' in Young, M.F.D. (Ed.), *Knowledge and Control,* pp. 47–69. London: Collier-Macmillan.

BERNSTEIN, B. (1977) *Class Codes and Control, Volume 3.* London: Routledge and Kegan Paul.

BERNSTEIN, B. (1986) 'On Pedagogic Discourse,' in RICHARDSON, J. (Ed.), *Handbook for Theory and Research in Sociology of Education*. Westport, Conn.: Greenwood Press.

BIDDLE, S. (1987) *Health Related Fitness*. London: Ling Publishing House.

BONNIFACE, M. (1987) 'The Changing Physical Education Curriculum.' Unpublished paper, Department of Physical Education, University of Southampton.

BURGESS, R. (1986) 'Points and Posts: A Case Study of Teachers in a Comprehensive School.' Paper presented to the British Educational Research Association Conference, University of London.

Centre for Contemporary Culture Studies (CCCS) (1981) *Unpopular Education*. London: Hutchinson.

CHITTY, C. (1987) 'The Comprehensive Principle under Threat,' in CHITTY, C. and LAWTON, D. (Eds), *Redefining the Comprehensive Experience*, pp. 6–28. Bedford Way Papers. London: Institute of Education.

CLARKE, J. and WILLIS, P. (1984) 'Introduction,' in BATES, T., *et al.* (Eds), *Schooling for the Dole?* pp. 1–11. London: Macmillan.

COLQUHOUN, D. and KIRK, D. (1987) 'Investigating the Problematic Relationship between Health and Physical Education: An Australian Study.' *The Physical Education Review*, 10 (2), 100–10.

CONNELL, R.W., *et al.* (1982) *Making the Difference*. London: George Allen and Unwin.

DEWAR, A. and INGHAM, A. (1987) 'Really Useful Knowledge: Professional Interests, Critical Discourse, Student Responses.' Paper presented at congress on Movement and Sport in Women's Life, University of Jyvaskgla, Finland.

DOYAL, L. (1979) *The Political Economy of Health*. London: Pluto Press.

EVANS, J. (1988a) 'Magic Moment or Radical Critique: The Rise and Rise of the New PE.' Paper presented to the Leisure Studies Conference: Leisure, Labour and Lifestyles, University of Sussex, June/July.

EVANS, J. (1988b) *Teachers, Teaching and Control in Physical Education*. Lewes: Falmer Press.

EVANS, J. (in press) 'Swinging from the Crossbar: Equality and Opportunity in Physical Education.' *British Journal of Physical Education*.

EVANS, J. and CLARKE, G. (1988) 'Changing the Face of Physical Education,' in EVANS (1988b), pp. 125–45.

EVANS, J. and DAVIES, B. (1988a) 'Creating and Managing an Educational Crisis.' Paper presented to New Zealand Educational Research into Educational Policy Conference, 17–19 August, pp. 13–33.

EVANS, J. and DAVIES, B. (1988b) 'Teachers, Teaching and Control' in EVANS, (1988b), pp. 1–21.

EVANS, J. and WILLIAMS, T. (1989) 'Moving Up and Getting Out: The Classed and Gendered Career Opportunities of PE Teachers,' in TEMPLIN, T. and SCHEMPP, P. (Eds), *Socialization into PE: Learning to Teach*, pp. 235–51. Indianapolis, Ind.: Benchmark Press.

GIROUX, H. (1981) *Ideology, Culture and the Process of Schooling*. Lewes: Falmer Press.

GREGORY, J. (1987) 'Comprehensive Crusaders.' *The Times Educational Supplement*, 6 February.

HARGREAVES, DAVID (1986) *The Challenge for the Comprehensive School*. London: Routledge and Kegan Paul.

HARGREAVES, JOHN (1987) 'The Political Economy of Mass Sport,' in DALE, R., *et al.* (Eds), *Education and the State: Politics, Patriarchy and Practice*. Lewes: Falmer Press.

HARGREAVES, JOHN (1986) *Sport, Power and Culture*, Cambridge: Polity Press.

HILSUM, S. and START, K.R. (1974) *Promotion and Careers in Teaching*. Windsor: NFER.

KIRK, D. (1988) *Physical Education and Curriculum Study: A Critical Introduction*. London: Croom Helm.

LAUDER, H. (1987) 'The New Right and Educational Policy in New Zealand.' *New Zealand Journal of Educational Studies*. 22 (1), 3–23.

LAUDER, H. (1988) 'Traditions of Socialism and Educational Policy,' in LAUDER, H. and BROWN, P. (Eds), *Education in Search of a Future*. Lewes: Falmer Press.

MOORE, R. (1987) 'Education and the Ideology of Production.' *British Journal of Sociology of Education*, 8 (2), 227–42.

MORRISON, R. (1969) *A Movement Approach to Educational Gymnastics*. London: J.M. DENT and SONS.

MUNROW, A.D. (1972) *Physical Education*. London: G. BELL and SONS.

PALMER, R. (1977) 'A Matter for Debate.' *The British Journal of Physical Education*, 8 (2), 36–7.

PAYNE, S. (1985) 'Physical Education and Health in the United Kingdom.' *British Journal of Physical Education*, 17 (1), 4–9.

RANSON, S. (1988) 'From 1944 to 1988: Education Citizenship and Democracy,' in RANSON, S., *et al. Local Government Studies*, 14 (1), pp. 1–21.

SCRATON, S. (1989) Shaping up to Womanhood: A Study of the Relationship between Gender and Girls' Physical Education in a City-based Local Education Authority. PhD thesis, The Open University, School of Education.

SHERLOCK, J. (1987) 'Issues of Masculinity and Femininity in British Physical Education.' *Women's Studies International Forum*, 10 (4), 43–5.

SPARKES, A (1988) 'The Micropolitics of Innovation in the Physical Education Curriculum,' in EVANS, J. (Ed.), *Teachers, Teaching and Control in Physical Education*, pp. 157–79. Lewes: Falmer Press.

SYKES, P. (1988) 'Growing Old Gracefully? Age, Identity and Physical Education,' in EVANS, J. (Ed.), *Teachers, Teaching and Control in Physical Education*, pp. 21–41. Lewes: Falmer Press.

TALBOT, M. (1989) 'Equality, Education and Physical Education.' Open lecture, University of Southampton, Faculty of Education, April.

TINNING, R. (1985) 'Physical Education and the Cult of Slenderness. A Critique.' *ACHPER National Journal*, 103, 10–14.

WHITEHEAD, N.W. and HENDRY, L. (1976) *Teaching Physical Education*. London: Lepus Books.

WHITEHEAD, R. (1987) A Study into the Social History of the Development of the School PE Curriculum with Special Reference to Aspects Concerned with Fitness and Health, MA (Ed.) dissertation, University of Southampton.

WILBY, P. (1977) 'Education and Equality', *New Statesman*, 16 September, 358–61.

WILLIAMS, T. (1988) The Career Opportunities of PE Teachers, MA (Ed.) dissertation, University of Southampton, Faculty of Educational Studies.

WRAGG, T. (1988) *Education in The Market Place: The Ideology behind the 1988 Education Bill*. London: National Union of Teachers, Jason Press.

WRIGHT, J. (1977a) 'Total Health.' *British Journal of Physical Education*, 8 (3), 80–2.

WRIGHT, J. (1977b) Editorial in *British Journal of Physical Education*, 8 (6), 115.

YOUNG, M.F.D. (1971) *Knowledge and Control*. London: Collier-Macmillan.

Chapter 7

Challenging Hegemonic Physical Education: Contextualizing Physical Education as an Examinable Subject

Lindsay Fitzclarence and Richard Tinning

The introduction of physical education as an examinable subject in the post-compulsory years of secondary school (years 11 and 12) has been a relatively recent innovation in Australia. Broadly speaking, it has been only within the last decade and a half that examination courses in physical education have been available to secondary school students in some Australian states. As there has been no 'national' curriculum, each state has pioneered its own developments largely in isolation from each other. In the process of developing examination courses physical educators have had to address key issues which the profession has debated vigorously for half a century or more. Much of this debate has centred on the nature of essential or 'worthwhile' knowledge in physical education, the educational status of physical education as a school (or college/university) subject, and the place of physical activity within an examinable 'academic' subject. The programmes that have recently become established and accepted in secondary school physical education have much in common with what Connell *et al.* (1982) called the 'hegemonic curriculum', which among other things is characterized by a preponderance of propositional knowledge, particularly in the sciences, and forms of pedagogy and assessment that project the values of the ruling class. Part of the difficulty with such hegemonic physical education programmes is that they present physical education knowledge as factual, empirical and value free. However, we agree with Evans and Davies when they claim that

> Physical education...is inevitably a site of struggle, a contest of and for competing definitions about what is to count as worthwhile knowledge, what the body, the individual, school and society are and ought to be. These values, assumptions, and definitions held by individuals both within the profession and

outside it influence, guide, facilitate and constrain the work of teachers and shape their pupils' identities and practices. (Evans and Davies, 1986, p. 2)

They add:

Taking this perspective we can view recent debates about the physical education curriculum as part of a broader battle for ownership and control over what counts as valid educational knowledge, how this is produced, distributed and evaluated. In short it is the struggle over ownership and control of the labour process of teaching. (Evans and Davies, 1986, p. 9)

In this chapter we discuss the development of a new examination course for secondary school physical education in Victoria, Australia that explicitly set out to challenge some of the key notions on which hegemonic physical education programmes are typically based. This new Victorian Certificate of Education (VCE) course replaces the previous Higher School Certificate (HSC) course which was introduced into Victorian secondary schools in the mid-1970s and was extremely popular in terms of the number of schools which adopted it and the number of students who chose to do it. This chapter will include a critique of the previous course, which represented hegemonic physical education in a powerful form, and an outline of the new course. As we were both members of the writing team for the new curriculum, to this extent at least we write from the perspective of insiders. We will approach the issue of curriculum development as a process of cultural production, and focus on how knowledge about physical activity, as represented by the curriculum, has been selected, organized, appropriated, legitimated and evaluated. In so doing, we intend to provide an example of how school curricula are constructed, not by accident, but rather as the result of choices made between contesting points of view which represent different vested interests. Throughout we attempt to locate the development of the new curriculum within the context of what we consider to be major contemporary social and cultural influences on physical education.

A Cultural Backdrop

As a way of thinking about the cultural backdrop onto which contemporary physical education is projected, the following media advertisements are illuminating. In late 1985 the ANZ bank commissioned the production of three advertisements. Taken together they provide something of a narrative about social change and the role of physical activity as a part of that process. The following is a brief outline of the content of the three advertisements. We believe it is relevant to open with such an account because it sets physical activity within a changing framework of social relationships. This cultural framework sets new boundaries of social practice and requires new forms of interpretation. Such interpretation is useful for our understanding of more specific changes within physical education.

Three Images

1　A young caucasian male, an athlete, stands in a city street with his coach. The athlete is dressed in white and is holding an Olympic-style torch. The coach is dressed in an Australian track suit. The athlete is preparing to run. In another part of the street a number of athletes also prepare to run. They are a cosmopolitan group dressed in black track suits emblazoned with the insignias of different nations. The voice-over informs us that the year is 1984 and Australia has just deregulated the banking industry and is preparing for an invasion of foreign competitors. At the same time it becomes clear that our lone athlete represents not only Australia but more specifically the ANZ bank. He is preparing to take on the other countries on their own 'turf'. As the gun goes and the two sets of athletes run off, an aerial shot pans back to overlook the city street. The lone Australian athlete runs directly towards the athletes of the other nations. He passes through the middle of their ranks and moves on to other streets — in a Japanese city, then cities of the USA, Britain and France. It is an image of a counter-invasion.

2　We are informed that it is 1988, the year of the Olympic Games. A young female diver is climbing the high tower. We are told that previously this athlete had been part of a training scheme for promising performers and that this athlete was selected for a scholarship at the Australian Institute of Sport. As she reaches the end of her climb, the voice-over drops in tone. As she steadies herself on the edge of the platform we are informed that today she will be 'performing her best for Australia. At ANZ we know how that feels.' The camera pans in to a close-up of her face, she then drops backwards from the tower. From above we see her neatly enter the water.

3　Now we move to the year 1990. A young male tennis player enters a room and faces a massive TV screen highlighting a tennis court and net. The athlete serves at the screen and registers a fault; he grimaces and turns back. A second serve registers double fault and again we see the pained expression. The athlete changes court sides and serves again. This time the screen flashes 'ACE' and the server revels in the brief moment of glory as he signals victory. Against this image the voice-over informs us that in the future world of banking what will count will be 'good service'. We are told that 'it's all about service. At ANZ we are working on it.'

Taken together, the three advertisements condense a number of related themes. The text includes reference to nationalism, corporate efficiency, competitive edge, winning and the dawning of the information and service era. The subtext incorporates the additional themes of youth, individualism, superior physical performance and risk-taking. These examples clearly demonstrate the movement of 'the physical' onto the stage of central political strategy (McKay and Huber, 1988).

To interpret changes to education in general and specific aspects of the curriculum such as physical education in particular, it is necessary to take account of the juxtaposition of different, but related, elements: public-private, concrete-abstract, physical-mental, person-society. Contemporary society fuses many of these elements which were previously discrete. As White has noted, 'the educational system in modern technologically-advanced capitalism is not only part of the capitalist superstructure, but of the productive mechanism. It is the scene of the production of ideas and culture which in themselves are the source of the production of things...thought and action, intellectual and material production are inextricably linked in the modern world' (White, 1987, pp. 67–8). Our account of changes to the development of the new curriculum in physical education accommodates such a framework of elements. The rest of this chapter focuses on three linked questions: What are the factors influencing the contemporary physical education curriculum? What are the dominant assumptions being built into contemporary physical education? What sorts of responses are appropriate to the issues being raised?

Current Themes in Physical Education

To commence this analysis, we will examine the idea that changes in the physical education curriculum are related to the *themes* which were part of the examples we used in the cultural backdrop. That is, we will commence with an image of certain trends within the physical education curriculum; an image which requires an interpretation which takes account of changes in the wider culture. In this section we will be concentrating on the first question: what themes are influencing the contemporary physical education curriculum?

The first theme is the trend towards contemporary curriculum development as an example of the fusion of previously discrete elements of influence. Three examples provide concrete expressions of the trend noted previously by White. First, in the following statement by Barry Stanton, the former National President of the Australian Council of Health, Physical Education and Recreation (ACHPER), we can see the fusion of elements to produce a national orientation to a curriculum idea.

> The commitment to proceed with the publication and marketing of the Daily Physical Education Program heralded a new life for ACHPER. The whole process of development, the incredible effort and commitment by a large number of people made the dream of an Australian curriculum for primary schools in Physical Education a reality. The important by-products of this project — the association with a commercial sponsor, a major publishing venture impacting every school in the country — launched ACHPER into a new direction of truly national dimension. (Stanton, 1987, p. 3)

Stanton's comments demonstrate the way in which a professional association can act as a bridge between schools, tertiary institutions, the corporate sector, government departments and non-government organizations. Second, at the level of the individual student there is another idea embedded within Stanton's statement. The Daily Physical Education Program focused on achieving the outcome of 'fit, skilled children' (Owen, 1988, p. 17) who would be imbued with a capacity for lifestyle construction. To make this point quite explicit it is worth taking a single example of a curriculum initiative which highlights the consolidation of a number of different interests and demonstrates the lifestyle construction element. The *Body Owners Manual* is a document which has been prepared by an educator, a psychologist and a medical epidemiologist, with input by the CSIRO, the Menzies Foundation and the Health Development Foundation. This last organization has funding from the Commonwealth Departments of Recreation and Sport, Education and South Australian Health Commission. In the the book the intention is to prepare children for healthy lifestyle choices. The manual communicates a stress on personal construction and ownership, of ideas, values and in a material sense the manual itself. 'Ownership is important because of the family interaction the Manual was designed to generate... because the Manual involves a lot of personal information and family responses it is designed so that each student should have their own copy' (Coonan *et al.*, 1984, p. 2). Third, a final indicator of the increasing tendency to integrate health and fitness institutions within a coordinated national strategy is provided by John Brown, a former Federal Minister of Sport and Tourism. This theme is indicated in his noting of the federal government's promotion of fitness via books, videos, ACHPER's Physical Education Week, the Australian Health and Fitness Survey, Australian Fitness Award and the Australian Fitness Accreditation Council. In offering a summary of these developments Brown asserted, 'I think you will agree that the Government has shown a continuing interest in having people physically fit for life generally apart from being fit to play sport' (Brown, 1987, p. 8).

Another theme which was noted in the advertisements, and which can be detected in statements about the physical education profession, appears in a recent comment by John Miller, the Executive Director of ACHPER and Editor of the *ACHPER National Journal* in 1987. The stress on corporate efficiency can be detected in the editorial of the summer edition of the journal in 1987. Miller noted that:

> climate for educational innovation is becoming decidedly drier. Across Australia, Education Departments are cutting back consulting and advisory services...as Education Departments abrogate responsibility for innovation, new players will enter the field.... Professional associations like ACHPER, will be called on to initiate and foster a climate of innovation at the chalk face, and tailor their professional development programs accordingly. There will be a trend toward privatization of professional development with individuals and faculties paying for advice and service. In the long run fee-for-service professional development may lead to more effective teacher support services. (Miller, 1987, p. 2)

This statement highlights a trend towards privatization and away from direct state patronage for educational delivery. The stress on corporate efficiency is plainly expressed in Miller's statement. The state in this scenario emerges as the overall managing and coordinating structure.

It is important to affirm that in prior times the state had direct control over the central ideas associated with the physical education curriculum. For example, in the period up to the Second World War and immediately afterwards the various Departments of Education within Australia relied heavily on the Board of Education in Britain for curriculum publications. In the period following the war physical education staff within the different states produced their own resource material as the basis for curriculum ideas. For example, within Victoria a book entitled *Physical Education for Victorian Schools* was produced in 1946 and used throughout most of the 1950s as a curriculum for both primary and secondary schools. As late as the early 1970s the Physical Education Branch within Victoria produced a suggested *Course of Study* for primary school physical education and a number of accompanying curriculum guides. It has been only in the last ten to fifteen years that a new order of curriculum development and support has been put in place. This trend has been described in examples cited above as a new arrangement of associations at the national level. Increasingly, the state Education Departments have united with a growing range of associated institutions to set the agenda for curriculum developments within physical education. This is the general background to the specific changes in the physical education curriculum. In our consideration of the development of the new Victorian Certificate of Education curriculum in physical education we have deployed these themes as a framework for analysis.

The Consolidation of Hegemonic Physical Education in the Post-Compulsory Years of Secondary Schooling: A Brief History

It was not all that long ago that for most teachers, and also most members of society, the idea of physical education as an examinable subject at year 12 (the final year of secondary education) would have seemed ludicrous. Physical education was concerned with practical activity like sport and games and certainly not a field of academic pursuit worthy of examination and entry to tertiary study. The fact that there were other subjects in the curriculum which, at least in part, were practical in nature, like art, music and the manual arts (technical drawing, domestic science/home economics) and which did have examinations, was not considered relevant in the case of physical education.

In the 1960s matriculation in Victoria was essentially an academic screening device to sort students with respect to university entrance. The curriculum was examined in an externally set and marked three-hour exam at the end of the academic year and an individual's future would largely depend on her/his performance on that particular day. Throughout the 1970s there was considerable criticism of this examination system and alternatives began to appear. Questions relating to the social justice of the system spawned changes to the matriculation requirements and created alternatives for those students who had no intention of going on to tertiary education. The HSC (Higher School Certificate) replaced the old matriculation examinations and began to include some school-based assessment which had the effect of reducing the 'make or break' consequences of the final year exam.

Within the HSC two groups of subjects were offered. Group 1 subjects were the traditional matriculation subjects and these subjects 'counted' for university selection purposes. Group 2 subjects were part of the attempt to create alternatives for the 'less academically-oriented' students who wanted to complete year 12 but not seek to enter university. Group 2 subjects included school-based assessment and were not considered for university selection purposes. Group 1 and Group 2 subjects represented two divisions in the academic status game. Given the 'common-sense consensus' (Kirk, 1988) that, since physical education's subject matter involves physical activity it is less cognitive and therefore less academic than other 'intellectual' subjects, the most likely place for physical education was as a Group 2 subject suitable for the less 'academically-oriented' student.

These changes in the upper secondary school curriculum were not happening in isolation from other changes to the education system. Tertiary education was undergoing massive change in the 1970s. As part of the federal Labor Government's policy to increase the availability of tertiary education to Australian youth, the 1970s saw the extensive development of the Colleges of Advanced Education (CAE) sector. New institutions were created and, in general, these colleges took in students who would otherwise not have gone on to tertiary education. As these new institutions developed, so did the range of the programmes they offered. Many programmes were included which did not find a place in the traditional university curriculum (e.g. chiropractic, art and design, tourism, recreation and so on). While there had been some limited programmes in physical education at a small number of universities in the early 1970s, usually as a diploma or as part of an education or arts degree, it was in the new colleges that physical education degree programmes proliferated in Australia.

Because there were no postgraduate programmes in physical education within Australia, the faculty who were employed to develop the undergraduate physical education degree programmes in these new institutions had gained their postgraduate qualifications at overseas universities, typically in North America, and they brought with them to their new posts the models of programmes which they themselves had experienced. In terms of the 'subdisciplines' of physical education, these new programmes offered courses in biomechanics, sociology of sport and physical education, exercise physiology, anatomy, history of sport and physical education, and psychology of sport. Programmes differed in their emphases (biological science or social science) depending on the influence of the planning faculty, but as a rule the biological sciences were most commonly stressed.

In Victoria these new tertiary programmes were developing at the same time as the restructuring of year 12 secondary education was taking place. As the HSC curriculum expanded in relation to its Groups 1 and 2 subjects, a small group of physical educators worked as a designated subject committee on the development of a year 12 physical education subject. Although it would have easily been accepted as a Group 2 subject, this was not the goal of the subject committee. They recognized the status game with respect to the subject groupings and desired that physical education be a Group 1 subject. To give physical education the academic credibility they desperately wanted, the subject committee created a programme which virtually excluded all physical activity and which echoed the pedagogy of high status academic subjects of the hegemonic curriculum, emphasizing in particular propositional knowledge that had an empirical and scientific flavour. Students studied exercise physiology and the human muscular system, biomechanics and schema theory in relation to the acquisition of motor skills. The social science aspects of physical education were available only as an option and it was abundantly clear that it was 'scientific knowledge' which was most highly valued. Such scientific knowledge was also the dominant element in the professional training of many of the newly graduated teachers from the CAEs. Since many of their degree programmes had emphasized the biological and physical sciences as the basis of knowledge about physical activity and the human body, programme graduates readily accepted and identified with the new HSC physical education curriculum. Although there was some criticism that the HSC curriculum was nothing more than a watered down version of CAE degree programmes, and that it had virtually eliminated physical activity, there was still a good deal of support for the course from teachers themselves.

But support for the HSC curriculum was based on more than perceived status gains and a familiarity with the emphasis on biological and physical science knowledge about physical activity. It was also based on the fact that the new curriculum embraced the logic of technocratic rationality which was itself being absorbed into the fabric of our educational logic (Rizvi, 1986) and which underpinned modern images of professionalism (McKay, Gore and Kirk, in press). As a form of 'scientific functionalism', technocratic rationality is an ideology which pervades contemporary thought in general and the physical education profession in particular (Tinning, 1987). It is manifest in the separation of theory from practice, in the separation of fact from value, in the application of reductionist thinking which results in the fragmenting of knowledge into separate supposedly discrete entities, and in concerns with efficiency which artificially separate concerns for means from ends. Technocratic logic also lends itself to a consideration of propositional knowledge ('knowing that') (Polanyi, 1969) as most appropriate since it can be readily assessed by means of tests or examinations.

Seduced by the subtle but pervasive influence of technocratic rationality as a mode of thinking, the developers of the HSC curriculum believed that the knowledge which constituted the new subject was in fact the *essential* knowledge of the field of physical education. Knowledge about the body was seen as the most important body of knowledge for physical education. It should be noted that emphasizing the technical and scientific was at the expense of social and interpretive ways of knowing. Propositional knowledge about the body in physical activity was believed to be more worthy than interpretive acquaintance-type knowledge which would be acquired through participation in physical activity. But even within propositional knowledge it was technocratic rationality which dominated the thinking. For example, learning about the energy systems involved in aerobic exercise was considered to be more important than learning about the way in which aerobics as a modern exercise phenomenon has the potential for both liberating and oppressing its participants. Learning about the biomechanics of throwing was seen to be more important than learning about the social significance of violence in sport. Learning about which muscles are involved in running was seen to be more important than learning about the way in which the media represent the body (of women in particular) and how unrealistic and damaging such representation can be for many individuals.

Significantly, since its introduction, the year 12 HSC course in physical education has become increasingly popular with students. It would seem that for adolescent youth, learning about one's body is an intrinsically interesting thing to do. But the popularity also is socially facilitated. There is no doubt that the consciousness of youth (and adults as well) has been significantly influenced by the media in the last thirty years. In the 1960s young people's consciousness was influenced by a limited exposure to such media shows as 'The Quiz Kids' and 'The Adventures of Hop Harrigan' on the radio and 'The Mickey Mouse Club' and 'Leave It to Beaver' on the new marvel called television. But it was more than the television image which was seen as black and white. Social issues themselves were seen to be black or white. History was essentially one-sided with Australia and the British Empire as the 'good guys'. McDonald's Hamburgers and Kentucky Fried Chicken were unknown in Australia, and football was only played on Saturday. Teachers represented authority and authority generally was unchallenged. But even more relevant for physical education was that this was an era before the advent of organized children's sport, and before the massive media interest in physical activity as a marketable commodity. Today the media are a pervasive intruder in our lives and a powerful and ubiquitous influence on our consciousness. In particular, for many young people life is a continuous round of TV, the radio (FM of course), and organized competitive kids' sport. Children (and adults) are bombarded with messages about physical activity, sport and bodies. As the American cultural analyst Stanley Aronowitz has claimed, 'the degree to which mass audience culture has colonised the social space available to ordinary persons for reading, discussions, and critical thought must be counted as the major event of social history in our time' (Aronowitz, 1981, p. 285). So it is that physicality and the corporeal are constantly impacting on our consciousness. Given such pervading mass culture, a course in physical education which emphasizes knowledge about the body would seem to be highly attractive to adolescent youth.

The HSC and the Blackburn Report

In June 1983 the then Victorian Minister for Education, Robert Fordham, commissioned a review of the post-compulsory years of schooling. The review was headed by Jean Blackburn and the report, released in May 1985 and known as the *Blackburn Report*, had a profound influence on Victorian secondary education. Blackburn was concerned with issues of social justice, particularly access and equity, and the extent to which the secondary school curriculum represented a preparation for life and not just for tertiary entrance. Among the *Report's* recommendations was the setting up of a Victorian Curriculum and Assessment Board (VCAB) which had overall responsibility for accreditation and certification at the senior secondary level, and the introduction of a single, common certificate, the Victorian Certificate of Education (VCE), to mark the completion of secondary schooling. The VCE was to be taken in years 11 and 12 and was to replace the one-year (year 12) HSC.

In developing the new VCE, VCAB policy required that courses of study include a balance of theory and practice, that the curriculum be geared to contemporary social and economic needs, and that there be flexibility of access for students in the course. On these three issues alone there were grounds for seriously doubting the chances of the HSC physical education course becoming a study in the new VCE. If physical education were to be included in the VCE, it had to be reconceived to satisfy VCAB policy.

Within the newly conceived subject groupings for the VCE physical education was to be grouped with health education, home economics and outdoor education and together the four studies would comprise the field of study known as 'human development'. Subjects in this field were to be developed from two key principles. First, they were to emphasize practical action related to everyday life. Practical action, sometimes known as 'practical problem-solving', should involve students in the consideration of issues which are significant to people, which involve students in the development of judgments, and the carrying out and reflecting on action. Practical action involves consideration of 'ought' and 'should' questions as well as 'how to' and 'why' quesitons. It requires thinking and action which challenge technocratic rationality as the logic of knowledge acquisition which focuses on means while ignoring ends, and which separates theory from practice and fact from values. Second, the studies were to have a common focus on the way in which individuals influence, and are influenced by, a range of interacting factors (particularly physical, hereditary and ecological factors, and social and cultural factors) which in various ways limit, direct and enhance the lives of individuals. Analysis of the content and pedagogy of the HSC course in physical education revealed that it would fail to adhere to these fundamental principles of the field of study. Physical education could no longer stand alone with its own propositional knowledge about the body in physical activity; it had to conform to principles which would integrate each of the four studies in the human development field of study.

The HSC course involved little if anything of what is embodied in the notion of practical action. Knowledge about the body was essentially non-problematic received knowledge. It involved little consideration of moral or value questions. For instance, the issue of physical fitness was presented in technocratic form. Fitness was seen as a non-problematic good and the focus of its study was on technical issues such as how to assess fitness and how one can get fit. Students learned a good deal about the components of fitness and the physiological adaptations of the body in the process of getting fit; they learned little about the reasons why fitness is such a key issue within our culture at this time in our history and whose interests are served by this concern. They learned little about how people have differing opportunities to get fit should they desire to, because of different economic status, ethnicity, gender or disability. The focus on physical activity in the HSC course was heavily biological and stripped of its social and cultural context. It gave students limited propositional knowledge without empowering them in any way to understand the social conditions which influence the place of physical activity in their own lives or the lives of other people. Another of the criticisms of the HSC course was that it was perceived to be (even if in reality it was not so) mainly for males who were physically competent. Although the course had no physical activity requirements in its curriculum other than some optional 'laboratory' activities, its image dissuaded those who considered themselves to be less motorically competent from doing it. The curriculum 'spoke' more to sporting males than it did to other adolescents. Given these shortcomings, if physical education were to receive a place in the new VCE, it would have to be a reconceptualized new course. It would have to be a curriculum which actively presented greater access opportunities for groups previously underrepresented, in particular ethnic adolescents, girls and less motorically competent boys.

The Conception of the VCE Study in Physical Education

In developing the physical education study we had to address three different trends: first, that VCAB was involved in a process of structural change partly in recognition of the fact that there was a larger number of students staying on at school through to years 11 and 12; second, that a more comprehensive view of the curriculum was required to cater for students who would not proceed to tertiary education, since previously the post-compulsory years of schooling were linked with an orientation to tertiary education; third, there had been much that had been achieved in establishing HSC physical education which was of high academic standard, and we wished to retain the best of what had been developed.

As writers, we were attracted to the notion developed by Blackburn that there was an urgent need for an education which provides students with a means for interpreting and acting on a developed understanding of the wider cultural fabric (Blackburn, 1985, pp. 15, 21). That is, we built into our work an assumption that students are entitled to an education that promotes a developed sense of common cultural patterns. We were concerned with the trend in physical education to define the subject in increasingly narrow and fragmented ways with knowledge drawn primarily from the biological/physical sciences. Our response was to place such biological/physical science understandings alongside knowledge drawn from sociocultural understandings. We were also concerned with increasing access to the subject for students with a broad range of backgrounds and aptitudes. This meant, among other things, not including activities which are the preserve of the most motorically competent individuals, or which can only be pursued by individuals with adequate financial resources. In preparing the curriculum we were aware that we were not starting with a clean slate. We were concerned with incorporating the best of the previous HSC course and locating it alongside a sociocultural perspective. This was essentially political, although we considered some of the HSC content to be worthwhile in itself. Politically it was important since the teachers who would have to teach the new VCE were those (at least in the beginning) who were familiar with the biological/physical sciences content and who would need some time to accept the significance of the changes included in the new curriculum.

One major concern throughout the development of the physical education study design was the relationship between abstract theoretical knowledge and academic status. There was no doubt that the HSC course had gained considerable status for physical education because it emphasized theoretical propositional knowledge at the expense of practical knowledge. Moreover, it emphasized science rather than sociocultural knowledge and this further contributed to the status of the subject. Within the new VCE we wanted to incorporate different 'ways of knowing' (Polanyi, 1969) about physical activity and this would of necessity limit the emphasis on propositional knowledge. We also wanted to place science-oriented knowledge alongside sociocultural knowledge and this had further implications for perceived status. In addition, the VCE was to be designed to include students who might otherwise not have stayed on at school until year 12. By retaining such students and by broadening the study beyond simply a preparation for tertiary study we ran the danger (in the eyes of some people) of 'watering down' the content in ways which would make it 'mickey mouse'. For some elements of the physical education profession the status issue is a major consideration and transcends considerations of equity, access, social relevance and epistemology.

The VCE Physical Education Draft Study Design

In 1988 VCAB produced its first stage of the new course in physical education. The initial public image of the course is captured in the following statement outlined in the draft design.

> Physical education examines the biological, physical, social and cultural influences on participation in physical activity. The role of physical activity in the study is to enhance understanding of those influences, and provides the means by which theory and practice are integrated. By expecting students to engage in the development and improvement of physical activity skills, the study provides the opportunities for them to reflect on and dis-

cuss factors which affect performance and participation. (VCAB, 1988, p. 1)

The content of the course was developed within four units, each unit being half a year in duration or fifty to sixty hours of class time. The units and particular areas of study outlined in the draft course were:

Unit 1: Physical Activity and Lifestyle (body image, patterns of living, health-related factors, innovations in physical activity);

Unit 2: Analyzing Physical Activity (understanding skill, learning a physical skill, technique and technology, biomechanical principles);

Unit 3: Perspectives on Fitness (understanding fitness, fuel for the body, training, changing horizons);

Unit 4: Physical Activity: A Biosocial Analysis (social change and physical activity, types of experience in physical activity, social influences in participation, the biosocial nature of participation in physical activity).

While units 2 and 3 retained a link to the former HSC course, the other two units mark a break with tradition. The content of units 1 and 4 can be thought of as innovatory in terms of making a contribution to the scope of a general definition of what is meant by the term 'physical education'. The pedagogical framework for the units was constructed around the notion of 'work requirements'. The five types of work requirements were physical activity learning and analysis classes, introductory exercises, laboratory activities, logbook and project. The mandatory inclusion of physical activity within the work requirements was a significant departure from the academic content of the HSC course. The study design, in following general specifications for the VCE, was to be thought about as a structure within which each school would develop a specific course. At the time of writing this chapter the course was half-way through the development phase with final accreditation due in 1990 and introduction into schools for year 11 and year 12 students due to occur in 1991.

The Process of Curriculum Change and the Implications for Teacher Education

Understanding the contextual complexities of curriculum development is one thing, having a new curriculum adopted by teachers is another. We know that the history of curriculum innovation is littered with the corpses of 'failed' attempts to change teachers' practice. In the case of the VCE physical education curriculum it has had to be 'approved by' tertiary faculty in addition to teachers in schools. VCAB have attempted to incorporate teachers' and academics' ideas and opinions into the development of the VCE study designs by having both teachers and academics as members of the writing teams and by the use of an extensive consultation process with schools and tertiary institutions. In this process draft versions of the study design were distributed to schools, colleges and universities and meetings were arranged to discuss reaction to the draft documents. Part of the initial resistance of some teachers was a reaction to the general philosophy of the VCE itself and represented a desire to maintain a meritocratic form of curriculum in the post-compulsory years of schooling. If the essence of such resistance had been accommodated in the study design, it would have resulted in physical education failing to be approved as a subject in the new VCE structure. However, as writers, we were enthusiastically supportive of the thrust of the new VCE and did not develop a 'complaint' (to the VCE policy) curriculum simply out of expediency (that is, to have physical education accepted).

As a result of the feedback received from the various consultation sessions the study design was modified within the boundaries of the possibilities of the VCE policy. The extent to which some teachers continue to reject the very assumptions on which the new curriculum is based will remain to be seen when the study design is implemented in schools around Victoria. We do know that 'fidelity of implementation' is in the hands of individual teachers and to this end we can predict that some teachers at least may accommodate the new curriculum into their existing HSC curriculum using a process which Sparkes (1987) has called 'strategic rhetoric'. In this process the language or rhetoric of the new curriculum is adopted but the actual practice goes essentially unaltered. It is hoped that the VCE work requirements in general and the 'common assessment tasks' (CATS) in particular will enhance the implementation of the spirit of the study design in the face of certain oppositional pressures from factions representing the dominant, hegemonic culture in physical education, which is individualistic, competitive and meritocratic.

Changing the curriculum is not without implications for the tertiary programmes which prepare the teachers to teach in the post-compulsory years of schooling. There is a two-way interaction between the tertiary institutions and the new VCE curriculum. The HSC secondary school curriculum in physical education had been influenced by the visions of physical education which are championed in the tertiary institutions, and, as indicated earlier, the VCE curriculum in physical education attempted to incorporate the best of the old HSC curriculum into a broader more culturally related new syllabus. On the other hand, the tertiary institutions will need to respond to the VCE in terms of adaptations to their programmes if they are to prepare teachers who are competent to teach the new curriculum. Programmes which remain examples of the propagation of the 'divided curriculum' (White, 1987), which continue to graduate teachers who champion fragmented specialized knowledge, individualism, competition, a meritocratic view of society and knowledge of the body as *the* body of knowledge for physical education (Tinning, 1987) will create considerable difficulties in terms of implementing the new VCE curriculum. A new teacher education capable of adequately preparing teachers to teach the VCE will need purposefully to contextualize physical education within the contemporary culture, to integrate the biological-physical and the sociocultural. It will need to be a biosocial curriculum.

An Interpretation and Conclusion

We have attempted to sketch an image of the processes and thinking associated with an attempt to reform one part of the physical education curriculum. The story, as we have constructed it, involves an account in which more general developments within curriculum thinking have played an important role in shaping the structure produced in the reform. In developing an interpretation of the curriculum changes noted here we are conscious of the need to extend the frame of reference for thinking about the curriculum. More specifically, we have been influenced by recent developments in curriculum theorizing that argue for the curriculum to be placed within a comprehensive theory of society which involves a cultural analysis (see Fitzclarence, 1987a). Here we turn full circle in this account as we attempt to think about developments within physical education within the context of broader social trends.

The Intellectual, Interpretive Framework

Physical education has been developed historically within a framework of what might be called 'public education'. Since the idea of universal public education started to unfold as a political reality it has been caught within the jaws of a fundamental contradiction. On one hand, the dominant Australian ideology has espoused the notion of public education as an aspect of egalitarian ideals and practices, while the social reality has continued to move forward around the differences produced by a class differentiated society. That is, a dual system of privilege counterposed to limited access to social wealth was presented as egalitarian, while offering access and attainment to the most 'worthy'. The ideology was one of an open, competitive and meritocratic society. The dominance of this ideology for about a century, until the 1960s, was not without challenge and question. The progressive education movement in the 1920s was one such example, but we can now trace that to an elite vanguard position which was demanding rapid deployment of the advances in the then new psychology of educational theory. As such, it can be seen as part of the orthodoxy of the meritocratic and competitive ideology. Within this espousal of egalitarianism the curriculum was presented as value free, and success or failure was linked to the individual.

Tangible social contradictions such as those highlighted by the nuclear threat, environmental concerns, ethnic differentiation and challenges to different examples of cultural imperialism and the modern phase of the women's movement became a major aspect of social and intellectual life in the 1960s and 1970s. They contributed to the emergence of new forms of intellectual understandings; ideas which found their way into the frameworks which have acted to challenge the dominance of conventions of the meritocratic and competitive ideology. For example, the 'new sociology of education' of the 1970s introduced questions and ideas which challenged the status of a value free notion of education (Bates, 1981). Apart from highlighting issues of 'winners' and 'losers' of the schooling process this emerging tradition placed important research questions on the academic agenda. These questions offered insights into the significant points of intervention in the curriculum process, intervention in terms of: What counts as worthwhile school knowledge? How is school knowledge organized? How is what counts as school knowledge transmitted? What kind of cultural system does the structure of the curriculum legitimate? Whose interests are served by the curriculum structure?

This critical tradition of educational scholarship was able to open the way to attention being turned to the structural elements of the social form which are produced, reproduced and transformed. Subsequent work has extended the analysis such that other issues about the curriculum can now be thought about in a systematic way. For example, *theories of knowledge form* introduced questions about the relationship between theory and practice, the balance between mental and manual, and concrete and abstract factors. *Theories of knowledge content* introduced a focus on the balance between the science and the arts, and the self-conscious recognition of the need to represent a range of social perspectives (for instance, is the curriculum one that looks out to other cultural traditions or is it always drawn inwards?). Finally, *theories of classroom social relations* focused on a balance between dependence and independence, and on being self-conscious of whose interests were being represented by the dominant pedagogical structures in use. Research in Australia, Britain and the USA, such as that represented in *Making the Difference* (Connell *et al.*, 1982) and *Learning to Labour* (Willis, 1976), highlighted how students learn class-specific behaviour which orients them to the world of work and the larger society. Taken together, these different perspectives on schooling helped educationists extend their thinking about the curriculum and to be more self-conscious of the outcomes of the curriculum process. Instead of thinking about the curriculum in the politically neutral terms of former times, it is now possible and indeed necessary to recognize that 'students appear to be developing a potential relationship to different forms of work, including domestic labor, and in so doing they are acquiring a specific form of symbolic capital' (Fitzclarence and Giroux, 1984).

As we have tried to demonstrate in this chapter, we have been influenced by the range of work developed within a critical tradition of curriculum theorizing. For example, within the VCE physical education the relationship between physical activity and theoretical knowledge was taken into consideration to offset the progressive weighting of the theoretical ways of knowing in physical education. We resolved to unite the practical and theoretical and the concrete and abstract by developing tasks that focused on physical activity, activity that the students would be expected to undertake, then reflect on (*theories of knowledge form*). Also we wanted to redress the progressive weighting of the physical and biological sciences in HSC physical education, at the expense of the sociocultural (*theories of knowledge content*). We wanted to employ a frame which allowed students to have some power in interpreting and acting on the social context which is developing with regard to body image and the commodification of the physical. We have also structured the work on the progressive independence of the student (*theories of classroom social relations*). From units that are worked around some particular frameworks of thinking (about culture, the physiology of the body, the mechanics of movement) we have moved progressively towards a more independent major project, a time when more personal and local aspects of physical activity can be connected to the wider intellectual and cultural frame. Accordingly, when we reflect on where we have travelled in working through this project, we acknowledge the contribution of the emergence of the critical tradition in curriculum theory. This work has provided us with a new language with which to think about and act on the curriculum; words such as 'equality', 'relevance' and 'social responsibility' have formed the lexicon of our curriculum vocabulary.

The Meta-Political Process

At this point we wish to pause. As we have reflected on the curriculum development work outlined here and the attempts to redress perceived flaws in the previous curriculum, we are also aware of another trend. Can we really be confident that this work has been part of a rational process in which a contribution has been made in moving education and society towards a more just, equitable and stable form? It is not possible to give an unequivocal answer to such a question. The very methodology employed in working through this project turns our attention outwards, away from the knowledge frame of physical education in order to seek an answer. From the point of view of a cultural analysis that attempts to link history, geography, customs and values, we are provoked to consider the work outlined here as part of the *meta-political process* of the restructuring of the nation-state. Increasingly, the old national boundaries have been weakened as the market processes of international capitalism have been extended. As this process has accelerated, the focus of our shared and private lives has been stretched. Old ties and associations have weakened and been replaced with more abstract forms of relationships, via the world of the telephone, fax, video and television. Within this expanding context the state takes on an increasingly significant role as coordinator and manager of collective social life (see White, 1987). As our examples of the ANZ advertisements in the introduction to this chapter highlight, the various state apparatuses promote the absorption of more and more of the images and practices of everyday life into the frame of the 'controlled society'. Writing of this trend, Marcuse notes:

> Contemporary society seems to be capable of containing social change — qualitative change which would establish essentially different institutions, a new direction of the productive process, new modes of human existence. This containment of social change is perhaps the most singular achievement of advanced industrial society; the general acceptance of the National Purpose, bipartisan policy, the decline of pluralism, the collusion of Business and Labor within the strong State testify to the integration of opposites which is the result as well as prerequisite of this achievement. (Marcuse, 1964, p. xii)

We would contend that the curriculum reform outlined in this chapter needs to be read at a number of related levels. It should be seen as an attempt to redress some of the apparent contradictions associated with the former divided and abstract curriculum (White, 1983). We will require more time to understand how it fits into the framework of the coordinated nation-state noted by Marcuse, and the extent to which the curriculum itself gives expression and legitimacy to the cycle of commodification of knowledge and social practices.

Postscript

If the argument of this chapter is at all correct, the redefinition of the status of Australia as a nation-state, in a changing context of other nations, will have direct implications for educators. Instead of physical education as a dimension of the efforts of the state to 'gear up' for military campaigns, contemporary physical education is drawn increasingly into the struggles to secure a footing in the international market place. As we indicated in our introduction, the idea of a strong and competitive marketing nation can be seen to be at the centre of many political strategies. Education, as always, is part of the skilling and legitimizing process associated with this political strategy. Accordingly, the physical education profession would be well advised to be self-consciously reflective about its role in the new politics. Without a developed understanding of the cultural processes at work, physical educators are in danger of being coopted by stronger and more persuasive lobby groups. This point can be demonstrated by reference to a recent article published in *The Australian*. Sports journalist Jeff Wells (1989) argued that if Australia is to have a realistic hope of competing with other sporting nations, what is required is a rethink of government policies for physical education. 'We should not even begin to think of competing on equal terms until mandatory daily physical education for all Australian primary school children is in place. Only then can we expect the rejuvenation of our prowess and the kind of performance our climate and standard of living should guarantee' (Wells, 1989, p. 21). No doubt Wells' comments will be applauded by many physical educators who have conducted a long struggle to secure the status of the subject. The question remains, though, whether such moves are part of a rational political strategy or just a dimension of the overall struggles of the international market place. We would contend that recent preoccupations with economics and retrenchment in public spending are limited ways to think about culture in general or to influence educational practice in particular. Increasingly, education is seen as synonymous with the 'economy'. What is required of physical educators is some critical debate about the new political processes and the attempt to secure some reflective independence from the ideological juggernaut which is rolling on through our various public institutions. In the short term this requires some hard thinking about a new definition of physical education in the post-modern world of the international market place. We take it that our work as described in this chapter is part of that process.

References

ARONOWITZ, S. (1981) *The Crisis in Historical Materialism.* New York: Bergin.

ARONOWITZ, S. and GIROUX, H. (1987) *Education under Siege.* South Hadley, Mass.: Bergin and Garvey.

BATES, R. (1981) 'New Developments in the New Sociology of Education'. *British Journal of Sociology in Education,* 1 (1), 67–80.

BLACKBURN, J. (1985) *Report of the Ministerial Review of Post-Compulsory Schooling,* Blackburn Report, Melbourne.

BROWN, J. (1987) 'In Profile: John Brown, MHR.' *ACHPER National Journal,* p. 8.

CONNELL, W., *et al.* (1982) *Making the Difference.* Sydney: Allen and Unwin.

COONAN, W., WORSLEY, A. and MAYNARD, E. (1984) *Body Owner's Manual.* Melbourne: Life Be in It Publications.

EVANS, J. and DAVIES, B. (1986) 'Sociology, Schooling and Physical Education', in EVANS, J. (Ed.), *Physical Education, Sport and Schooling: Studies in the Sociology of Physical Education.* Lewes: Falmer Press.

FITZCLARENCE, L. (1987a) 'The Physical Education Curriculum: A Cultural Perspective,' in *Teaching Physical Education Reader.* Geelong: Deakin University.

FITZCLARENCE, L. (1987b) 'The Physical Education Curriculum: The Right Direction?' *Education and Society,* 5 (1–2), 79–85.

FITZCLARENCE, L. and GIROUX, H. (1984) 'The Paradox of Power in Educational Theory and Practice.' *Language Arts,* 61 (5), 462–77.

KIRK, D. (1988) *Physical Education and Curriculum Study: A Critical Introduction.* London: Croom Helm.

McKAY, J. and HUBER. D. (1988) 'Swan Sport and Ideology.' *Arena,* 83, 117–29.

McKAY, J., GORE, J. and KIRK, D. (in press) 'Beyond the Limits of Technocratic Physical Education.' *Quest.*

MARCUSE, H. (1964) *One Dimensional Man.* Boston, Mass.: Beacon Press.

MILLER, J. (1987) Editorial, *ACHPER National Journal,* 118, p. 2.

OWEN, N. (1988) 'Physical Education, Health Education and the New Public Health.' *ACHPER National Journal,* p. 17.

POLANYI, M. (1969) *Knowing and Being.* London: Routledge and Kegan Paul.

RIZVI, F. (1986) 'Bureaucratic Rationality and the Democratic Community as a Social Ideal.' Paper presented at the Annual Meeting of the American Educational Research Association, San Francisco.

SPARKES, A. (1987) 'Strategic Rhetoric: A Constraint in Changing the Practice of Teachers.' *British Journal of Sociology of Education,* 8, 37–54.

STANTON, B. (1987) 'President's Column.' *ACHPER National Journal,* December, p. 3.

TINNING, R. (1987) 'Physical Education in Victoria through Rose and Other Coloured Glasses.' Keynote address to the Physical Education Teacher's Annual Conference, Monash University, December.

VCAB (1988) *Human Development Field of Study: Physical Education.* Melbourne: Victorian Curriculum and Assessment Board, June.

WELLS, G. (1989) 'Just Bashing His Head against the Boofheads.' *The Australian,* 24 July, 21–2.

WHITE, D. (1983) 'After the Divided Curriculum', *Victorian Teacher,* 12 (1), 6–7.

WHITE, D. (1987) *Education and the State: Federal Involvement in Education.* Boston, Mass.: Beacon Press.

WILLIS, P. (1976) *Learning to Labour.* Farnborough, Hants: Saxon House.

Chapter 8

Winners, Losers and the Myth of Rational Change in Physical Education: Towards an Understanding of Interests and Power in Innovation

Andrew C. Sparkes

'You see, to get the changes I want introduced I have to convince them. If I can convince them they will introduce the changes. I could make them but they wouldn't do it properly or as well as they could. They need to be convinced.' These are the words of Alex, a newly appointed departmental head, who is a central character in the story of teacher-initiated innovation that is the focus of this chapter. His words reveal an implicit belief in curriculum change as a rational process. This is not surprising since the world of education has long been dominated by the 'scientific management' or 'objectives' approach instigated by Tyler (1949), that takes the management of change to be a rational and technical process. Indeed, the work of contemporary curriculum theorists, such as Arnold (1985, 1988), Jewett and Bain (1985) and Siedentop (1983), bears testimony to the ongoing influence of the objectives approach upon our thinking about life in schools. At the heart of this approach is a view of change as a rational, linear and value free process. Commenting upon the innovator who adopts such a view, Nicholls notes:

> He is likely to consider his colleagues to be rational human beings; he is convinced of the benefits of the proposed innovation and believes that if he communicates these to his colleagues they, too, will be convinced and therefore willing to adopt the innovation. It is, however, a deceptively simple approach, especially in relation to innovations which require people to change their behaviour. (Nicholls, 1983, p. 29)

The rationale that underlies the objectives approach is deceptively simple and it has been conceptually critiqued on numerous occasions.[1] The purpose of this chapter is not to replicate in detail these critiques, but rather to raise questions concerning this dominant approach by looking at what happens when these assumptions operate in action within a physical education department involved in change. This is why Alex is so central to the story. He genuinely believed in change as a rational process and with the best of intentions operated on this basis with his staff. By documenting the impact of these beliefs upon those within the department and their subsequent reactions to Alex's proposals for change I hope to reinforce the point made by Fullan (1982) that change is never a wholly rational process. Furthermore, the following empirically grounded account attempts to disturb the prevalent ideology of school-centred innovation that fails to acknowledge the presence and importance of conflict and struggle between different teachers and subject departments in the process of educational change. At best, this view treats the value conflicts that surround the idea of change in a very superficial manner while, at worst, it takes such conflicts to be pathological in nature. However, as Dalton (1988) reminds us, conflict, negotiation and compromise are all taken, given, challenged or negotiated. Fullan (1982, p. 91) sums it up well when he argues that disagreement and conflict are 'not only inevitable but fundamental to successful change. Since any group of people possess multiple realities, any collective change attempt will necessarily involve conflict.' Therefore, by focusing directly upon such disagreements and conflicts in the context of the messy realities of school life, this chapter attempts to make problematic the view that change is, or can be, a rational and value free process.

Beyond Neutrality: Costs and Rewards in the Process of Innovation

One of the major weaknesses of the rational view of change is its incongruence with the real world of teaching and life in schools. In this respect Shaw (1988, p. 270) comments that 'the excessive application of rationality to complex problems of policy and planning runs headlong into two difficulties: people and change.' People and change make up a combustible mixture because, in terms of the subjective realities of those involved, innovation and change are rarely, if ever, neutral. As Ball notes:

> They [innovations] tend to advance or enhance the position of certain groups and disadvantage or damage the position of others.

Innovations can threaten the self-interests of participants by undermining established identities, by deskilling and therefore reducing job satisfaction. By introducing new working practices which replace established and cherished ways of working, they threaten individual self concepts. Vested interests may also be under threat: innovations not infrequently involve the redistribution of resources, the restructuring of job allocations and re-direction of lines of information flow. The career prospects of individuals or groups may be curtailed or fundamentally diverted. (Ball, 1987, p. 32)

For those involved in any change there are personal costs and rewards. There is evidence to suggest that despite the changing nature of work in schools it is the intrinsic rewards of teaching that sustains teachers. These include student learning and attainment, collegial stimulation and support, the 'glow' of service, the craft pride generated by evidence of successful teaching and the sheer enjoyment of being with young people (see Lortie, 1975; Feiman-Nemser and Floden, 1986; Poppleton, 1988; Sikes, Measor and Woods, 1985; Templin, Sparkes and Schempp, in process). However, it would be wrong to assume that all teachers will respond to the same incentives in a similar fashion regardless of personal idiosyncracies. Teachers will subjectively assess the ratio of investment to return for themselves in relation to their own personal value systems. Consequently, they will perceive and value rewards in different ways depending upon, among other things, their age, experience, present career position, family situation, circumstances beyond school, race and gender. As such, innovations should not be seen as reified entities that have an objective existence that is independent of the individual's perception or construction of reality.

Furthermore, it needs to be recognized that what is defined as rewarding to a teacher at a certain time may well become a cost at a later date as the life circumstances of the individual change (see Sparkes, 1988a). Teacher 'A' may define (at a given time) a change as rewarding, while teacher 'B' will define the same change as a high cost exercise. For instance, a teacher holding 'elitist' values is likely to have a very different view of any given innovation when compared to a teacher holding 'egalitarian' values. Even when the goals of an innovation are expressed in the most general way, for instance, 'to facilitate the learning of children', the different educational and political values that teachers hold will influence them to approach the task in a number of ways. Thus different value positions have a pervasive influence upon the practice of teachers in schools and they also inform the way that they subjectively assess the costs and rewards of change.

In terms of the costs and rewards involved in the change process a range of interests is at stake. These interests take various forms and Ball (1987) talks of vested, ideological and self-interests. Vested interests focus upon the material concerns of teachers in terms of their working conditions, rewards from work, career development and promotion. Here access to and control of the finite resources available within the school are crucial. These include time allocation (the amount of time given to a subject, the number of timetabled lessons or free periods a teacher is given, the allocation of high or low ability pupils to the subject), materials, capitation allowance and additional monies, personnel (control of job specifications and appointments) and territory (specialist subject rooms, laboratories, playing fields on site). There is also a range of professional or ideological interests that can operate within any given school or department. According to Ball (1987), these refer to matters of value and various forms of philosophical commitment. These positions are most in evidence in staffroom conversations or in staff meetings where teachers articulate their preferred view of educational practices and school organization. As an example, proposals to introduce mixed-ability grouping into a school that streams pupils by ability are likely to initiate a heated debate over the advantages and disadvantages of these forms of social groupings. Very often this kind of debate will highlight the differing and competing ideological positions of subjects as individuals in the school seek to define and maintain their's as the dominant viewpoint.

The case study by Ball (1981) of Beachside Comprehensive School provides a good example of this inter-departmental contestation. In the public debate of the staff meeting the languages and maths departments argued *against* the introduction of mixed-ability grouping on 'educational' grounds ('the needs of the pupil and the interests of the child'). The geography department argued *for* mixed-ability on similar grounds. The same study indicates how differing conceptions of both subject pedagogy and subject paradigm can exist within the same department (see Ball and Lacey, 1984). The former refers to the manner in which teachers view the content of their subject, while the later refers to the systems of ideas and organization of learning in the classroom under specific conditions, that is, appropriate method rather than content.

Finally, there are personal or self-interests. These are intimately linked with vested interests on such issues as status, promotion and working conditions, yet they are not often voiced as self-interests in public debate. Another important aspect of self-interest is the sense of identity or self that the teacher aspires to, that is, what kind of teacher or person do they want to be? Do they define themselves as subject specialist, administrator, sports coach, traditionalist, progressive or visionary?

Depending upon the manner in which they define themselves teachers will find differing satisfactions from working in schools with particular kinds of pupils in specific settings (Sparkes, 1989). Here we need to differentiate between the substantial self and the situational self (Nias, 1984). The latter concerns those social identities that change with time, place and role, and involves the multiple selves that we learnt to present to others depending upon the situation (Goffman, 1959). The former is made up of the individual's most valued views of and attitudes to self that are constantly defended and highly resistant to change. It is in terms of the substantial self that teachers engage with the curriculum at a deep personal level as they attempt to create and maintain a work setting that allows for congruence between their substantial self and their interaction with the school curriculum (Nias, 1985; Sparkes, 1988b; Woods, 1984).

Unfortunately, while it is possible to isolate a range of interests for analytical purposes, it is often more difficult to separate them in reality as they are interactive in nature. What is certain is that these vested, ideological and self-interests are ever present in schools and departments as deep rooted and often implicit 'subterranean issues' (Lacey, 1977). During periods of innovation and change they rise forcefully to the surface as teachers mobilize their resources to protect their interests. Within this process there will be winners and losers. Winners will be those who perceive themselves as currently experiencing more gains than losses from the changes or who anticipate doing so in the foreseeable future. In contrast, the losers perceive the losses (potential or actual) to outweigh the gains and the price of change as not worth paying. In addition, there may well be some teachers who are 'sideliners' (Roskies, Liker and Roitman, 1988), who define themselves as neither winners nor losers. They do not view the change as positive or negative for them, they may not consider it personally relevant to their lives; for instance, a supply teacher, a temporary teacher, a teacher about to retire or move to a new post may feel this way. The main point is that winners and losers, at both the individual and departmental level, are a fundamental reality in the process of change which cannot be ignored.

Power and the Centrality of Micropolitics

Once it is accepted that there will be winners and losers in the process of change, then the rational planning model begins to creak at the seams. Of course, all would be well if consensus prevailed and change were a politically neutral process. But, as many case studies have highlighted, change simply does not work that way. These studies strongly suggest that if we are to understand the limits and possibilities of educational change, then schools and departments should be regarded as 'arenas of struggle', that is, contexts in which power is unevenly distributed among members and in which there are likely to be ideological differences and conflicts of interest. As Gronn points out:

> Confronted by competition for scarce resources and with ideologies, interests and personalities at variance, bargaining becomes crucial. Political exchanges, which can occur at all organizational levels and in all spheres of management, formal and informal, comprise negotiation and definitions governing the content and conduct of action. Conflict between the actors takes a number of forms. It can be manifest, hidden or latent. (Gronn, 1986, p. 45)

These conditions make it appropriate to conceive of educational organizations as political systems, both internally and in their external relationships (Bacharach, 1988). Consequently, we have to ask such questions as 'who wins and who loses and how does this come about?' Questions of this kind force us to focus on the nature of power and its use in schools. Bacharach and Lawler (1980, p. 1) define politics in organizations as the 'tactical use of power to retain or obtain control of real or symbolic resources'. Power, according to Morgan (1986), is the medium through which conflicts of interest are ultimately resolved, that is, power influences who gets what, when and how. Consequently, any attempt to understand educational change must accept the dynamics of these power struggles as an integral part of its analysis.

Unfortunately, power remains an elusive concept in the literature. Bacharach and Lawler (1980), in their detailed and comprehensive analysis of the nature of power in organizations, differentiate between two types of power, authority and influence. The former is that kind of power which stems from the legal right to make decisions governing others and is the static, formal and structural aspect of power. In contrast, the latter is the multidirectional, fluid, informal, dynamic and tactical aspect of power that is a key resource in micropolitical activity. Rational models of change are secure and even credible when dealing with the 'authority' dimension of power. However, they become increasingly uncomfortable and less convincing when they have to confront the 'influence' dimension and the manner in which this interacts with authority in schools as part of the change process. Accordingly, the rational framework studiously ignores the domain of micropolitics that, according to Hoyle (1986, p. 126), consists of those 'strategies by which individuals and groups in organizational contexts seek to use their resources of authority and influence to further their interests'.

In the domain of micropolitics it is the implicit rather than the explicit, the outside rather than the inside, of formal structures and procedures, and the informal resources of influence rather than authority that determine the fate of innovation and change. This leads Ball (1989, p. 232) to view power as 'an active penetrating and flexible concept...it does not involve reference to position or capacity as such but to performance, achievement and struggle.' Such a view allows for a consideration of winners and losers and how they are created by acknowledging that power is above all else about outcomes that are produced in the course of the practices of agents, which according to Hindness (1982, p. 501) 'are always subject to definite conditions and obstacles, which often include the practices of other agents.' Consequently, as Blase (1988, p. 126) notes, 'micropolitical discussions of organizational life have stressed the interactive, dialectical, multidirectional, strategic, ideological, conflictive, situational, and interpretive processes in organizations associated with the use of power.' As micropolitical studies begin to penetrate the underside of organizational life, the idealized image of change as a rational, linear and value free process begins to fracture as a more realistic picture of how change takes place in school emerges.

Power Plays in Action: Examples from a Case Study

How does all this work itself out in schools and departments? How do competing interests, ideologies, perspectives and visions interact as teachers engage in their daily working lives? Here we have a problem since as Ball (1987), Blase (1988) and Hoyle (1986) have pointed out, very few studies exist of the everyday micropolitical interactions in the school setting, particularly from the perspectives of teachers. Furthermore, despite the emergence of the school-based curriculum development (SBCD) movement, Hargreaves reminds us that

> depressingly little is known about the exact quality and nature of teachers' participations in programmes of SBCD...there is a special need to be cautious and sceptical when reading the SBCD literature for little of it is research based, and very often amounts to little more than an ideology of teacher participation and grassroots democracy. A substantial and constructive contribution to such a sceptical approach would be varied ethnographic study of the dynamics of the decision making process in different educationist contexts. (Hargreaves, 1981, p. 305)

With this in mind I intend to focus exclusively upon the educationist context, that is, the arena of school life that involves the discussion of school politics and draws selectively and consciously on educational theory and research (Keddie, 1971). This includes staff meetings, departmental meetings and teachers' encounters with influential others and inquisitive outsiders. My attention will be given to the manner in which decisions were made at a series of departmental meetings by a group of seven physical education specialists involved in a range of teacher-initiated innovations. This focus is chosen because the decision-making process forms one of the primary arenas of political conflict as individuals and groups attempt to maximize their specific interests by ensuring that the decision outcomes reflect their own interests (Bacharach, 1988). I hope to illustrate how members of a department had differential access to resources of power and the manner in which this severely limited the ability of a single individual or group to have its interests represented in the decision-making process. In essence, the following shows how talk is a key resource in the process of control, domination and struggle that allows a departmental head to push through a crucial decision concerning a series of curriculum changes against the wishes of some of the members of his department. It is an example of micropolitics in action.

The data presented are a small part of a three-year (1983–86) case study of teacher-initiated innovation in a physical education department at a large, English, co-educational, comprehensive school called Branstown. Here a newly appointed departmental head, called 'Alex', attempted to introduce structural changes in physical education which involved the abolition of streaming by ability in games lessons in favour of mixed-ability grouping and the inclusion of more individual activities at the expense of team sports. In addition, he attempted to reorient the educational philosophies of those in his department towards his own. The confusions, anxieties and conflicts caused by these proposals for change were witnessed by me during the fieldwork phase of the research which began in September 1983. During this academic year I adopted the role of 'researcher-participant' (see Gans, 1982) within the department and used 'reflexive' interviews (Hammersley and Atkinson, 1983) to focus on the adoption phase of the innovation process when Alex began to conceive of changing the curriculum and started to introduce his ideas to the department. From September 1984 to September 1986 reflexive interviews were used to enhance and develop my interpretation of the adoption phase and to examine the consequences of the innovations for the teachers involved once the changes had been implemented.

It is notoriously difficult to provide all the contextual information required to make sense of an extended case study and details of this study are available elsewhere.[2] Of importance for this discussion is the mode of thought that dominated the department prior to the arrival of· Alex. Before Alex arrived the department had operated within a sporting ideology. This was subject-centred, concerned with the development of high level physical skills and the maintenance of 'standards' within a meritocratic system. The focus of attention was on the elite performer and more able pupils who formed the nucleus of the successful school teams that acted as a barometer for the achievement of the physical education department within the school. The most visible expression of this ideology in action was the organization of the games lessons in physical education. Here both boys and girls were streamed by ability and the physical education specialists took the most able pupils in 'top group' which contained the potential school team players. The less able were taken in these lessons by non-specialist teachers. The boys' curriculum in particular was heavily 'skewed' (Glew, 1983) towards the major team games at the expense of individual activities in the quest for inter-school sporting success.

The arrival of Alex introduced a new ideological position into the department which may best be described as 'idealist' in nature. This was child-centred, egalitarian and concerned with the personal and social development of all children via individual self-paced activities, such as educational gymnastics and swimming. Essentially, the idealist ideology was anti-elitist and anti-traditional. While this ideology is not unusual among the teaching profession, it was the first time that any physical educator at Branstown School had held such a view. Therefore, within the department there were 'competing systems of interpretation' (Silverman, 1970) which differed with regard to the nature of physical education as a subject, what should be included in the curriculum and how it should be taught. These competing systems of interpretation clashed throughout the study as each struggled for domination. This struggle revealed a range of interests in operation and provided insights into the tactical use of the differential power resources available to those involved.

The innovations were instigated by Alex due to a complex interaction of a range of self and vested interests, only a few of which will be considered here. In particular, after a short period in the school Alex realized that the curriculum he had inherited on taking over the department was capable of negating his sense of self. Commenting on his early involvement with this curriculum, he noted:

> I had that terrible experience of that Autumn term, and I really did start to struggle there. I just couldn't accept that form of system — I was definitely under increased pressure — how can I

put it? Internally I was under pressure. It was totally against my philosophy. I couldn't cope with it — I felt I couldn't live with myself because it was so bad, it was so elitist. Honestly, I would come back in after a games lesson and some of the teaching made me despair. I felt like crying sometimes. I would come home and I'd be angry and I was desperate — 'What can I do?', 'Where do I go?', 'Do I change everything — or what?' (Alex, interview transcript)

Besides the need to create a work setting that was congruent with his substantial sense of self there were additional pressures on Alex which related to his career aspirations. He commented:

I think that the Headmaster thought the department was a mess, and a bit too traditional and not moving in the direction he wanted. There was a mess, and no real direction in the curriculum, it was a bit behind and needed updating and bringing into line with school policy — and obviously I was under pressure to do that.... I was appointed for my philosophies and beliefs, and I like to think that they fit it with the comprehensive ideal. If I didn't end up with the majority of my ideals and philosophies within the department, then I wouldn't have done my job, and been seen to be doing my job properly. (Alex, interview transcript)

Alex had a great deal to gain by introducing change to the physical education curriculum. His sense of self as an educator would be enhanced and the introduction of changes in line with the policy of the school management team would carry favour with this powerful group and further his career interests. In this sense Alex would be a winner in the process. However, it needs to be recognized that the members of his department who held, to a greater or lesser degree, the sporting ideology were also engaged with the curriculum at a deep personal level and had their own career aspirations. In many respects they had a great deal to lose since their own sense of self was bound up with the maintenance of school teams and sporting success which they believed had a direct bearing on their career prospects within the educational system. For several of these teachers the introduction of mixed-ability groupings into the games lessons was taken to act against the production of successful school teams and this would serve to reduce the status of the subject within the school. As one teacher commented:

I do think that school teams are important, and this new fangled thing that's coming around where school teams ought to be dropped and we concentrate on everyone. I don't really think that is a good idea at all...I think that if you dilute it too much, and you keep the good ones together with the less able ones and you do a course that is for everybody, without concentrating on the elite at some stage. I think that's doing a disservice to the good kids. (interview transcript).

In the summer term of 1983, during which the members of the department became 'orientated' (Sparkes, 1986) to each other, it gradually became evident that different ideologies were operating within the department. These differences were highlighted during the autumn term of the same year when the major team games dominated the physical education curriculum. Commenting on two of the men who held strong sporting ideologies, Alex said:

If you were to ask Simon and Peter what a successful PE department was, they would talk in terms of school teams and how well they were doing, and they would talk about how well certain activities were developed within the school. I think that the basic difference between, not the two schools of thought, but the two philosophies. One you develop the activity and you develop as many pupils as possible within that activity, and hope that the other things, the educational aims and objectives come along with it, and the development of the child comes along with it. Or, you think of the individual first. You think of each individual pupil, and you think how you can develop as many of these as possible by giving them meaningful experiences, and develop a positive attitude towards physical activity so that it continues after school. (Alex, interview transcript)

Simon, contrasting his own view with that of Alex, commented, 'I see the skill as being the major formal point of a lesson and the other things are a by-product. I mean they have got five years to pick up a sense of social responsibility.... But Alex turns that on its head, he would say the responsibility first and the skill second. (Simon, interview transcript)

As I have argued elsewhere (Sparkes, 1988b), at their extremes these two ideologies were worlds apart with neither understanding or accepting the views of the other. Three members of the department held strong sporting ideologies and three held the same ideology in a weaker form. In such a situation Alex believed that he would have to convince his staff that his own particular idealist ideology was the 'right' one before introducing changes to the curriculum. If he could convince his staff of the 'rightness' of his views, then he felt that major structural changes could be introduced into the curriculum in a conflict free, step-by-step and efficient manner. The initial change he required was the removal of the streamed top group in games lessons and the introduction of mixed-ability grouping. Alex genuinely believed that such a change involved a value free and rational process. Consequently, he felt that one of his primary tasks was to provide relevant information and articulate a coherent rationale so that his staff would 'understand' and, therefore, 'accept' his views. Once they accepted his views he believed that they would also alter their practice of teaching in the classrooms. Alex seemed unaware that this change was far from neutral for those involved and that it acted as a major threat to the sense of self and the career aspirations of many in his department.

Alex was aware that he had the formal authority to impose change but did not wish to utilize this element of his power. This decision was, in part, related to his belief that change would best be achieved by rational debate and dialogue. He commented, 'if I just change it they'll do it, but they won't do it as good as they could do it.' Consequently, he chose to utilize the weekly departmental meetings to act as the main platform for informing his staff about his educational philosophies and the need (in his eyes) for curriculum change in the department. These meetings were to be part of an 'open' democratic department that Alex wished to create on his arrival at Branstown. However, it became clear early in the autumn term of 1983 that because he held such a strong vision of where he wanted physical education to go in the future within the department, Alex would find it very difficult to accommodate the views and interests of others. His following comment gives a hint of this: 'I have tried to make it clear to my department. If they disagree with anything I say I would rather they come out and say it, discuss it, and if I'm wrong I will say I'm wrong. If six of them say something and I still feel I'm right, I will still carry on thinking the way I do, because in the end I have to accept responsibility. I might make a decision that goes against the six, but I would still give them the opportunity to argue against me' (Alex, interview transcript). Furthermore, Alex made it clear that he was prepared to utilize his formal authority when necessary. For example, he informed the men that the prevailing practice of utilizing educational gymnastics lessons as an additional games lesson was to cease and they would all have to teach this form of gymnastics. Therefore, his visions of democracy were tempered with autocracy. The latter gradually became more dominant as Alex met with resistance to his proposals for change that he did not expect, did not understand, and which he saw as slowing down his progress towards the idealized curriculum that he wanted to be implemented in the next academic year (1984–85).

The first sign of this resistance was encountered by Alex at a school in-service day early in the autumn term of 1983. Here he presented the members of the department with a detailed breakdown of the activities taught on the curriculum which he believed showed clearly that team games were given too much emphasis and that there was a need for more individual activities to be introduced. He claimed that this was particularly so for the boys who needed to be provided with an educationally balanced programme. The handout that Alex gave to each member of the department stated that the first year boys only had 35 per cent individual activities. Unfortunately for Alex, not all the members of the department agreed with his interpretation of the nature of the activities. Those holding the strong sporting ideology argued that a great many individual skills were taught in rugby, football and cricket, so the curriculum was in fact dominated by individual activities rather than a team orientation. This led to a heated debate throughout the day as each side tried to convince the other to no avail. It also gave me as the researcher my first inkling of the passions that were to arise as the competing ideologies came into direct conflict. After the meeting during lunch Peter was considering the breakdown of the activities presented by Alex; he commented to Simon, 'So we've been totally fucking wrong have we? Totally fucking wrong for the last ten years, that's just bloody ridiculous.'

After this day Alex was more aware that his views were threatening to his staff but could not understand why they disagreed with his interpretation regarding the nature of the activities on the prevailing curriculum in terms of balance. The members of his department were rational beings so how could they not agree given the figures that he provided them with? After the in-service day he raised the issue again at several of the weekly departmental meetings only to be met with the same reaction. This led Alex to feel frustrated and bemused. It also steadily increased his hostility to the sporting ideology.

> With some of them I feel that I've got to put it in black and white, in two different areas, individual and teams. I'm not sure whether it's staring them in the face and they want to ignore it, or they are just that blind that they can't see it. I might do some bar charts to set it out more obviously. Set it out, so that it smacks them in the face really, that its 'wrong' what they are doing, and this is the way to do it 'right'. (Alex, interview transcript)

> The things stopping us from doing that at the moment [having a balanced curriculum in Alex's terms] is the fact that people want to keep the half-year games group, and the only reason that has

been put forward for it is that they like to have the top group together, the people that they will have in the teams. To give that reason is so elitist...other than being personal [to Simon] and saying 'You haven't a clue what you are on about, and the whole emphasis of your teaching is wrong.' (Alex, interview transcript)

The resistance he met over this issue confused Alex. Why was his department not convinced by his rational arguments that he felt were based on sound and proven educational principles? To him it was simple — his ideological position was right and their's was wrong. Democracy is a frustrating and time-consuming process with no guarantee of getting what you want. Yet Alex needed to get his idealized curriculum 'agreed' upon quickly so that it could be implemented at the start of the next academic year (1984–85). Indeed, the time structure of the school year provided an additional source of pressure on the form that the change process took because decisions needed to be arrived at by June or July in any given year so that the timetables could be arranged for the coming year. This meant that Alex had less than a year to introduce the initial changes he desired. This pressure, coupled with a need to create a curriculum that would allow for his own expression of self and further his career interests, meant that despite his early aspirations regarding democracy and openness his actions and tactics began to take on a more autocratic tone as the school year progressed. Having faced resistance to his proposals for change, Alex commented, 'I tell you what I see phasing out in this school, is half-year games and the top-group for the sake of getting teams out, and skills practices related to matches with the top-group. I see these being phased out. It's going to be by subtle means.' These subtle means involved the strategic use of his power resources to ensure that crucial decisions were made in his favour at those departmental meetings that focused on his proposals for change. Morgan (1986) has identified a range of sources of power that individuals can use to shape the dynamics of organizational life. The following sections deal with but a few of these to illustrate how Alex ensured that his proposals for change were 'accepted' during the academic year 1983–84.

Formal Authority

Despite Alex's attempts to play down the formal authority invested in him as departmental head, which in Weber's (1947) terms allowed for the possibility of rational-legal domination, the rest of the department recognized that Alex could 'have the final word' if he so wished. As Peter commented, 'I think that Alex will do what he wants to do whatever

Simon and myself want I must admit. If he makes a decision as Head of Department then there's not a lot that we can do really. He's the Head of Department, he's got the authority to push it [his desired changes] through, which I'm sure he will' (Peter, interview transcript). Before one departmental meeting Alex invited the staff to put down on paper their views on half-year games so that they could be raised for discussion. Regarding this invitation Simon noted, 'I will put something down. I don't think it will make the slightest bit of difference. I think that we are going to do it, and I think that he [Alex] wants us to do it, to run for a year and see how it goes' (Simon, interview transcript).

Rachel, a probationary teacher in the department , was very aware of the authority that Alex had. 'He's very forceful. I think that as a Head of Department he will get what he wants done, that's why he's Head of Department isn't it?' There was a general atmosphere in the department that, despite the rhetoric of Alex regarding open discussion and negotiation, at the end of the day he would do what he wanted and at some point he would let them know when. These perceptions were framed by the structure of the authority relationships that already existed in the school whereby the senior management team was seen to take the important decisions regarding organizational issues. As a consequence the department expected to be told what to do, as the following extract from a departmental meeting indicates. The issue under consideration was the allocation of facilities once the top group in games was abolished.

Alex: I will allocate the facilities and it is up to you to allocate what you feel is the right balance to the curriculum.

Peter: What else are you going to do in that outdoor session?

Alex: Well, you can choose to do two sessions of rugby, cross-country or football.

Peter: I thought that you were going to lay it down now what kind of sessions we are going to do.

Alex: No, I'm not going to tell you exactly what you have to do.

Peter: I thought that's what you were going to do.

Alex: No, I'm just covering the areas that you should cover...would you prefer a more rigid structure?

Peter: I just thought you were going to say it that's all. That we had to do this, this, and this.

In many ways this was not an unrealistic expectation because the other sources of power that Alex had at his disposal during departmental meetings, and which he used skilfully, meant that rarely did the outcome of the decision-making process go against him.

Control of Decision-Making Premises

The ability to influence the outcomes of the decision-making process has attracted considerable attention in the literature on organizational theory (Sathe, 1985; Schein, 1985). This form of influence has as much to do with preventing crucial decisions being made as it has with fostering desired outcomes. At the departmental meetings Alex controlled the issues to be included on the agenda and, therefore, had control over the decision-making premises, that is, the issues that were to command attention. Those that commanded attention were defined as important while other concerns were marginalized and defined as trivial. With regard to those departmental meetings that concerned his proposals for change, Alex invariably defined the issues for consideration. For example, at one of these meetings he opened the meeting by asking the staff for their opinions on the advantages and disadvantages of the present system of half-year games. At another he defined the main issue for the meeting as the lack of awareness on the part of the physical education staff regarding the overall aims and objectives of the school which were in agreement with his rationale for change.

Alex even maintained control on those occasions when he could not attend the departmental meetings himself. The following list of prepared points was given to Monica (head of girls' physical education) for her to raise as the key areas for discussion in a meeting that she was to chair when Alex was absent.

1 Are we producing the type of pupil with the right attitude to physical activity, health, and fitness?
2 If 'yes', are we producing enough of them?
3 A look at the present fifth year will help you here.
4 If we are not producing enough of them with the right attitude, how can we change the content of the curriculum to help them?
5 What we should be trying to do is — not producing only good games players (it could be argued that this is all that we do at present), but allowing pupils (through teaching pupils activities and concepts that have some personal meaning i.e. they understand the values and enjoy the activities) to leave school with a positive attitude towards participating in physical activity, combined with an understanding of the benefits of it.
6 I would advocate that in our teaching we need to construct our aims and objectives in relation to the experiences and challenges that I mentioned last week.

7   Please bring to the next meeting any alternative structure that you feel would be a better alternative for your pupils. Bring it on paper and justify your system.

Even though he was not at this meeting, Alex was able to control the main issues that were to be discussed. The manner in which these issues were formulated and framed also acted to undermine the position of those holding the sporting ideology by implying that it was deficient in terms of the range of experiences it offered to pupils. Furthermore, the 'right' way, that is Alex's way, is indicated by referring back to a framework that he provided in a previous meeting. The staff are then asked to challenge him openly by providing an 'alternative' structure within a context where he had already defined the only acceptable structure.

Control of Decision-Making Processes

As departmental head who acted as chairperson at meetings, Alex was also able to control the decision-making process which included when to make a decision and how the decision was to be reported. As a consequence it was Alex who decided at which departmental meetings during the year key issues regarding his proposals for change would be discussed and decisions made. He also controlled the order of voting at these key meetings. For instance, in the critical departmental meeting in December 1983, when he was pressing to get the top group system in games voted out, he chose to use an open verbal vote and selected the order in which he asked members of the department to speak. This tactic did not go unnoticed by Simon who was the only one to vote against the change in the absence of Peter who also disagreed.

> I thought that the way that the voting went in the meeting was very contrived. It just wanted a show of hands. It was 'Jeremy, what do you think?'...The first time was 'Jeremy, can you tell me?' You put somebody like Jeremy under pressure like that and he will say 'Yes, I'll go along with you.' Then it was Monica, then Rachel. Well, that's three down already. That leaves you with Catherine, and I was the last one to be brought into vote. So by that time it was all over and it wouldn't have made any difference I suppose.... I just said, it's obvious it's passed but I would like it minuted that someone disagreed with it.' (Simon, interview transcript).

When I questioned Alex about this tactic, he confirmed that he believed Jeremy to be a crucial vote and that he had made a decision prior to the meeting to place him under some pressure by asking for his views first. He had gained agreement from two of the women, who held weak sporting ideologies, regarding the vote prior to the meeting. It was clear that Simon would vote against the change so Alex did not want him voting first because he did not want this to influence Jeremy in any way. Rachel, a probationary teacher, was third in the voting line. She held a strong sporting ideology but, having seen both Jeremy and Monica (head of girls' PE) vote for the change, her vote was also in favour of the changes, even though during interviews with me Rachel expressed her opposition to them.

Control of Knowledge and Information

Every member of the department recognized that Alex was well read and up-to-date regarding curriculum issues. As Catherine commented, 'he is red hot in arguing his case. I think that it has helped Alex being so articulate and knowing his papers and spending time reading. He is obviously very keen.' Alex did read widely and this had been motivated by his application for the position of departmental head in the months prior to his appointment at Branstown. He was able forcefully to articulate his ideas and call upon educational theory to substantiate his claims. In this sense Alex was accustomed to operating in the 'discursive' mode of consciousness. Catherine noted, 'I think that Alex is very up-to-date on things because he has been applying for jobs, and that is one of the leading questions. You have got to know your aims and objectives, and you have to be well read in this, that, and the other, because on that he has looked at the theory quite a bit' (Catherine, interview transcript).

In addition, just after his arrival Alex had been selected as Chairperson for the Lower School Curriculum Working Party. This committee had been set up to evaluate recent trends in the school curriculum at a national level and to relate these to the future curriculum at Branstown School. Membership of such a committee gave Alex access to many recent government documents concerning the curriculum that the members of the department did not have access to. The contacts with the other staff on this committee (usually other departmental heads and the school senior management team), the access to recent educational material and the reading done to prepare him for job applications in the past meant that Alex was operating with an expanded information field. In contrast, it was noticeable how little the rest of the members of the physical education department read the educational literature. Their reading was confined almost exclusively to books and articles that dealt with the coaching of sport and how to teach skills. In this sense they operated within a restricted information field. Alex recognized this situation within the department: 'I appreciate that, not their knowledge, but their reading is very limited. Because I am involved in this other area as well (Lower School Curriculum Working Party), and because I have done a bit more reading than they have, things to me fall into place more easily than it does for them' (Alex, interview transcript).

During departmental meetings Alex utilized his expanded information field and his ability to operate in the discursive mode of consciousness constantly to define the realities of the decision-making process in his terms. That is, he invariably called upon his department to operate and articulate their views within his frame of reference. By making the discursive mode of consciousness the primary domain for communication the meetings reaffirmed his 'expert' knowledge in relation to the restricted information available to his staff. Again, this allowed Alex to define, frame and refocus issues to his advantage. For example, during one meeting the discussion had strayed away from the issue that Alex wanted to concentrate on. He redefined the issue in terms of his 'expert' knowledge and called attention back to his frame of reference. 'But going back to the aims of education and the aims of the school. The general aim of education in most recent documents in simple terms is, they say "to enrich the life of the pupils, to actually improve the life of pupils". So when they leave school, in basic terms, you have improved the quality of life for that person' (Alex, interview transcript).

The above also provides an example of the manner in which Alex acted as a 'gatekeeper' who filtered, summarized and analyzed information from a range of sources that were not available to the rest of his department. The interpretation was then presented to the department in a form that favoured his interest and supported his rationale for curriculum change. The access that Alex had to the members of the school senior management team enhanced his ability to define boundaries between segments of the school and interpret the actions of significant others for his department. The following provides an example of how the views of the deputy headteacher (Clarke Kent) underwent such a transformation during a departmental meeting when Alex was justifying his claims for curriculum change.

This also ties in with what's happening within the school at the moment. Each department is being asked by Clarke Kent, who is in charge of the curriculum in the school, to identify the needs of pupils, and to identify the aims and link them with the needs of the pupils. And he wants them to be specific, and he wants them to be linked to their current needs and their needs over the next ten years. (Alex, interview transcript)

The control of knowledge and information enabled Alex to exert strong pressures upon his staff to conform to his view of reality in the school and was closely linked to his strategic use of contrastive rhetoric in departmental meetings.

The Use of Contrastive Rhetoric

The forms of influence available to Alex enabled him to dominate the departmental meeting in terms of direction, content and outcomes. This ability was enhanced significantly by his use of contrastive rhetoric. According to Hargreaves, this form of language refers to 'that interactional strategy whereby the boundaries of normal and acceptable practice are defined by institutionally and/or interactionally dominant individuals or groups through the introduction into discussion of alternative practices and social forms in stylized, trivialized, and generally pejorative terms which connote their unacceptability' (Hargreaves, 1981, p. 309).

At Branstown School the 'alternative practices' were in fact those that operated in the prevailing curriculum, which Alex, the institutionally and interactionally dominant individual, was attempting to change. That departmental meetings were regarded as a platform from which to polarize issues to highlight and reinforce his own viewpoint is made evident in Alex's comment that 'through departmental meetings I have tried to get the department to understand my views. First of all, I'll give them my opinions of what I think is right and wrong.' This strategy involved the continual juxtapositioning of educational issues within a framework of meaning that made clear to his staff the view that Alex favoured. The following is an example of this taken from a meeting where he wished to gain agreement that the extant curriculum was not balanced and also that individual activities were superior to team games for 'educating' pupils.

As I have said, everything that we teach in PE is through experiences. Where do the children gain most? Is it through individual activities where we can gain the maximum benefit from what we have to offer them in regards to experiences, because we would know exactly what we are offering them. . . . Or is it in a games situation where they are part of a team, and there are fifteen out there and you are playing a game, or going perhaps through a skill practice, and then teach them for a lot of the lesson through that games situation? Where are they going to get the most benefit? Where can we have the most control over the experiences they have? Is it through the individual activities where we can set them tasks, be it open or closed, whether in formal gym, dance, or educational gymnastics or swimming? Where do they get the most benefit?...In a games situation we do give sometimes vague outlines of what we are getting over in that situation...but we have more control of it and we have more chance to give them these experiences in individual lessons. That's why I would like to see a change in the balance of the curriculum to give more individual work for boys. (Alex, interview transcript)

The ability to use contrastive rhetoric was another resource that was available to Alex which enabled him to influence the reality of the department. The range of resources at his disposal that were not available to his staff highlights the differential access to the cultural resources underlying the decision-making process that existed within the department. This differential access ensured that Alex held not only de jure institutional power but also possessed de facto interactional power which in combination allowed him to dominate departmental meetings and ensured that his proposals for curriculum change were voted in against the wishes of several in the department. However, having claimed that Alex was the institutionally and interactionally dominant individual at the departmental meetings should not be taken to imply that he met with no resistance from other members of the department. During departmental meetings various forms of resistance emerged.

The Exclusion of Educational Theory and Non-Classroom Events

Alex constantly attempted to get the department to operate within his frame of reference which involved the discursive mode of consciousness that drew upon 'abstract' educational theory. It became evident during the meetings that the members of the department were either unable or unwilling to operate within his particular framework in order to assess the validity of his proposals. The following conversation is taken from a meeting where Alex was attempting to focus attention on a range of concepts defined as important in recent government documents. These included 'self-directed learning' and 'taking responsibility for one's own actions', which, according to Alex, could best be achieved via individual activities rather than team games since the latter (in his opinion) turned a great many pupils off physical activity in general. These conceptual issues were given in list form to the meeting and Alex tried to focus upon them in an abstract manner.

> *Rachel:* How do you measure any activity because a child may be analyzing a game, not actually getting stuck in, but standing back and thinking about it?
>
> *Alex:* In an objective way it is very difficult but in a subjective way I think that you can look at his involvement...the way he keeps up with the game, and getting involved in that particular aspect of the sport, but I think that we all know the ones that will sit back.
>
> *Simon:* The extreme of that is we have got people who are below what we call the top-band. The ones that are less able. If you take someone like James Wright, he's an extreme of his type, less able or whatever. If you look at his involvement, his presence in the group, and the way you then teach the group because one individual changes it completely. So, are we saying which end do we aim for? Or are we supposed in a mixed-ability group to aim at the top-band, aim for the middle, or do we spend our time with the bottom ones?...When in a lesson you inevitably change your teaching methods by the fact that he's in there.
>
> *Alex:* OK, well, I've got my opinion on that but I would rather other people get involved.
>
> *Monica:* I would have thought that someone like James Wright is physically less able but not mentally. But quite often when we band our kids in games, I mean how are we banding them, physically, mentally or less able?
>
> *Simon:* I'm not criticizing his presence there, the fact that he's in there. I'm just saying that he takes part in it mentally and physically but he finds it very difficult. But the teacher teaching the lesson a lot of the time is teaching towards him at the lower end, and so, the top kids lose out to a certain extent.
>
> *Monica:* That's one advantage of individual activities isn't it?
>
> *Alex:* [Sounding very agitated and frustrated] The question 'E' poses, 'insufficient emphasis on the whole person'.

The extract indicates how, in this instance, Simon introduces a practical example into the discussion based on his own classroom experience that the rest of the department are able to relate to in terms of their experiences of dealing with low ability pupils in mixed-ability settings. Indeed, he trades on and appeals to a shared set of cultural assumptions among his colleagues regarding low ability pupils so that the meaning and the point of the example he gives are obvious to all involved. During the meetings the members of the department drew predominantly *not* upon the logic and principles of educational theory but upon their own classroom experience. They rarely turned to evidence beyond this form of experience to justify their own personal preferences. Concrete personal experience, not 'abstract' educational theory, governed their reaction to Alex's proposals for change (see also Jackson, 1968; Lortie, 1975). My interviews with the staff confirmed that they did not value educational theory as a systematic and coherent body of knowledge containing insights that might have some relevance to their classroom teaching and life in school. Consequently, this form of knowing was not an acceptable part of departmental discussions and so was culturally excluded. Considering this in his 'cultural exclusion thesis', Hargreaves notes:

> The exclusion, it seems, derives less from the ignorance of the relevance of nonclassroom matters than from the cultural pressures and assumptions as to what constitutes an acceptable account in classroom discussion. In *that* context, it was the immediate, practical situation of the classroom that mattered most of all. This was the testing ground, the court of appeal against which all claims to truth and feasibility were publicly measured. (Hargreaves, 1984, p. 250)

This, in part, helps to explain why the attempts by Alex to get the members of the department to operate within the discursive mode of consciousness and justify their views in abstract terminology failed. His appeals were transformed into practical issues relating to their own concrete experiences which had the effect of creating resistance to Alex in the meetings. The exclusion of educational theory also functioned continually to refocus the content of the meetings away from the issues that Alex wanted to gain agreement on. Intimately linked to this exclusion of theoretical evidence to substantiate proposals for change was the introduction of questions into the conversation that served to divert attention away from the issues that Alex wanted to focus on. Both of these continually deflected the issue and allowed the department to partially redefine the debate in their terms. The net effect was systematically to produce circularity within the departmental meetings; they became speculative and tangential, so that clearly defined points of agreement rarely emerged. For Alex, with his belief in change as a rational process, this circularity was bemusing and frustrating. Because he felt that he had articulated a convincing and coherent case for change, he could not understand why his department did not simply agree with him. As a consequence, he defined their contributions in these meetings as a form of resistance and felt that they were deliberately erecting obstacles to thwart him: 'I'm finding it very difficult. I'm finding it very difficult because it's such a simple thing to understand, and I think that people are deliberately ignoring it and I can't work out why.'

The Use of Silence

According to Hargreaves (1981, p. 315), 'non-responses, like silences, are highly ambiguous social events. Their meaning depends very much on the context of their occurrence.' In the context of the innovative process at Branstown School silence tended to indicate disagreement. Prolonged silence was taken to indicate active non-cooperation. Peter, who held a strong sporting ideology, utilized silence to great effect in several meetings. During the morning session of an in-service day this tactic was used and it created an atmosphere of tension and animosity. The following is an extract from my field notes on this meeting.

> The meeting had been in session for forty-five minutes and Peter was still refusing to be drawn into any discussion. He had said nothing since the meeting started, despite Alex's attempts to gain a response by looking directly at him when he asked a question. Peter's reaction was to lower his eyes and continue to doodle on a note pad in front of him. He smiled openly at some of the issues raised and the ensuing comments and nodded his head in disapproval at others. At other times he gave a quiet laugh but never gave a direct response. As the meeting progressed it was obvious that due to the circularity of the discussion in which Alex could not get any form of agreement, and the non-response of Peter, that Alex was losing his composure. The tone of his voice had changed noticeably, there was an edge to it that indicated that he was attempting to contain his anger. His face was red and he was sweating more than normal. The atmosphere within the meeting was very tense, and the rest of the staff were aware that Alex was in a state that they had never seen him in before. Towards the end of the meeting Alex was considering a technique in basketball in order to clarify a point, at which Peter made his one and only comment of the meeting 'Not really, no.' Alex stopped talking in mid-sentence, turned to Peter and said acidly 'It talks!' The room was silent and nobody laughed. It was obvious to everyone that Alex was in a state of anger. (Extract from field notes)

The next day when they were together to organize some school matches, Monica and Catherine noted that this was the first time that anyone in the department had seen Alex lose his temper. Alex, in a telephone conversation with me on the same evening as the meeting, jokingly mentioned that if Peter had been sitting closer to him, he would not have been accountable for his actions. He admitted that he had left the meeting 'bloody well raging'. In a reflective consideration of this incident in 1984 he commented, 'they either didn't want to see the point or couldn't see the point, and I became more and more upset about it, because I thought that I had put it in black and white.... That's when I began to lose my temper.' Once again this provided an example of the frustration that Alex felt when he could not get those in his department to agree with him on a 'rational' basis. Significantly, after this meeting in November 1983 Alex began gradually to increase his domination of those departmental meetings that centred on his proposals for curriculum change.

Concluding Remarks

Clearly, this is a partial picture of the change process that took place in the physical education department at Branstown School. However, it does raise some questions regarding the assumptions of curriculum change as a rational, linear and value free process. Furthermore, it illustrates the problems encountered when an individual operating with these assumptions attempts to introduce curriculum change in a school. Indeed, the issue of change at Branstown School was value laden for those involved, which means that the departmental meetings that I have described were not characterized by consensus or rationality in the idealized sense. Tensions, misunderstandings and anxieties emerged within them as this group of teachers attempted to protect and enhance a range of interests within the decision-making process. The departmental meetings acted as an arena of struggle in which future winners and losers, with different and competing value systems, ideologies and power resources, clashed in the innovative process.

It was only when, in 1984–86, he enrolled for a diploma course in management at a local polytechnic that Alex realized how his own assumptions regarding the change process had acted against his visions of democratic leadership and informed the autocratic stance he ended up taking. As part of this course he had to reflect on his attempts to innovate and this included him interviewing members of his department concerning their views on the change process that he had initiated at Branstown

School. In a series of reflective essays on his management approach he commented:

> Halfway through the year I introduced my ideas for curriculum change. My first and biggest mistake on reflection. There was agreement by some members and a revealing silence from others. In the months that followed there was more conflict between myself and other members than at any other time in the two years that I have been there. . . . It was a time of great concern. I was initially trying to develop a comfortable and friendly atmosphere and ended up taking an autocratic line. . . . Having given them the opportunity to become involved [in decision-making] with no results, I became frustrated and began to introduce changes with a tendency to steamroller them through meetings. On reflection, and again from feedback from interviews, this was the worst possible strategy I could have adopted at the time. I was putting up a front, stating that I wanted them to contribute ideas, and yet quite blatantly pushing through my own ideas. This period saw me at my lowest ebb in this school. I could not understand why there was an atmosphere of distrust behind what was a show of conformity.

By engaging in individual in-depth interviews with his staff regarding their personal views on the innovative process Alex came to realize that there was a range of costs and rewards for those involved. He began to realize that their ideological stance regarding the nature of education and the teaching of physical education was very different from his. Importantly, Alex was able to see how their sense of self, career aspirations and feelings of professional competence, that is, a range of self, professional and ideological interests, were bound up in these differing value systems and the manner in which his proposals for change threatened these at a deep and profound level. It became clear to him that several of his department had a great deal to lose in terms of the curriculum changes that, for him, would be very rewarding. As such, their resistance needed to be seen as part of the intelligent action of teachers in the context of their working lives rather than as a pathological form of behaviour that required suppression by autocratic measures. Alex recognized how he had invited symbolic participation at departmental meetings, that is, he had been involved in creating the illusion of participatory democracy in the decision-making process without ever giving any indication to his staff that he was prepared to relinquish control over this process.

Prior to these interviews with his staff, and guided by his belief in the assumptions of rational curriculum change, Alex had not been aware of the multiple realities that existed. Indeed, his use of the power resources at his disposal acted to deny these realities. In Lightball's (1974) frame of analysis these assumptions had operated to prevent Alex from conceptualizing the department as having $n+1$ dimensions. Here n relates to the number of group members and $+1$ constitutes the objective reality of which they are a part, that at once includes them and provides the context for their distinctive and always partially overlapping realities. However, for Alex during the academic year 1983–84 there could be only one acceptable reality and that was his, and the major task was seen in terms of converting his department to this reality by 'rational' means. As I have indicated, this approach was self-defeating because if communication is conceived to be a process whereby two or more people *mutually* enlarge the commonality of their separate realities, then little communication took place in the departmental meetings which were characterized by a pooling of collective ignorance that denied the plurality of value systems that the teachers held.

Essentially, Alex dominated the departmental meetings in order to impose his reality on the staff. His was the only acceptable reality, it was the 'right' one and their's was wrong. In doing so, the fears and anxieties of his staff were glossed over in the belief that once they 'understood' the change these concerns would disappear and the resistance to his proposals cease. This did not happen. Furthermore, since it was his department who had to carry the educational goals and images of his reality into action, that is, to make much of his reality their's at a practical level, and since no person responds to realities other than his/her own, then Alex's adoption of a one-way form of communication in departmental meetings, based on his belief in rational change, was doomed to failure. For his reality to become their's, he would have had to make part of their's his, but this could not happen because their reality was defined as 'wrong' and marginalized in the meetings by the use of various power resources.

Since the realities of his staff were 'wrong', Alex used the departmental meetings as a platform to articulate his personal rationale for change and to provide a range of answers for his staff so that they would fully understand his proposals and then be supportive of them. Unfortunately, the 'solutions' provided by Alex were answers to 'problems' defined by himself. Little attention was given to the nature and components of the problems as conceived by the rest of the department who held an educational ideology that differed greatly from his own. For many, in their n individual realities, the problems that Alex defined did not exist for them in their daily lives. However, since reality exists in the

n and not the $+1$ reality, then for the members of the department to invest their energies in a problem, it had to come to exist for them in their n realities. For those holding the strong sporting ideology this simply was not the case. The extant curriculum at Branstown School allowed them to enhance a range of vested, ideological and self-interests. Indeed, the curriculum at Branstown School prior to the arrival of Alex was a direct expression of this particular ideology. Therefore, Alex ended up employing a problem-solving process that consistently ignored the question: 'Whose problem are we solving?' As a consequence, the costs and rewards for those involved did not become a central focus in the departmental meetings. This being the case, Alex was unable to unfold the realities of his staff from the private domain to the public arena, and was forced to cope blindly with the private realities that guided his staff during the year.

In closing, I wish to emphasize that Alex was a well-meaning individual. My intention has not been to portray him as the villain of the piece, as a power-wielding ogre who did not care about his staff. Nothing could be further from the truth. The events described at Branstown School caused Alex a great deal of personal anguish precisely because he did want to work closely with his staff and provide them with a supportive atmosphere for change. The real issue is the manner in which a belief in change as a rational, linear and value free process guided his actions and the way in which this affected his relationships with the other members of the department. The rational view of change finds it hard to tolerate ambiguity, conflict and the plurality of value systems that operate in schools both between and within departments. The response often involves the use of a range of power resources to ensure that the linearity of the process is maintained. Consequently, change is imposed upon people, which means that they rarely gain any sense of personal ownership of the very process in which they are central. However, since the realities of individuals are enlarged by exchange and not domination, the change process guided by the assumptions of the rational framework is self-defeating. It ends up contributing to the very thing it wishes to deny, that is, the presence and centrality of conflict and struggle. Furthermore, as the events at Branstown School indicate, the notion of rational change fails to match the realities of life in schools. Here change as a dynamic process is characterized by conflict, struggle, negotiations and compromise as individuals and subject areas strive to enhance their interests. Once this is accepted, then we are in a position to move beyond the myth of rational change to understand how interests and power operate in the process of innovation.

Notes

1 The following are but a few who provide critiques of the 'objectives' or 'rational' approach to curriculum planning and change: Barrow (1984), Eisner (1985), Giroux (1981), Holt (1987), Hoyle (1986), Kirk (1988a), Kirk and Smith (1986), Lawton (1989), Olsen (1982), Stenhouse (1975).
2 Aspects of this work are provided in Sparkes (1989, 1988a, 1988b, 1987a, 1987b, 1986). See also Kirk's (1988b) study for a similar treatment of teacher participation in school-centred innovation in physical education.

References

ARNOLD, P. (1985) 'Rational Planning by Objectives of the Movement Curriculum'. *Physical Education Review*, 8 (1), 50–61.

ARNOLD, P. (1988) *Education, Movement and the Curriculum*. Lewes: Falmer Press.

BACHARACH, S. (1988) 'Notes on the Political Theory of Educational Organizations' in WESTOBY, A. (Ed.), *Culture and Power in Educational Organizations*. Milton Keynes: Open University Press.

BACHARACH, S. and LAWLER, E. (1980) *Power and Politics in Organizations*. San Francisco, Calif.: Jossey Bass.

BALL, S. (1981) *Beachside Comprehensive: A Case-Study of Secondary Schooling*. Cambridge: Cambridge University Press.

BALL, S. (1985) 'School Politics, Teachers' Careers, and Educational Change: A Case-study of Becoming a Comprehensive School,' in BARTON, L. and WALKER, S. (Eds), *Educational and Social Change*. London: Croom Helm.

BALL, S. (1987) *The Micro-Politics of the School: Towards a Theory of School Organization*. London: Methuen.

BALL, S. (1989) 'Micro-politics versus Management: Towards a Sociology of School Organization,' in WALKER, S. and BARTON, L. (Eds), *Politics and the Processes of Schooling*. Milton Keynes: Open University Press.

BALL, S. and LACEY, C. (1984) 'Subject Disciplines as the Opportunity for Group Action: A Measured Critique of Subject Sub-cultures,' in HARGREAVES, A. and WOODS, P. (Eds), *Classrooms and Staffrooms*. Milton Keynes: Open University Press.

BARROW, R. (1984) *Giving Teaching Back to Teachers: A Critical Introduction to Curriculum Theory*. Brighton: Wheatsheaf.

BELL, L. (1986) 'Managing to Survive in Secondary School Physical Education.' in EVANS, J. (Ed.), *Physical Education, Sport and Schooling: Studies in the Sociology of Physical Education*. Lewes: Falmer Press.

BENYON, J. (1985) 'Career Histories in a Comprehensive School.' in BALL, S. and GOODSON, I. (Eds), *Teachers' Lives and Careers*. Lewes: Falmer Press.

BLASE, J. (1988) 'The Everyday Political Perspective of Teachers: Vulnerability and Conservatism.' *International Journal of Qualitative Studies in Education*. 1 (2), 125–42.

DALTON, T. (1988) *The Challenge of Curriculum Innovation: A Study of Ideology and Practice*. Lewes: Falmer Press.

EISNER, E. (1985) *The Art of Educational Evaluation: A Personal View*. Lewes: Falmer Press.

EVANS, J., LOPEZ, S., DUNCAN, M. and EVANS, M. (1987) 'Some Thoughts on the Political and Pedagogical Implications of Mixed Sex Grouping in the Physical Education Curriculum.' *British Educational Research Journal*, 13 (1), 59–71.

FEIMAN-NEMSER, S. and FLODEN, R. (1986) 'The Cultures of Teaching,' in WITT-ROCK, M. (Ed.), *Handbook of Research on Teaching*. London: Collier Macmillan.

FULLAN, M. (1982) *The Meaning of Educational Change*. New York: Teachers College Press.

GANS, H. (1982) 'The Participant Observer as Human Being: Observations on the Personal Aspects of Fieldwork,' in BURGESS, R. (Ed.), *Field Research: A Sourcebook and Field Manual*. London: Allen and Unwin.

GIROUX, H. (1981) *Ideology, Culture and the Process of Schooling*. Lewes: Falmer Press.

GLEW, P. (1983) 'Are Your Fixtures Really Necessary?' *British Journal of Physical Education*, 14, 126–28.

GOFFMAN, I. (1959) *The Presentation of Self in Everyday Life*. New York: Anchor Books.

GRONN, P. (1986) 'Politics, Power and the Management of Schools.' in HOYLE, E. and McMAHON, A. (Eds), *World Yearbook of Education, 'The Management of Schools'*. London: Kogan Page.

HAMMERSLEY, M. and ATKINSON, P. (1983) *Ethnography: Principles in Practice*. London: Tavistock Publications.

HARGREAVES, A. (1981) 'Contrastive Rhetoric and Extremist Talk: Teachers, Hegemony and the Educationist Context.' in BARTON, L. and WALKER, S. (Eds), *Schools, Teachers and Teaching*. Lewes: Falmer Press.

HARGREAVES, A. (1984) 'Experience Counts, Theory Doesn't: How Teachers Talk about Their Work.' *Sociology of Education*, 57 (October), 244–54.

HINDNESS, B. (1982) 'Power, Interests and the Outcomes of Struggle'. *Sociology*, 16 (4), 498–512.

HOLT, M. (1987) *Judgement, Planning and Educational Change*. London: Harper and Row.

HOYLE, E. (1986) *The Politics of School Management*. London: Hodder and Stoughton.

JACKSON, P. (1968) *Life in Classrooms*. New York: Holt Rinehart and Winston.

JEWETT, A. and BAIN, L. (1985) *The Curriculum Process in Physical Education*. Dubuque, Iowa: Brown.

KEDDIE, N. (1971) 'Classroom Knowledge.' in YOUNG, M. (Ed.), *Knowledge and Control*. London: Collier MacMillan.

KIRK, D. (1988a) *Physical Education and Curriculum Study: A Critical Introduction*. London: Croom Helm.

KIRK, D. (1988b) 'Ideology and School-Centred Innovation: A Case Study and a Critique.' *Journal of Curriculum Studies*, 20 (5), 449–64.

KIRK, D. and SMITH, S. (1986) 'How Objective Are ROSBA Objectives? A Critique of Objectivism in Curriculum Design.' *Curriculum Perspectives*, 6 (2), 32–6.

LACEY, C. (1977) *The Socialization of Teachers*. London: Methuen.

LAWTON, D. (1989) *Education, Culture and the National Curriculum*. London: Hodder and Stoughton.

LIGHTBALL, F. (1974) 'Multiple Realities and Organizational Nonsolutions: An Essay on Anatomy of Educational Innovation.' *School Review*, 18 (February), 255–93.

LORTIE, D. (1975) *Schoolteacher: A Sociological Study*. Chicago, Ill.: University of Chicago Press.

MORGAN, G. (1986) *Images of Organization*. London: Sage.

NIAS, J. (1984) 'The Definition and Maintenance of Self in Primary Teaching.' *British Journal of Sociology of Education*, 5 (3), 267–80.

NIAS, J. (1985) 'A More Distant Drummer: Teacher Development and the Development of Self,' in BARTON, L. and WALKER, S. (Eds), *Education and Social Change*. London: Croom Helm.

NICHOLLS, A. (1983) *Managing Educational Innovations*. London: George Allen and Unwin.

OLSEN, J. (1982) 'Classroom Knowledge and Curriculum Change: An Introduction,' in OLSEN, J. (Ed.), *Innovation in the Science Curriculum*. London: Croom Helm.

POPPLETON, P. (1988) 'Teacher Professional Satisfaction: Its Implications for Secondary Education and Teacher Education.' *Cambridge Journal of Education*, 18 (1), 5–16.

RISEBOROUGH, G. (1981) 'Teacher Careers and Comprehensive Schooling: An Empirical Study.' *Sociology*, 15 (3), 355–81.

RISEBOROUGH, G. (1988) 'The Great Heddekashun War: A Life Historical Cenotaph for an Unknown Teacher.' *International Journal of Qualitative Studies in Education*, 1 (3), 197–223.

ROSKIES, E., LIKER, J. and ROITMAN, D. (1988) 'Winners and Losers: Employee Perceptions of Their Company's Technological Transformation.' *Journal of Organizational Behavior*, 9, 123–37.

SATHE, V. (1985) *Managerial Action and Corporate Culture*. Homewood, Il.: Irwin Press.

SCHEIN, E. (1985) *Organizational Culture and Leadership*. London: Jossey Bass.

SHAW, K. (1988) 'Rationality, Experience and Theory.' in WESTOBY, A. (Ed.), *Culture and Power in Educational Organizations*. Milton Keynes: Open University Press.

SIEDENTOP, D. (1983) *Developing Teaching Skills in Physical Education*. Palo Alto, Calif.: Mayfield.

SIKES, P., MEASOR, L. and WOODS, P. (1985) *Teachers' Careers: Crises and Continuities*. Lewes: Falmer Press.

SILVERMAN, D. (1970) *The Theory of Organizations*. London: Heinemann.

SPARKES, A. (1986) 'Strangers and Structures in the Process of Innovation,' in Evans, J. (Ed.), *Physical Education, Sport and Schooling: Studies in the Sociology of Physical Education*. Lewes: Falmer Press.

SPARKES, A. (1987a) 'Strategic Rhetoric: A Constraint in Changing the Practice of Teachers.' *British Journal of Sociology of Education*, 8 (1), 37–54.

SPARKES, A. (1987b) The Genesis of an Innovation: A Case Study of Emergent Concerns and Micropolitical Solutions. Unpublished doctoral thesis, Loughborough University of Technology.

SPARKES, A. (1988a) 'Strands of Commitment within the Process of Teacher Initiated Innovation.' *Educational Review*, 40 (3), 301–17.

SPARKES, A. (1988b) 'The Micropolitics of Innovation in the Physical Education Curriculum.' in EVANS, J. (Ed.), *Teachers, Teaching and Control in the Physical Education Curriculum: Studies in the Sociology of Physical Education.* Lewes: Falmer Press.

SPARKES, A. (1989) 'The Achievement Orientation and Its Influence upon Innovation in Physical Education.' *Physical Education Review*, 12 (1), 36–43.

STENHOUSE, L. (1975) *An Introduction to Curriculum Research and Development.* London: Heinemann.

TEMPLIN, T., SPARKES, A. and SCHEMPP, P. (in process) *Physical Education Teachers: A Cross-Cultural Analysis.* Indianapolis, Ind.: Benchmark Press.

TYLER, R. (1949) *Basic Principles of Curriculum and Instruction.* Chicago, Ill.: University of Chicago Press.

WEBER, M. (1947) *The Theory of Social and Economic Organization.* Oxford: Oxford University Press.

WOODS, P. (1984) 'Teacher, Self and Curriculum,' in GOODSON, I. and BALL, S. (Eds), *Defining the Curriculum.* Lewes: Falmer Press.

Chapter 9

Images of Healthism in Health-Based Physical Education[1]

Derek Colquhoun

There can be no doubt that in the last two decades we have seen an increased societal interest in health matters. This is reflected in many cultural arenas, not the least of which is a growing trend to refocus physical education towards health-based issues. Health-Based Physical Education (HBPE) is becoming firmly established as the new orthodoxy in primary, secondary and tertiary education institutions in North America, Britain and parts of Australia. Health in itself has become a concept through which we structure our symbolic meanings and associations in our daily experiences. As with the body, health is socially defined and, as Crawford (1986) suggests, 'it is a category of experience that reveals tacit assumptions about individual and social reality.' Since many aspects of our day-to-day living are influenced by issues pertaining to health, and there is an ever growing discourse on the subject, we need to understand the symbolic meanings which people associate with health and all that this entails.

Health is something which we all experience either physically or socially (however it is defined) and therefore we all have some understanding of what it means to be healthy or to be ill. 'Health is a "key word", a generative concept, a value attached to or suggestive of other cardinal values. "Health" provides a means for personal and social evaluation' (Crawford, 1986, p. 62). Building on and extending the work of Crawford (1986), I will illustrate and highlight how health is presented in the process of schooling and how the ideological meanings and values associated with this presentation are accepted and worked through by teachers, pupils and the writers of curriculum materials, particularly as they relate to physical education. I will show how culturally determined messages are translated into the school context and will question some of the taken-for-granted assumptions about the nature and presentation of health.

Healthism as Ideology

To focus on the individualistic nature of the increased health consciousness, Crawford (1986) has coined the term 'healthism'. For Crawford
healthism involves

> the preoccupation with personal health as a primary — often *the*
> primary — focus for the definition and achievement of personal
> wellbeing; a goal which is attained primarily through the mod-
> ification of lifestyles...healthists will acknowledge in other words
> that health problems may originate outside the individual, e.g. in
> the American diet, but since these problems are also behavioural,
> solutions are seen to lie within the realm of individual choice.
> Hence they require above all else the assumption of individual
> responsibility. (Crawford, 1986, p. 368, original emphasis)

Healthism acts as an ideology by reducing the complex causes or
etiology of diseases to simple behaviour or lifestyle factors. An increase in
the amount of aerobic exercise, for example, is often posited as a major
strategy recruited to combat coronary heart disease (Cooper, 1968). Because of the emphasis given to exercise, other avenues for improving
health are often ignored or neglected. As an ideology, healthism serves to
depoliticize other attempts at improving health. It appears 'natural' and
'given' that individuals should take responsibility for their own health.
Self-responsibility for health is a major facet of healthism which may
serve as an illusion 'that we can as *individuals* control our own existence,
and that taking personal action to improve health will somehow satisfy
the longing for a much varied complex of needs' (Crawford, 1986, p.
368, original emphasis). As I will show later in this chapter, healthism is
the dominant ideology in health education in schools and is a central
construct in the new trend towards HBPE which is now developing in
Britain, the USA and Australia (Kirk and Colquhoun, 1989).

In an examination of the presentation of health in the school curriculum it is possible to adopt the framework developed by Crawford (1986).
In 1981 Crawford embarked on an ethnographic study of sixty adults
(who were mainly white, middle-class and female) in an attempt to
discover how these people perceived health. The 'foreshadowed problems' in his study were described as follows.

> I did not come to these interviews with the idea of 'testing' a
> particular theoretical proposition. I did not know what I would
> find. In the interviews I attempted...to remain open to unantici-
> pated avenues of discussion. This approach, of course, needed to

be balanced against the need to address a consistent set of concerns. I wanted to know how people describe their health; how they define the term and what concepts are employed (each interview began with the questions, Are you healthy? How do you know?). I also wanted people to talk about their explanations for their state of health: what they identify about themselves or their physical or social environments as important; what they perceive as a threat to their health; and what, if anything, they believe they can or should do to protect or enhance their health. (Crawford, 1986, p. 64)

To analyze his data Crawford used a grounded theory approach (Glaser and Strauss, 1967) which enabled the generation and development of two central explanatory conceptual categories. Accepting that most people described their health in the 'prevailing medical idiom' using popular medical discourse and that health was viewed as dynamic or transient, Crawford developed the concepts of 'health as self-control' and 'health as release'. It was to these two mandates that Crawford turned to explain how health was given its expressive form by the individuals in his study.

Healthism, Self-Control and Schooling

According to Crawford, intrinsic aspects of health as self-control include ascetic self-denial, self-discipline and will-power. Modern Western culture is presented as possessing an inviting, tempting and often hazardous magnetism for the unwary. The individual is constantly bombarded with 'unhealthy' options such as smoking, drinking alcohol and overeating. For the individual there must be a commitment to health since, in this discourse of consumption, health does not come naturally. Individuals must develop a health ethic which involves making sacrifices of time and effort to 'work' on their health, perseverance to maintain their practices and habits, and a motivation to curb their interests, excesses and inclinations.

This health ethic is summed up in the following quotes from his interviewees.

To be healthy takes a little more discipline.

I have to go back and take a look at my lifestyle. I have to find time for it...I think I have to be more concerned or excited about being healthier.

We both belong to a private club that allows us to do more for our health as far as exercise is concerned. It's just fitting it into that bloody schedule. Right now it's difficult. It's like saying I don't have time to be healthy. (in Crawford, 1986, p. 68)

The feeling of guilt for our personal failings is a crucial aspect of interpretations of health as self-control. This is no more evident than in our relationship to food which, as Chernin (1981) has suggested, is often exhibited through constant dieting and overeating.

Diet has almost always been a fundamental, underpinning principle in the practices of powerful social institutions like medicine and the church. Turner (1982), for example, cites the work of George Cheyne in the eighteenth century who was concerned with 'dietetick management' and was based on control in which individuals had a 'religious duty' for their own health and the health of the social body. This religious calling, self-responsibility and duty were accepted in precedence to medicine — the reverse of which is perhaps the case today. Tinning (1985), in his critique of 'Physical Education and the Cult of Slenderness', suggests that the physical education profession is complicit in reinforcing messages which emphasize a 'socially desirable body image'. To be fat is to be socially unacceptable and often people find fatness repugnant. Crawford suggests that people are frequently judged by their weight or appearance; 'within a second you make a judgement saying this person is healthy or not' (Crawford, 1986, p. 70). Crawford argues that thinness is equated with self-control, discipline and will-power, a matter of mind over body. A lack of self-control was frequently cited, for example, by Suler and Bartholomew's (1986) case study of 'Overeaters Anonymous', a self-help group established to help people cope with their perceived overeating. Overeaters are influenced by the current 'cultural fanaticism' for the socially trim body and therefore often feel guilty for their overeating and subsequent obesity. Indeed, it is important to note that obesity has become a medicalized issue. This is evident from a content analysis of *Index Medicus* conducted by Kohler Reissman (1983). Prior to 1960 obesity was rarely mentioned in the medical literature. However, by 1981 there was a considerable increase in the literature concerning all aspects of obesity.

For many, a cycle of overeating, guilt and more overeating is often the result of an obsession with food and culturally determined images. These tendencies are portrayed as a lack of self-control and will-power. 'Who wouldn't be obsessed with food after being told that all her problems are due to her not being in control of food?' (Aldebaran, 1975, cited in Tinning, 1985, p. 1). Typically, the exercising of self-control and will-power is a replacement for a lack of control over their immediate environment and daily experiences. Feelings of political impotence are often associated with the individual's explanation of health as self-control. 'When the macro-conditions that affect health appear out of control, self-control over the considerable range of personal behaviours that also affect health is the only remaining option' (Crawford, 1986, p. 74). In the next section I will expand on this analysis of health as self-control and explore and illustrate the presentation of health as self-control within the process of schooling. School is, of course, part of the wider social matrix and is vulnerable to the various meanings, significations and interpretations which are associated with the concept of health. I will examine the ways in which health is presented, legitimated and accepted within schools and also how the messages associated with health are contested, refracted and transformed.

Health, Self-Control and Schooling

Health as self-control emerges as a major focusing concept in school health education through two prevailing messages: first, a mechanistic conception of the human body; and second, a reliance on the closely related controlling devices of 'self-responsibility' and 'habits'.

The Human Body as a Machine

You know the model of your car,
You know just what its powers are,
You treat it with a deal of care,
Nor tax it more than it will bear,

But as to self — that's different;
Your mechanism may be bent,
Your carburettor gone to grass,
Your engine just a rusty mass,
Your wheels may wobble and your cogs
Be handed over to the dogs
And then you skip and skid and slide
Without a thought of things inside.

What fools indeed, we mortals are,
To lavish care upon a car,
And ne'er a bit of time to see
About our own machinery.
(John Hendrick Hangs, cited in Howell and Howell, 1983, p. 277)

I have already mentioned that the body is a culturally and socially determined object associated with meanings, beliefs and values. However, self-control is a dominating idiom dictating the presentation of the body in health education and in the new HBPE. The message is one of precision and control (Linder, 1970), where the body is portrayed as a machine needing regular servicing and maintenance.[2] The mechanistic model of the body developed from Cartesian rationality presented the body as a 'statue or machine of clay' (Turner, 1982). According to Turner, it was Harvey's work on circulation which suggested that the body was 'an Hydraulic Machine, fill'd with liquor' and that 'the health of this system of pipes, pumps and passages could only be maintained by appropriate supplies of food and liquid.'

Nowhere is this message made more clear in school health education literature than in *The Body Owners Manual* (BOM) which was written by some of the researchers involved in the development of the Daily Physical Education Program in Australia (Coonan, Worsley and Maynard, 1984).[3] BOM was designed to 'complement' the Daily Physical Education Program and as such was a workbook for students to reinforce theoretically the practical daily physical education work. BOM included sections on 'Health and Lifestyle', 'Body Systems', 'Fitness', 'Rest and Relaxation' and 'Nutrition'. Within each of these sections there were numerous activities for the children to complete. The manual was 'extensively reviewed, evaluated and revised' as a result of empirical work which showed that children 'acquired a sophisticated knowledge of epidemiology, lifestyle, and health relationships. In addition, they exhibited changes in food beliefs and lunch-time dietary behaviours e.g. reduced consumption of energy-rich foods' (Coonan, Worsley and Maynard, 1984, p. 1). The relationship here between the body and machines is clear. 'The body is like other machines (e.g. cars) and animals. In order to move they all need ENERGY.' The analogy of the motor car lends itself nicely and uncritically to the human body, as these extracts from BOM illustrate.

> In cars, petrol is mixed with air and burnt to produce energy to be used for movement. In people, our 'petrol' comes from digested food we eat. It is also mixed with air.
>
> The blood takes the fuel to our millions of motors (our cells). Some is used for movement.
>
> In a car, petrol and air are burnt in the engine to produce energy which works the motor and turns the wheels and moves the car along the road.
>
> Petrol + Air → Energy for Movement + Exhaust fumes + Heat

In the body, oxygen (part of the air breathed in through the lungs) is mixed with nutrients (food) in the blood. In the cells this is used to produce energy which enables muscles to move our arms, legs and other body parts.

Oxygen + Food → Energy for movement + Wastes + Heat

Unlike a car which has only one engine, the body has millions of small, energy, producing cells in all systems of the body. (p. 95)

Not only does the title of the workbook, *Body Owners Manual*, imply notions of self-control and self-responsibility but so too do the headings of the individual modules within the book.

Module 7 — You've got to work on your health right now.
Module 9 — Your good health depends on you.
Module 10 — Taking control.
Module 43 — Taking control of your diet.

It is within Module 10, 'Taking Control', that we find the classic and 'Sad Tale of Neville Winfield and His Custom-Made Motor Car'.

Neville's eyes twinkled as he looked over his new red, custom-made sports car. Just the thing, he thought, to set off his image as a busy young up-and-coming businessman. . . .
His car soon fitted into his busy lifestyle. As he rushed from job to job, he would screech into the station, 'Fill 'er up' he would shout, and then, with tyres screaming, he would screech off to his next appointment.
It was six months later and Neville was running late as usual, his car radio blaring, a cigarette smouldering as he sped to his Thursday night businessman's get together. Suddenly the funny engine noise which had started two weeks before, became a roar, then a loud thump as the motor stopped dead and the car limped to a halt.
Neville was furious! His face reddened and he banged his fist against the car. . . . **'Stupid***Machine!!'** he shouted. 'There is no way I'm getting stuck with a hopeless machine like this, especially as it costs so much,' he thought.
Neville rang the auto club and had the car taken back to the dealer. The next day the car dealer listened quietly as Neville, partly hidden behind a cloud of smoke, but still red in the face, complained about the poor quality of the car, and about his rotten luck in getting such a bad model. He made up his mind. The car had to be fixed at the dealer's expense or be replaced by a new

model. The dealer politely agreed to have his mechanics inspect the damage and told Neville to come back the following day, to hear the diagnosis.

When Neville heard the diagnosis he nearly blew a gasket. **The diagnosis**....
1 a failure to add oil or water
2 bald tyres
3 a melted motor. The car was a complete mechanical mess. Worse news was still to come. The car dealer flatly refused to fix up the damage. **'The fault'**, he said, **'was not with the car, or due to bad luck, but it was due to your utter stupidity!'** In other words the diagnosis is bad car maintenance.

Neville was furious. 'I'll take you to court!' he yelled. Unfortunately Neville was the third stupid driver the dealer had confronted for the week. The dealer intended Neville to be the last. 'Get out you twit!' yelled the dealer, his patience exhausted. 'From the look of your red face and all your coughing and spluttering, I would say you are in worse shape than your car. **If you cannot look after yourself — how can you expect to look after a car?'**

Neville's main problem was that he failed to take control and organise a regular maintence check for both himself and his car....

To Take Control
(1) You need knowledge about how things work.
(2) You need knowledge about the needs of the parts.
(3) You need skills to maintain those parts.
(4) You need a regular maintenance plan.

Being Healthy...means all systems 'Go'.
...and requires regular checking of each system.
(Coonan, Worsley and Maynard, 1984, pp. 57–8, original emphasis)

The messages from this sad tale are obvious. Individuals need to look after themselves and they need a certain amount of self-control to be able to organize regular servicing and maintenance. Indeed, regular servicing and maintenance are desirable and essential. If an individual does not subscribe to his/her maintenance schedule, then 'the fault' is theirs — a reinforcement of the 'your fault dogma' and victim blaming approach (Crawford, 1978). Luck plays little role in maintaining good health —

this is something which needs to be worked on and striven for, or in Almond's case it needs to be achieved:

> it must be pointed out that this concern for health makes it an *achievement* word. It is not something that is done just for a few weeks in order to store the benefits in the bank and picked up again when the mood suits one. It is an *achievement* that only comes about because people incorporate frequent physical activity into their lifestyles and maintain it on a regular basis. This is an important point to remember. (Almond, 1988a, p. 2, original emphasis)

This might suggest that Almond sees health as a 'product', as an end point, in contradiction to an ongoing and dynamic process. Of course, health may be viewed as a product which still needs working on. This is where we find the idea of healthy habits useful.

Healthy Habits: Maintaining the Servicing Schedule

Here is the link between the Cartesian mechanistic conception of the body and the controlling devices of 'self-responsibility' and 'habits'. Individuals need self-control, self-discipline and will-power constantly to upgrade and maintain the body. To achieve health they need to go out and work for it — luck or serendipity will not bring it their way. Individuals cannot store health and fitness, and each needs regular attention. 'The goal is achieving regular exercise patterns. Due to the transient nature of health related fitness ('use it or lose it'), it requires regular participation if fitness levels are to be maintained' (Biddle, 1987, p. 47). To develop regular servicing which the body needs, one requires self-responsibility — 'this book [*BOM*] is based on evidence that young Australians can make good choices, and become responsible for their own health...and if given the chance can teach their families 'Good Health Habits''' (Coonan, Worsley and Maynard, 1984, p. 4) — and intelligence — 'the Body Owners Manual is a personal challenge, not only to the intelligence of body owners but to their bodies as well...' (Coonan, Worsley and Maynard, 1984, p. 5). Whether it be self-responsibility or what the Australian Better Health Commission (1986) terms 'self-reliance', the message is clear; individuals have a moral duty to themselves and to society to make these intelligent decisions concerning their health. It is through this notion of self-responsibility that the ideology of healthism is so pervasively presented in health education materials such as the *BOM*.

A major determinant in the debate between individual freedom for health and environmental determinism is the notion of 'healthy habits'. This is the idea that there are certain habits which, if pursued daily, would reduce the incidence of elected diseases such as coronary heart disease. These healthy habits developed from the work of large-scale epidemiological studies (see Morris *et al.*, 1953; Paffenbarger and Hale, 1975; Keys, 1970). From these studies 'risk factors' were identified (inactivity, obesity, smoking, hypertension) and to reduce the effects of these risk factors individuals were encouraged to participate in lifestyle changes or healthy habits. For example, the writers of Module 4 of *BOM*, entitled 'Lifestyle Can Be a Health Hazard', suggest that 'the way most Australians live today is a health hazard i.e. not enough physical activity, too much of the wrong foods, often not enough sleep, too much stress. To be healthy we need to understand what is wrong with our present lifestyle, what causes the problems and how to do something about it' (Coonan, Worsley and Maynard, 1984, p. 27). Many health educators would readily espouse the notion of 'healthy habits'; a cursory glance at any health education textbook would be able to identify at least seven of these daily habits. However, the authors of *BOM* are not satisfied with this. In Module 9, 'Your Good Health Depends on You', the healthy habits become more forceful and are called the 'Rules of Healthy Living'.

Rule 1 regular, vigorous activity
Rule 2 eating more fresh fruit and vegetables and wholegrain foods
Rule 3 eating less sugar and sugary foods
Rule 4 eating less fatty foods
Rule 5 eating less salt and salty foods
Rule 6 learning how to relax and how to deal with stress
Rule 7 getting plenty of rest
Rule 8 not smoking
Rule 9 not misusing drugs like alcohol, caffeine (tea, coffee, cola) and pain killers
(Coonan, Worsley and Maynard, 1984, p. 53)

An important point to bear in mind with these principles is not just that they are expressed as rules, but rather that five out of the nine involve some notion of abstinence or temperance. They subscribe to a 'thou shalt not' mentality which reinforces the self-control mandate along the lines of will-power, and, therefore, failure to live by the rules can do nothing but increase feelings of guilt and profligacy for lack of responsibility and moral and social concern. This 'thou shalt not' mentality does not rely on individuals having a guilty conscience for simply breaking the rules for breaking the rules sake. Rather, it is a guilt formed by a realization that something has been lost. In the case of exercise, or rather lack of exercise, what is lost in the long term is protection from coronary heart disease, as one example.

This 'futuristic perspective' is supported by the claims that coronary heart disease is now a pediatric problem, a point which is readily utilized by the advocates of the new HBPE (see Armstrong, 1984). Following this line, practising healthy habits will reduce significantly the incidence of coronary heart disease in adulthood. This futuristic perspective was evident in the comments of pupils who participated in the study I made of healthism and daily physical education in Queensland primary schools (Colquhoun, 1989). The study involved qualitative interviews and observations of over fifty teachers in four Queensland primary schools as well as interviews with pupils, and took place between 1985 and 1989; it also involved an analysis of curriculum materials in use in schools. The four schools were Birra, Bonnyvale, Fourtown and Kullambeel. All the names of schools and teachers have been changed to maintain confidentiality.

Exemplifying the futuristic perspective, the Kullambeel pupils remarked:

DC: Why do you think you do Daily Fitness?
Pupils: To keep fit... *not to be too fat*... you need to exercise to use all the food up... have a good time... *to keep your heart healthy* when you're young.
DC: Why is that important?
Pupils: So you don't have a *heart attack* when you are older... or *blood clots*. (emphasis added)

Metaphorically, we can apply the notion of 'health as investment' where individuals have a certain perception of 'the bank of life' where adhering to healthy habits, for example, doing physical education daily, is like taking out and maintaining an insurance policy or putting money into the bank for a 'rainy day' (old age). The premium isn't too high; only a small sacrifice now will pay big dividends later in life.

For many teachers, getting the children into healthy habits was a crucial aspect of their teaching. Some teachers suggested that the habitual nature of daily physical education undoubtedly helped their acceptance of the curriculum programme.

Teacher 1:   The children were only told a couple of times and they now know the routine.
Teacher 2:   Once the kids get into the routine it's fine. Some of the kids have got to the stage where they've had it for six years ... they expect to do daily physical education.

Some teachers felt that health is definitely something that needs to be achieved, and often the process can be quite painful and involve hard work, as a classteacher from Kullambeel suggested, 'daily fitness is teaching them to get into a routine and to suffer a little for a good cause and to learn self-discipline. . . . We do the fifteen minutes and that's the exercise for their body and I try to make it appear that it's just something they have to do' (Teacher 3). This teacher hinted in her interview that she really did think that often children could not have fun and improve their fitness at the same time. This idea was endorsed by another Kullambeel teacher:

DC: How do your kids find your daily fitness?

Teacher 4: It's mixed — there are those children who can't stand any type of fitness or physical sport. Most of the children like doing the health hustles — they don't regard that as fitness so that's a fun activity.

DC: Why do you think that is?

Teacher 4: We all have to do things in life we don't want to do and 'fitness' is for the children's health.

However, another teacher at Fourtown was not so enthusiastic about getting into a routine: 'if you do it [daily physical education] often enough you get sick and tired of it, it just becomes a duty and there is no pleasure in it' (Teacher 5). The idea that healthy habits are something which must be constantly worked at is reinforced by *BOM*.

The challenge that BOM offers you is not an easy one. Some things may be hard to do. Some things might be uncomfortable for a while. **To get fit you must work fairly hard.**
For the first few weeks of your DPE programme, you might feel a bit uncomfortable, and you might get sore muscles.
But!
After about two months you'll feel fantastic.
In fact, you would probably miss the nice feelings you get from exercise if, for some reason you couldn't do it.
This is the BOM's challenge.
Can you work hard enough to develop Good Health Habits?
How do you meet challenges? By **Self-Control**. By **Personal Action** or **Do you avoid them?**
Personal action and doing things for yourself - is the **best way to Good Health**.
If you are **mature** enough to **work hard** at this course, you

can be sure that you are well on the way to becoming a healthy adult. (Coonan, Worsley and Maynard, 1984, p. 11, original emphasis)

So far the message is clear: work hard, meet the challenge, be mature and intelligent, have self-discipline, take responsibility and health will come your way. The authors of *BOM* make the point even more attractive to children through the use of cartoons. Trixie Toogood, for example, is a 'superlative person — e.g. kicks football the length of pitch and catches it; does 150 pressups before breakfast.' A polar example (the bad guy), is represented by The Late Mort Smallpiece who 'died of a coronary when he was 41.... A nice chap, but he never got around to doing anything about altering his unhealthy habits. Full of good intentions to the end!'

As in Crawford's (1986) study, feelings of guilt were often associated with non-compliance to the healthy habits, or in this case not doing daily physical education or daily physical activity:

DC: So you could fit in half an hour health lesson and that would give you the maximum of three hours [the time gazetted by the Queensland Education Department for Health Education].

Teacher 6: Thank you, yes we could and we will be starting next week [laughing]. It is important, I suppose it is terribly pushed aside. I feel guilty when I see Ben's [the specialist physical education teacher] board down in the staffroom and I read the topic for this week. Gosh, I'm awful. (Kullambeel)

Teacher 7: What they were doing in Adelaide was unbelievable compared to up here and I've changed completely since I've started. I never used to keep myself fit and now I've got to the stage where I feel guilty if I haven't done something for say two days...it's really got to the stage where I had this real syndrome of feeling guilty. I've given up things like sugar, I won't take salt anymore, I watch what I eat, I've become really...maybe health conscious. (Fourtown)

Perhaps these feelings of guilt were exaggerated and exacerbated by the fact that many teachers saw daily physical activity as natural — 'sometimes the kids are really itching for some physical activity' (Teacher 8, Kullambeel) — and necessary — 'there has to be some physical activity during the day' (Teacher 9, Fourtown). However, the teachers were not alone in their feelings of guilt. Some of the grade 7 children at Bonnyvale also felt this way when they did not exercise.[4]

DC: When you get home do you think 'Oh, I haven't done any sport today, I haven't done any exercise today, I haven't ridden my bike today. I think will I go out and play footie or netball or skipping or whatever'? Does anybody think in those sorts of terms?

Pupils: Yes, everytime I get home I do an hour's skipping ...just normal straight skipping and double skips and triple unders and that.

DC: What's that skipping for then?

Pupils: Just to get quick on your feet.

DC: For what sport?

Pupils: Soccer.... My mum does because she plays tennis every weekend and if she misses out she sort of feels err...

DC: Does everybody else think like that if you don't exercise?

Pupils: Like I go for jogs at night with my friend and if I miss a jog I think 'Oh, I'm going to get fat'...you sort of feel different because you are used to doing it every night and that feels like a slob.

For many children, the most tangible and immediate experience of health and fitness was body shape. Using teachers as examples, the grade 7 children from Birra described how health equates with a 'good body', while ill-health equates with fatness.

Pupils: Fitness is like looking after your body and keeping it in good shape and then health is say you eat all the right foods and keeping yourself healthy.

DC: OK, when you say fitness is keeping your body in good shape...can anybody help her out by what she means by that?

Pupils: Not to get too fat and keep the right size and not be too skinny.

DC: Can anybody give me an example of a teacher here who they might say is the right size or the right shape? What about Mr. Collier [their classteacher]?

Pupils: No, Mr. Collier is too skinny — too tall and skinny.

DC: What about Mr Finch [the physical education teacher]?

Pupils: [laughing] The opposite.

DC: So what might make a teacher unfit? Can you recognize somebody if they're unfit by just looking at them?

Pupils: Yes.

DC: What sort of things do you look for?

Pupils: A belly [laughing].

The grade 6 pupils at Fourtown also had a particular perception of health and fitness:

> *DC:* So can anybody tell me why you actually do Daily Fitness?
> *Pupils:* So you keep in good shape.
> *DC:* Keep in good shape?
> *Pupils:* So you don't grow up like Norm.[5]
> *DC:* So you don't grow up like Norm?

The pupils used body shape as an indicator of an unhealthy teacher: 'She always smokes and she doesn't do much exercise. Mrs Fern is pretty unhealthy because she smokes all the time and she doesn't do any exercise. She's fairly fat too.' The Bonnyvale pupils held the same view.

> *Pupils:* I've never seen her [the librarian] do any sport, she's in the library all day...her favourite hobby is reading and watching TV. She's big and fat.
> *DC:* Are you saying big people are unfit?
> *Pupils:* They look unfit because they are so big... It [being healthy] makes them look better as well. If you are unfit you sort of look slobby.... We just go out — we go skipping every morning. I like to think about it when Mrs Clements or Mrs Smith comes past because you think, 'We are here skipping and they're just big and horrible.'[6]

These attitudes form part of what Tinning (1985) has called the 'cult of slenderness' or a preoccupation or obsession with a 'socially desirable body image'. The mesomorph (such as Sally Sandshoe, Simon Sandshoe and Davo Toogood in *BOM*) is the 'correct' body shape which is the appealing result of practising healthy habits, while the ectomorph (such as Narene and Neville Winfield in *BOM*) is the unwanted and undesirable product of neglect and abuse. These images permeate society at large and are evident in books, television and the media, children's toys and advertising in particular. John Hargreaves (1986) suggests that the images associated with the mesomorphic body are more significant than we normally assume.

> The mesomorphic image resonates strongly with ideologically conservative notions concerning achievement, drive and dynamism, discipline, conformity, cleanliness, efficiency, good adjustment, manliness and femininity. On the other hand, ectomorphic images connote weakness, lack of adjustment and neuroticism, antisocial tendencies, unattractiveness and coldness; and en-

domorphic images connote laziness, inefficiency, self-indulgence, unhealthyness and unattractiveness. (Hargreaves, 1986, p. 170)

Even though I have illustrated how self-control surfaces in schooling, what is unclear at this stage is the exact reason why such a mandate should exist in the first place. Earlier I mentioned Crawford's (1986) suggestion that feelings of political impotency in health matters lead people to give greater attention to their lives which they can actually get to grips with, namely their bodies, and to some degree their lifestyles or behaviours. Another explanation, perhaps one allied to this, is the suggestion that self-control is part of the current crisis of contemporary Western capitalism. It is tempting to suggest that associated with the development of modern capitalism there was a need for a docile, controllable and malleable workforce. Typical analyses of such a relationship between the body and control have tended to focus on how the body has been manipulated by domination of various subgroups classified by sex, class, race and age. These analyses usually attempted to draw explicit links between capitalism and methods of controlling the social body. Hargreaves (1987), for example, suggests that in the nineteenth century

the model normal individual knew his place and was positively committed to the established social order. Body images, discourse and practices figured prominently in the grand design for improvement. An upright posture with no hands in pockets, a clean well-washed body, a simple neat and tidy appearance, teetotalism, no smoking, no 'self abuse', no sex outside marriage, active participation in organised sport, frequent and regular exercise, fitness and good health, and above all a 'hard' body — constituted the God-fearing, obedient, hard working, respectable individual. (Hargreaves, 1987, p. 146)

This is a caricature — individuals in the nineteenth century would rarely conform to these ideals. However, what is significant is that the aspirations of the social body were reflected in the symbols of individual lifestyle and behaviour. The need for a manageable workforce is only one aspect of capitalism which serves to encourage the notion of self-control. Another facet of capitalism which will prove useful in this discussion to elucidate the intricacies of the problem is that of 'consumerism'. First, however, I will expand on the concept of 'healthism as release', since a knowledge of this concept allows an analysis of how the two mandates of release and control are dialectically linked and how they affect and are affected by consumerism and therefore the capitalist order.

Healthism, Release and Schooling

Instead of being concerned with ascetic self-denials, Crawford's (1986) second mandate, 'health as release', is organically concerned with instrumentalism, freedom from constraints and pleasure seeking. Those who extol the virtues of health as release are concerned with well-being, contentment, fun, hedonism, narcissism and enjoyment; 'if it feels good then it can't be all that bad' (Crawford, 1986). A prerequisite for such a view is to be a non-worrier free from stress. There is a feeling of 'live for today' — a sense of immediate gratification or indulgence unlike the delayed gratification of the exponents of health as control which has a futuristic perspective. In fact, for the advocates of health as release present self-denials cannot be justified by hoped-for gains in the future since these self-denials may lead to a 'fetishization of self-control' where almost any behaviour is perceived as harmful (Crawford, 1986). Alternatively, release may be seen as an acknowledgment of a lack of self-control — a reaction to the 'thou shalt not' mentality, a release of 'long suppressed desires' (Featherstone, 1982).

Presentations of health as release have an important part to play in the justificatory rhetoric of the new HBPE. For Whitehead and Fox (1983), physical education can offer the school curriculum the two unique aspects of motor competence and lifetime fitness.

> The benefits that physical activity offers which are *unique* and *essential* to all students in helping them lead a full and healthy adulthood are as follows;
> 1. It is the means by which we learn to create and control our body movements.
> 2. It is the way that we keep physically fit. Exercise is vital to looking good, feeling good, and protecting ourselves against 'modern' diseases. (Whitehead and Fox, 1983, p. 22, original emphasis)

This dichotomy of skills and fitness is implicated in the development of health-related fitness which, for Almond (1983), revolves around the central ideas of 'encouraging and promoting an active lifestyle' and 'making the most of oneself'. Both of these central aspects appear to subscribe to the mandate of health as release in various forms. They both have notions of 'contentment' and 'enjoyment' at their heart. Clearly, 'making the most of oneself' does involve a modicum of self-control, but the prevailing message is one of contentment.

> The message for schools from my questioning of the slogan 'adopt an active lifestyle' may be that we should attempt to

generate 'feeling good' from activity...I am trying to make a much stronger point because it may be more important to generate 'FEELING GOOD' as a result of activity than keeping young people engaged in vigorous activity for most of their lessons. The point may be too subtle but 'FEELING GOOD' places a responsibility on the teacher to really think about the effect of content on young people and their motivations for finding physical activity a satisfying experience. (Almond, 1985, p. 90, original emphasis)

Instead of concentrating on the controlling nature of physical activity (in terms of controlling coronary heart disease), Almond is concerned with the idea that physical activity promotes and enhances 'the quality of life': 'by taking part in regular, purposeful physical activity the body's organs and systems adapt to function in a more enhanced state, producing energy to enrich life, and generating personal feelings of well-being' (Almond, 1988a). Bray (1987) also suggests that an improvement in the quality of life can be attained from regular physical activity: 'in addition to the traditional pursuit of skills, today's pupils need to have a greater focus on health and begin to understand that continued participation in physical activities will enhance the quality of life ahead of them' (Bray, 1987, p. 9). Ken Cooper (1968), the doyen of aerobics, agrees with Almond and Bray but states his case slightly differently and with a little ingenuity, claiming that 'as one man who enjoys life...as much as anyone, I maintain exercise is one essential that not only helps you enjoy the life you have but can help you to have more life to enjoy' (Cooper, 1968, p. 160).

Health and fitness then are instrumental, a means to an end. Many children adhere to a 'gospel of self-fulfilment' (Crawford, 1986) which means they have a good time and simply enjoy themselves in their physical education lessons. Recently, Sparkes and Dickenson (1987) have quoted children as saying, 'it's [physical education] fun, enjoyable, a laugh' and 'you have a great laugh — it makes you happy.' In the study schools several children equated health and fitness with fun.

> *Pupil:* It's fun, it's good for you. It helps you get your mind off things. (Kullambeel)
> *Pupil:* I like sport because it's good for you and it's fun (Kullambeel)
> *Pupil:* Fitness can be fun and not painful if you are fit but like me when I started [exercising] I hated it and it was very painful. I am fit now and enjoying it like mad. (Bonnyvale)
> *Pupil:* Health and fitness is part of your long lasting life. The more healthy and fit you are the more fun you will have in

your life. Also, health and fitness is really fun to me and it should be fun to everyone. (Bonnyvale)

For many, health as release is the more important of the two mandates.

Gone are the days of self-inflicted GBH to get into shape. Relax and enjoy — this is the age of easy exercise....

At last, *at last*, it's been discovered that drastic health regimes are not good for you. Now is the time for No Sweat Fitness.... The British are a race of extremists. Just as we scorch ourselves skinless on Mediterranean beaches, so we go for the 'burn' in exercise studios. But compulsive exercise is as unhealthy as compulsive eating....

A body that looks good but doesn't look as though it's tried too hard is what we're after. (Alexander, 1987, pp. 21–2, original emphasis)

The mandates of health as self-control and release allow us to identify the meanings and messages associated with health. As such, they are necessarily simplistic in that they make an almost false distinction between the two so that analysis can take place. However, in reality individuals work through the messages and meanings using both mandates. Bray (1987), for example, accommodates the notion of dual mandates when she suggests that 'it is important that through an exciting and stimulating programme of physical education children have achieved some success, had some fun, learnt to manage their bodies with some control and so developed confidence in themselves. It is vital that children associate physical activity with pleasure if they are to choose to devote a part of their precious leisure time to physical activity' (Bray, 1987, p. 16). Some of the teachers in the study also engaged the notion of dual mandates in their rationalization of the links between health and physical education. 'Both are educating for a healthy life, a longer life and more enjoyable life, and they are teaching children the capabilities of their bodies and how to be physically skilful, to be socially able and how to develop a positive self-concept' (Wimala, itinerant physical education teacher).

For another itinerant physical education teacher,[7] the link between the mandates was very clear, albeit at a subconscious level: 'The most important point is to encourage the children into a healthy pattern of living. I try to show them by example and by teaching them how to look after their bodies, about fitness and respecting and getting the most out of their bodies. If they grow to enjoy being active and healthy they won't want to jeopardise that with unhealthy practices' (Teacher 11). This teacher's interpretation of health and fitness suggests that individuals need a degree of self-control to facilitate or act as a precursor to release. Also, according to some teachers, once individuals have attained self-control, then they will not want to abuse their bodies by losing control and 'poisoning' themselves.

Health, Fitness and Consumerism

> Ours is an age obsessed with youth, health and physical beauty...the dominant visual media churn out persistent reminders that the lithe and graceful body, the dimpled smile set in an attractive face, are the keys to happiness, perhaps even its essence. (Kern, 1975)

Another point of access to the debate, and one which pulls many of its various strands together, can be made through consumer culture. This involves

> the impact of mass consumption on everyday life which has led to the gearing of social activities around the accumulation and consumption of an ever increasing range of goods and experiences. New modes of cultural representation ensure the proliferation of images which saturate the fabric of social life with a melee of signs and messages which summon up new expressive and hedonistic definitions of the good life. (Featherstone, 1983, p. 4)

Consumer culture largely involves the analysis and decoding of messages which bombard the individual's consciousness, messages which ultimately lead to the consumption of consumer goods whether they be tents, tea-pots or tennis shoes. A person's lifestyle reflects his/her 'individuality' in terms of his/her appreciation of 'goods, clothes, practices, experiences, appearance and bodily disposition' (Featherstone, 1987). Consumerism induces self-improvement and self-expression by focusing on idealized representations of lifestyle and all it involves, be it material goods such as cars, hi-fis, or surf boards to less tangible aspects such as good personal care and grooming or simply associating goods with good health,

> Consumer culture latches on to the prevalent self-preservationist conception of the body, which encourages the individual to adopt instrumental strategies to combat deterioration and decay (applauded too by state bureaucracies who seek to reduce costs by educating the public against bodily neglect) and combines it with

the notion that the body is a vehicle of pleasure and self-expression. Images of the body beautiful, openly sexual and associated with hedonism, leisure and display, emphasise the importance of the 'look'. (Featherstone, 1982, p. 18)

The 'look' or 'the shapely and well muscled torso' (Hoberman, 1984) has other uses, of course. Hoberman (1984), for example, has extensively shown how the notion of 'form is power' has been enthusiastically adopted by fascists to enhance the 'body politic'. Fascist leaders such as Mussolini continually attempted to associate themselves with sporting heroes and the typical mesomorphic profile.[8] In addition, the body is applied metaphorically to the health of the economic system and we quite often hear of economies 'flexing their muscles' (see Emmison, 1986).

Consumerism, or what Crawford (1986) terms the 'science of satisfactions', and health as release are linked through the craving to atone some desire or need. For the sake of consumerism these needs are attached to goods and materials and it is the achievement of these needs which for health as release are mediated through contentment and serenity. 'This is the world of men and women who quest for the new and latest in relationships and experiences, who have a sense of adventure and take risks to explore life's options to the full, who are conscious they have only one life to live and must work hard to enjoy, experience and express it' (Featherstone, 1987, p. 59)

In attempting to locate the source of consumerism both Featherstone (1987), building on the work of Pierre Bourdieu, and Crawford (1986) look to the newly found interest in 'lifestyle' which in the past has been the preserve of sections of the middle class or what he calls 'the new petite bourgeoisie': 'the new conception of lifestyle can best be understood in relation to the habitus of the new petite bourgeoisie, who, as an expanding class fraction centrally concerned with the production and dissemination of consumer culture imagery and information, is concerned to expand and legitimate its own particular dispositions and lifestyle' (Featherstone, 1987, p. 57). In determining whose interests are being served by consumer culture with its symbol production and signification, Featherstone (1987) suggests that the petite bourgeoisie are 'natural consumers':

if we are to turn to the new petite bourgeoisie habitus it is clear that whereas the bourgeoisie has a sense of ease and confidence in his [sic] body, the petite bourgeoisie is uneasy with his body, constantly self-consciously checking, watching and correcting himself. Hence the attraction of body maintenance techniques, the new Californian sports and forms of exercise, cosmetics, health foods, where the body is treated as a sign for others and not as an instrument.

...The new narcissism where individuals seek to maximise and experience the range of sensations available, the search for expression and self-expression, the fascination with identity, presentation and appearance makes the new petite bourgeoisie a 'natural consumer'. (Featherstone, 1987, pp. 64–5)

Crawford (1986) takes a slightly different slant on the issue and suggests that the middle class needs some form of identity which it can attain from healthism.

It is the professional middle class, however — the social category least pressured by the economic crisis — that most readily adopts and displays the value of self-control, including its physical expressions....For the middle class, the evocation of self-control is a ritual of identity and justification. And in the face of class insecurity, the conspicious pursuit of health — jogging, not smoking, health fashion, etc. — becomes a rite of belonging. (Crawford, 1986, p. 80)

For Crawford (1986), the discourse on health and consumerism serves to illuminate the 'tyranny of consumption' and the inherent contradictions evident in the relationship between the two mandates. For example, he suggests that 'the culture of consumption demands a modal personality contrary to the personality required for production. The mandate for discipline clashes with the mandate for pleasure....Release extended to the shop floor is subversive. Self-control and self-denial extended to the market is equally subversive' (Crawford, 1986, p. 92). Shapiro (1988) has summed up neatly what Bell (1975) termed 'the cultural contradictions of capitalism':

These contradictions center on the demand for a Protestant ethic in the area of production, for a demand for pleasure and play in the area of consumption. The cultural underpinnings of production emphasize the values of work, sobriety, sexual restraint, and a forbidding attitude towards life.... By contrast, the culture of consumption is one in which the corporation, through its products and advertisements, promotes pleasure, instant joy, relaxation and letting go as well as hedonistic fantasy. All of this has left the culture with an extraordinary set of tensions and conflicts.... It is clear that the cultural contradictions of capitalism confront the modern consciousness with a bewildering set of conflicts and moral dilemmas: authority vs. freedom, restraint vs. indulgence, satisfaction vs. denial and so on. (Shapiro, 1980, pp. 428–9)

An obvious example of the contradictions which individuals are exposed to can be identified in the large-scale campaigns which attempt to promote health and fitness in the community. Such campaigns often use the media and carry a slogan to conceptualize the essence of the message to be conveyed to the public. These slogans are the source of confusion and contradiction. On the one hand the individual is told to 'look after yourself' (that is, exhibit self-control), while on the other hand and at the same time the individual is told that health can be attained through the slogan 'Life. Be in It' (that is, exhibit 'release' through enjoyment, fun and excitement).

Not only do the two mandates clash through various bodily experiences but they also exist and appear in differing degrees. As Alexander (1987) noted earlier, we are moving away from the dominance of ascetic self-denials; rather, the dominating theme of today is one of release, perhaps mediated through the pervasive consumer culture which is in turn an implicit part of Western capitalism. Hargreaves (1987) makes the relationship between self-control and release more explicit:

> Ponderous, repressive forms of control characteristic of respectable everyday life and work discipline during the emergence and subsequent development of industrial capitalism, are no longer dominant.... Negative forms of constraint are becoming recessive: the dominant form of control now is an expansive system of discipline and surveillance based on stimulation and satisfaction of desire.... The trend is most evident in the way the body is deployed in consumer culture, a culture which, above all, thematizes the primacy of the personal and satisfaction of individual desires.... The leisure, advertising, fashion and entertainment industries, not without the complicity of their clientele, are engaged in a constantly elaborating programme whose objective is the constitution of the modern 'normal' individual. Consumer culture discourse/practice structures and satisfies individual desire *so that individuals enthusiastically discipline themselves.* (Hargreaves, 1987, p. 141, emphasis added)

As the proliferation of consumerism continues, the number and types of images which promote the mandate of release will also grow and expand. Since consumer culture 'surrounds goods and activities with images which hold out the promise of self-expression, release and a fulfilled desire', it is of significance that 'advertising relies less on messages which reinforce existing stereotypes and more on fluid lifestyle images which offer more diffuse feelings of happiness and well-being' (Featherstone, 1983, p. 6). We need to be able to identify at any one historical moment which images are being presented and reinforced through consumer culture if we are to trace these messages into schooling. So far it appears that the images and messages associated with health in society seem to wax and wane over time and at the present moment release through notions of fun, hedonism and narcissism is in the ascendancy.

Conclusion

Crawford's (1986) conceptual categories of health as self-control and release have served a useful purpose in aiding the analysis of the presentation of healthism in Health-Based Physical Education. Through them, I have been able to highlight how healthism masks and renders unproblematic a number of notions about health and in particular how these are affecting and are affected by the new Health-Based Physical Education.[9] It is clear that the ideological messages and meanings associated with the current presentation of health in schools, such as viewing health as self-control, the use of imagery like the body as a machine, the adherence to healthy habits and through the guilt lack of control creates, all serve to support healthism. Health as self-control includes aspects of will-power, self-discipline, self-denial and restraint. Individuals need to develop a 'health ethic' since health cannot be inherited and must be worked at. Healthism encourages individuals to avoid 'self-abuse' by adopting healthy habits. Failure to do so means that the individual is immersed in guilt. The conceptual tool of release has made it possible to identify how the new Health-Based Physical Education uses images of well-being, contentment, fun, hedonism and narcissism in its justificatory rhetoric. Health as release is concerned with more than ascetic self-denials. It is concerned with immediate pleasures nurtured by consumerism which makes aspects of daily life appealing and attractive. In Health-Based Physical Education health as release is manifest in notions of 'feeling good' and 'quality of life'.

If we accept that we can identify ideological messages transmitted through the mandates of self-control and release, then we need to ask what are the sites of compliance and resistance for these ideologically charged messages? What is the scope or potential for resistance, bearing in mind the pervasiveness of consumer culture? Can we identify the hegemonic groups whose interests are being served by presenting health in such a way in the curriculum? Can we identify healthism through 'the dominant ideology thesis' (Abercrombie, Hill and Turner, 1980)? Are there class, sex, age, race and subgroup differences in the perception of health? How do the cultural contradictions of capitalism materialize in the school curriculum? These questions must be answered before we can adequately locate health in the school curriculum. Healthism, in particular as it is manifest in HBPE, is opaque and void of critical analysis in the physical education field. By asking these questions we can begin to open up to scrutiny the acquiescence, ambivalence and accommodation of teachers and curriculum writers to the values and messages presented to them in order to enable them to decode the various meanings attached to health.

Notes

1 The data in this chapter are from Colquhoun's (1989) unpublished PhD thesis, 'Healthism and Health-Based Physical Education: A Critique', University of Queensland.
2 See also Gillie and Mercer (1978).
3 I differentiate here between the concept of daily physical education and the curriculum package the *Daily Physical Education Program*. For a critique of daily physical education as a concept see Kirk (1989).
4 Grade 7 children are approximately 10–11 years old.
5 Norm was a character used by the Australian health promotion campaign 'Life. Be in It'. His lifestyle consisted of all the 'self-abusing' bad habits such as eating too much and exercising too little. Unfortunately for the promotion, individuals began to 'identify' with Norm so the character was subsequently dropped.
6 These comments were typical of the children from each school even though differences in their socioeconomic backgrounds were apparent. The groups of children interviewed at each school consisted of equal numbers of boys and girls and there were no discernible differences in their attitudes.
7 Itinerant specialist physical education teachers were based at one school (usually the largest) and serviced several schools — usually two, three or four in any one week.
8 It could also be argued that non-fascist political leaders also associate themselves with sporting heroes. Bob Hawke, the Prime Minister of Australia, for example, is often portrayed in the media attending sporting events, particularly cricket matches.
9 It is important to identify and examine the various messages and meanings associated with healthism and consumerism in terms of different agendas such as sexism, racism, ageism, class and disability.

References

ABERCROMBIE, N., HILL, S. and TURNER, B.S. (1980) *The Dominant Ideology Thesis*. London: George Allen and Unwin.

ALEXANDER, T. (1987) 'No Sweat.' *Time Out*, April, 870, pp. 21–2.

ALMOND, L. (1983) 'A Rationale for Health Related Fitness.' *Bulletin of Physical Education*. 19 (2), 5–10.

ALMOND, L. (1985) 'Health Based Physical Education: Some Critical Issues.' *British Journal of Physical Education*, 16 (3), 89–90.

ALMOND, L. (1988a) A Health Focus in Physical Education. Unpublished manuscript.

ALMOND, L. (1988b) Personal communication.

ARMSTRONG, N. (1984) 'Why Implement a Health Related Fitness Programme?' *British Journal of Physical Education*, 15 (6), 173–5.

BELL, D. (1975) *The Cultural Contradictions of Capitalism*. New York: Basic Books.

Better Health Commission (1986) *Looking Forward to Better Health*. Canberra: AGPS.

BIDDLE, S. (1987) 'Motivational Psychology and Exercise: Implications for Education, Health and Fitness in the Curriculum. *Perspectives*, 31, School of Education, University of Exeter.

BRAY, S. (1987) 'Health and Fitness in the Primary School: Health and Fitness in the Curriculum.' *Perspective*, 31, School of Education, University of Exeter.

CHERNIN, K. (1981) *The Obsession: Reflections on the Tyranny of Slenderness*. New York: Harper Row.

COLQUHOUN, D. (1989) Healthism and Health-Based Physical Education: A Critique. Unpublished PhD thesis, University of Queensland, Australia.

COONAN, W., WORSLEY, A. and MAYNARD, E. (1984) *Body Owner's Manual*. Melbourne: Life. Be in it.

COOPER, K.H. (1968) *Aerobics*. New York: Bantam Books.

CRAWFORD, R. (1978) 'You Are Dangerous to Your Health.' *Social Policy*, 8 (4), 10–20.

CRAWFORD, R. (1986) 'A Cultural Account of "Health": Control, Release, and the Social Body,' in MCKINLEY, J.B. (Ed.), *Issues in the Political Economy of Health Care*, pp. 60–103. London: Tavistock.

DODD, G. (1983) *Daily Physical Education Program*. Kingswood: ACHPER.

EMMISON, M. (1986) 'Visualizing the Economy: Fetishism and the Legitimation of Economic Life.' *Theory Culture and Society* 3 (2), 81–96.

FEATHERSTONE, M. (1982) 'The Body in Consumer Culture.' *Theory Culture and Society* 1 (2), 18–33.

FEATHERSTONE, M. (1983) 'Consumer Culture: An Introduction.' *Theory Culture and Society*, 1 (3), 4–9.

FEATHERSTONE, M. (1987) 'Lifestyle and Consumer Culture.' *Theory, Culture and Society*, 4, 55–70.

FOUCAULT, M. (1980) *Power/Knowledge*. Brighton: Harvester Press.

GILLIE, O. and MERCER, D. (1978) *The Sunday Times Book of Body Maintenance*. London: Michael Joseph.

GLASER, B.G. and STRAUSS, A.L. (1967) *The Discovery of Grounded Theory*. London: Weidenfeld and Nicolson.

HARGREAVES, J. (1986) *Sport, Power and Culture. A Social and Historical Analysis of Popular Sports in Britain.* Cambridge: Polity Press.

HARGREAVES, J. (1987) 'The Body, Sport and Power Relations,' in HORNE, J., JARY, D. and TOMLINSON, A. (Eds), *Sport, Leisure and Social Relations*, pp. 139–59. London: Routledge and Kegan Paul.

HOBERMAN, J.M. (1984) *Sport and Political Ideology.* London: Heinemann.

HOWELL, R.A. and HOWELL, M.L. (1983) *Foundations of Physical Education.* Brisbane: William Brooks.

KERN, S. (1975) *Anatomy and Destiny: A Cultural History of the Human Body.* New York: Bobbs-Merrill.

KEYS, A. (1970) 'Summary: Coronary Heart Disease in Seven Countries.' *Circulation*, 41–42, 186–95.

KIRK, D. (1989) 'Daily Physical Education Research: A Review and a Critique.' *Physical Education Review*, 12 (1), 21–30.

KIRK, D. and COLQUHOUN, D. (1989) 'Healthism and Physical Education.' *British Journal of Sociology of Education*, 10 (4), 417–34.

KOHLER RIESSMAN, C. (1983) 'Women and Medicalization: A New Perspective.' *Social Policy*, Summer, 3–18.

LINDER, S.B. (1970) *The Harried Leisure Class.* New York: Columbia University Press.

MORRIS, J.N., HEADY, J.A., RAFFLE, P.A., ROBERTS, C.G. and PARKS, J.W. (1953) 'Coronary Heart Disease and Physical Activity of Work.' *Lancet 2*, 1053–7, 1111–20.

PAFFENBARGER, R.S. and HALE W.E. (1975) 'Work Activity and Coronary Heart Mortality.' *New England Journal of Medicine*, 292, 545–50.

SHAPIRO, S. (1988) 'Beyond the Sociology of Education: Culture, Politics, and the Promise of Educational Change.' *Educational Theory*, 38 (4), 415–30.

SPARKES, A.C. and DICKENSON, B. (1987) 'Children's Activity Patterns: Treating the Problem and Not the Symptom.' Health and Physical Education Project Newsletter, Number 9, 1–3, in *British Journal of Physical Education*, 18 (6).

SULER, J. and BARTHOLOMEW, E. (1986) 'The Ideology of Overeaters Anonymous.' *Social Policy*, Spring, pp. 48–53.

TINNING, R. (1985) 'Physical Education and the Cult of Slenderness: A Critique.' *The ACHPER National Journal*, 107, 10–13.

TURNER, B.S. (1982) 'The Discourse of Diet.' *Theory, Culture and Society*, 1 (1), 23–33.

WHITEHEAD, J. and FOX, K. (1983) 'Student Centred Physical Education.' *Bulletin of Physical Education*, 19 (2), 21–30.

Notes on Contributors

Linda L. Bain is Professor of Kinesiology and Physical Education and Dean of the School of Communication and Professional Studies at California State University, Northridge. Her area of expertise is curriculum theory and development and she is co-author with Ann Jewett of the book *The Curriculum Process in Physical Education* (1985). Her research has focused on the hidden curriculum in physical education. Dr Bain is Fellow of the American Academy of Physical Education and has served as President of the Research Consortium of the American Alliance for Health, Physical Education, Recreation and Dance.

Derek Colquhoun lectures in health education at Deakin University. He has carried out research on the health benefits to children of participation in daily physical education, and the issues and problems in teaching health within the physical education curriculum. His most recent publications have consisted of a critique of healthism in health-based physical education.

Alison Dewar teaches sport sociology and pedagogy in the Physical Education, Health and Sports Studies Department at Miami University in Oxford, Ohio. Her work centres on feminist critiques of sports and physical education.

John Evans teaches the sociology of physical education and the sociology of education in the School of Education at the University of Southampton. He authored *Teaching in Transition: The Challenge of Mixed Ability Grouping* (Open University Press, 1985) and edited *Physical Education, Sport and Schooling* (1986) and *Teachers, Teaching and Control in Physical Education* (1988) both for Falmer Press. He also contributes regularly to the literature in the sociology of education.

Lindsay Fitzclarence teaches curriculum theory in the School of Education at Deakin University. His recent research has centred on the cultural context of curriculum change in physical education, on the commodification of the body and physical activity, and post-structural critique of education. He is co-author with Stephen Kemmis of *Curriculum Theorizing: Beyond Reproduction Theory* (Deakin University Press, 1986).

Jennifer M. Gore is currently completing her PhD in curriculum and instruction at the University of Wisconsin-Madison. She has taught in a number of tertiary institutions, most recently in the pedagogy section of the Human Movement Studies Department at the University of Queensland. Her current research interests include discourses of feminist and critical pedagogy, post-structural critique and Michel Foucault's notion of 'regimes of truth'.

David Kirk teaches in the School of Education at Deakin University. His research interests are in the fields of curriculum and the sociology of knowledge, with specific applications in physical education and health education. His book *Physical Education and Curriculum Study: A Critical Introduction* was published by Croom Helm in 1988. He has also published papers on curriculum innovation and research, teacher education and research on teaching, health-based physical education and daily physical education. His current projects include studies of the cultural construction of the body and body shape in the context of consumer society, and the part that school physical education materials and programmes play in this process.

Andrew C. Sparkes teaches physical education in the School of Education at the University of Exeter. He has published widely on the subject of curriculum innovation and change, with particular emphasis on the micropolitics of school-based curriculum development, on qualitative research methodology and on a variety of topics in school physical education.

Richard Tinning teaches physical education in the School of Education at Deakin University. His main teaching and research interests are in the areas of physical education curriculum/pedagogy and teacher education. His book, *Improving Teaching in Physical Education*, was published in 1987, and his most recent research has critiqued conventional practice in physical education and the notion of technical rationality in the teacher education process.

Index

Lightning Source UK Ltd.
Milton Keynes UK

173042UK00003B/23/A

9 781850 006756